KINGDOM *of* BAHRAIN
Political Review

Ahmed Khuzaie
Nour Zenaty
Meredith Sullivan
Lia Isono
Evgeny Kukharev

Copyright © KHUZAIE ASSOCIATES LLC 2020, 2021, 2022

e-Book ISBN 978-0-578-57405-9

Hardcover ISBN 979-8-9852646-1-6

Paperback ISBN: 979-8-9852646-0-9

Book Design: Husain Mahroos & Sayyed Mohammed Ali

Cover Photo: Abdulla Alkhan - Abdulqader`s Caf'e, Muharraq Souq - 1960, Bahrain

Library of Congress Control Number: 2019907942

KHUZAIE ASSOCIATES LLC

WASHINGTON, D.C.

UNITED STATES OF AMERICA

Contents

List of Illustrations

Acknowledgments

THIS REVIEW IS PRIMARILY BASED
on information researched and collected through publications, media
outlets, and personal interviews. Collecting the data was difficult, considering that some
of it were not previously documented.
This book was encouraged and supported by many who took the time to tell their stories
and referred us to resources that made this book a reality. We are hugely indebted to
Jamil al-Alawi, Jasim Murad, Ali Rabea'a, Saeed al-Asbool, Dr. Ali Fakhro, Taqi
al-Bahrana, Nawaf al-Sayyed, Fatima A al-Qatari, Dr. Mohamed al-Kuwaiti, Jamal
Dawood, Abdulhadi Marhoun, Dr. Taqi al-Zeera, and Sheikh Abdulla al-A'ali,
although they may not agree with all of the conclusions of this review, but without
whom we would have not been able to finish this book. .

Executive Summary

THIS BOOK AIMS TO PORTRAY THE POLITICAL HISTORY AND ITS IMPACT ON THE KINGDOM OF Bahrain. What differentiates it from other reports is the factual rather than the emotional approach it adopts, as well as the balanced instead of ideological, opinionated outlook. It is well known that the media played a significant role in the events from 2011 up to today as a source of information or by making the problems seem more significant than they were, depicting Bahrain like another Iraq. It is a known fact that the owners of these media outlets are either founded or financed by the Islamic Republic of Iran, a state that has been trying to take over the peaceful island as its fourteenth state.

Despite what most people presume, political unrest did not start in 2011 and was not occasioned by the regional conflicts but, instead, has been in the making for a long time.

This project was initiated to provide a comprehensive and factual retelling of the historical and current aspects of the political scene in the Kingdom of Bahrain. A thorough analysis has been made of all political societies and their ideologies, manifestos, affiliations, and stories. Also, it presents a broader study of Bahraini politics, including showcasing of all the elements involved in the political configuration of the Kingdom, such as the Government, its structure, Constitution, and the related bodies. The review presents a record of the Kingdom's political history, current situation, all factors involved in the political structure, & how successes and drawbacks have shaped today's political outcomes.

In the present age of the internet, it is very easy for people to sink into their own echo chambers of similar ideas. Those who subscribe solely to what is articulated in human rights organizations, for example, tend to restrict themselves to the news provided by these bodies. On the other hand, people who subscribe solely to Government media only pay attention to Government narratives. This review will stand out from those previously made by single organizations. It presents facts and data compiled by international researchers from Government entities, political societies, international organizations, and think tanks, among other sources. The objective is to provide an unbiased, fact-based, and, therefore, accurate historical timeline, political outlook, and recommendations.

This political review on the Kingdom of Bahrain was written to disseminate a well-rounded and unbiased account of events. It aims to help expose people to the truth no matter how much it conflicts with their personal views.

Timeline

1913

Britain and the Ottoman Government sign a treaty recognizing the independence of Bahrain, while the country remains under British administration.

1931

The Bahrain Petroleum Company (Bapco), a subsidiary of the Standard Oil Company of California (Socal), discovers oil at Jabal al-Dukhan and production begins the following year.

1939

Britain decides that the Hawar Islands, which lie in the Gulf of Bahrain between Bahrain and Qatar, belong to Bahrain, not Qatar.

1961

Shaikh Isa bin Salman al-Khalifa becomes ruler of Bahrain.

1967

Britain moves its main regional naval base from Aden to Bahrain.

1970

The Administrative Council becomes a twelve-member Council of State, headed by a president, the ruler's brother, late Shaikh Khalifa bin Salman al-Khalifa.

1970, May

Iran renounces its claim to sovereignty over Bahrain after a United Nations report shows that Bahrainis want to remain independent

1971, May

Bahrain declares independence and signs a new treaty of friendship with Britain. Shaikh Isa becomes the first Emir, and the Council of State becomes a cabinet.

1971, August

Bahrain gains formal independence from Britain.

1971

Bahrain and the U.S. sign an agreement which permits the U.S. to rent Naval and Military facilities.

1972, December

Elections are held for a Constituent Assembly. Only Bahraini males over twenty can vote.

1973, December

After the Constitution comes into force on December 6th, elections are held on December 7th for a National Assembly, a legislative advisory body, with fourty four members (fourteen cabinet members and thirty elected by male voters).

1975

Following complaints by Prime Minister Shaikh Khalifa bin Salman al-Khalifa that the National Assembly is impeding the work of the Government, the Emir dissolves the assembly and rules by decree.

1975, May

Bahrain joins the Cooperation Council for the Arab States of the Gulf, known as the Gulf Cooperation Council (GCC), which also includes Kuwait, Oman, Qatar, Saudi Arabia, and the United Arab Emirates.

1981, December

Seventy-three people, said to be members of the Tehran-based Islamic Front for the Liberation of Bahrain, headed by Shiite Iranian cleric, Sayyed Hadi al-Modarrissi, are arrested and accused of conspiring to overthrow the Government on December 16th, Bahrain's National Day.

1986, April

In April, Qatari troops occupy Fasht al-Dibal Island but withdraw in June after mediation by Saudi Arabia.

1986, November

Opening of the King Fahad Causeway, which links Bahrain to the mainland of Saudi Arabia.

1991, January/February

As part of the Gulf Cooperation Council (GCC) Peninsula Shield Force, Bahrain participates in the coalition Operation Desert Storm against Iraq (the Gulf War).

1991 July

Qatar takes its territorial claim to the Hawar Islands, Fasht al-Dibal and Qitat Jaradah before the International Court of Justice (ICJ) in the Hague, but Bahrain rejects the claims.

1991, October

Bahrain signs a defense cooperation agreement with the United States providing port facilities and joint military exercises.

1992, December

The establishment of a thirty-member Consultative Council, appointed by the Emir for a four-year term.

1994, November

Protests against a charity marathon led by Sheikh Ali Salman result in harming four British nationals, lead to the arrest of Sheikh Salman, which ignited the 90's unrest.

1994, December

Demonstrations follow the arrest on December 5th of Shia cleric, Sheikh Ali Salman.

1995, January

Sheikh Ali Salman is deported and seeks asylum in Britain.

1995, February

Bahrain rejects International Court of Justice (ICJ) mediation in its dispute with Qatar.

1995, June

After a reshuffle, the cabinet includes five Shia Ministers.

1995, September

A Shia cleric, Sheikh Abdulamir al-Jamri, who was arrested in April, is released from prison.

1996, January

After bomb explosions in Manama's business quarter, al-Jamri is arrested again on January 18th. A Sunni lawyer and poet, Ahmed al-Shamlan, is also detained on February 8th but released in April.

1996, June

The Government says it has uncovered a coup plot by an Iranian-backed group, Hezbollah-Bahrain. Bahrain recalls its ambassador to Iran and downgrades its representation to charge d'affaires level.

1996, September

The Consultative Council members increase from thirty to fourty.

1997, April

Bahrain acquires sole ownership of the Bahrain Petroleum Company Bapco.

1998, February

Shaikh Khalid bin Mohamed bin Salman al-Khalifa replaces British citizen, Ian Henderson, as Director of the Security and Intelligence Service (SIS).

1998, December

Bahrain provides Military facilities for Operation Desert Fox, the U.S. and UK bombing campaign against Iraq.

1999, March

The Emir, Shaikh Isa, dies and is succeeded by his eldest son, Shaikh Hamad. On March 9, Shaikh Hamad's son, Shaikh Salman, becomes Crown Prince.

1999, July
Sheikh Abddulamir al-Jamri is sentenced to ten years' imprisonment but is pardoned by the new Emir.

1999, December
The Emir of Qatar, Shaikh Hamad bin Khalifa al-Thani, visits. Both countries establish a committee to settle territorial disputes.

2000, August
Gulf Air airplane crashes on the way back from Cairo. All passengers die.

2000, September
Emir appoints the non-Muslims to the Consultative Council for the first time, including four women one of whom is a Christian and a Jewish businessman.

2001, February
Referendum on political reform; Bahrainis overwhelmingly back proposals under which Bahrain would become a Constitutional Monarchy with elected lower Chamber of Parliament and an independent judiciary.

2001, November
Political societies start to form to replace underground movements.

2002, February
Bahrain turns itself into a Constitutional Monarchy and allows women to stand for office in a package of reforms. Shaikh Hamad bin Isa bin Salman al-Khalifa transitions from Emir to King.

2002, May
Local elections are held, Bahrain's first poll for almost thirty years. For the first time, women vote and stand as candidates, but fail to win a seat.

2002, October
Parliamentary elections held, the first in nearly thirty years. Authorities announce the turnout was more than 53.48% despite a call by Opposition for boycott.

2003, May
Thousands of victims of alleged torture petition the King to cancel the law, which prevents them from suing suspected torturers.

2004, April
Nada Haffadh is made Health Minister, the first woman to head a Government Ministry.

2004, May
Nizar al-Baharna quits al-Wefaq and attempts to establish a new political society.

2004, May
Protests in Manama against fighting in the Iraqi holy cities of Najaf & Karbala. The King sacks the interior Minister after police try to prevent the protest.

2004, September
Bahrain and the U.S. sign Free Trade Agreement.

2005, March-June
Thousands of protest marchers demand a fully elected National Council.

2006, January
U.S. President George W. Bush signs a bill to enact the 2004 U.S.-Bahrain free-trade agreement after it is approved by the U.S. Congress.

2006, March
A tours boat capsizes off the Bahrain coast, claiming the lives of fifty eight passengers.

2006, November
The Shia opposition wins 40% of the vote in a general election. A Shia Muslim, Jawad bin Salem al-Urrayedh, is named deputy Prime Minister.

2006, September
The controversial report known as al-Bandar becomes known to the public by its writer

Salah al-Bandar.

2007, September
Thousands of illegal foreign workers rush to take advantage of a Government-sanctioned amnesty.

2008, May
A Jewish woman, Huda Nonoo, is appointed Bahrain's ambassador to the U.S. She is believed to be the Arab world's first Jewish ambassador.

2008, December
Authorities arrest several people who allegedly planned to detonate homemade bombs during Bahrain's national day celebrations.

2009, April
King pardons more than 170 prisoners charged with endangering national security, including thirty five Shiites being tried on charges of trying to overthrow the State.

2010, September
20 Shia opposition leaders accused of plotting to overthrow monarchy by promoting violent protests and sabotage arrested in the run-up to elections.

2010, October
Main opposition societies Wa'ad and al-Wefaq, make slender gains ahead of Parliamentary elections.

2011, February
Thousands of protesters gather in Manama, inspired by popular revolts that toppled rulers in Tunisia and Egypt. A security crackdown results in the death of several protestors.

2011, March
Gulf Peninsula forces are called in, following further unrest. Authorities declare a National Safety Law and clamp down hard on protestors. Protests continue, despite a ban on demonstrations.

2011, April
Ministry of Justice acts towards banning two political societies due to their role in political unrest.

2011, September
Low turn-out for bi-elections to replace MPs from the Shia opposition who quit Parliament objecting to the violent crackdown on demonstrators.

2011, November
Government concedes that excessive force was used by security forces in Bahrain against protesters.

2012, February
Police thwart opposition attempts to protest on the anniversary of the crackdown on previous year's mass demonstration on the site of the demolished Pearl Roundabout. Protests nonetheless resume through the spring.

2012, May
Abdulhadi al-Khawaja ends a three-month hunger strike. A military court jailed him for life in June 2011 for plotting against the State.

2012, June
Appeals court partially overturns long jail sentences on twenty medics for taking part in anti-Government protests. Nine are acquitted, and the rest were given much shorter sentences.

2012, August
Rights activist, Nabeel Rajab, is jailed for three years for taking part in illegal gatherings. Sporadic anti-monarchy protests continue.

2012, October
Protesters clash with riot police in Manama at the funeral of Ali Ahmed Mushaima, who died in Prison after being jailed for taking part in the revolution. The authorities indefinitely ban all protests and gatherings.

2013, February

National dialogue talks begin in an effort to end the unrest.

2013, March

King Hamad appoints his son, Crown Prince Salman bin Hamad bin Isa al-Khalifa, as deputy Prime Minister.

2013, September

Bahrain's main Shia opposition groups pull out of talks with the Government in protest of the arrest of a leading member of al-Wefaq, the main Shia opposition society.

2014, January

The Government suspends deadlocked reconciliation talks with the Shia opposition.

2014, July

Bomb blast kills police officer, the latest in a series of attacks on security forces.

2014, October

Al-Wefaq to seize their activities for three months, the court ruled.

2014, November

Parliamentary elections are boycotted by the Shia opposition as a farce.

2014, March

Bahrain, Saudi Arabia, and the UAE temporarily withdraw their ambassadors from Qatar after alleging it has been meddling in their internal affairs.

2014, December

Leader of al-Wefaq opposition society, Sheikh Ali Salman, is arrested. Protests and clashes between his supporters and security forces ensue.

2015, March

Bahrain and four other GCC states take part in Saudi-led airstrikes on Houthi rebels in Yemen.

2017, January

Bahrain executes three Shiites convicted of killing three policemen in a bomb attack in 2014—the country's first execution in six years.

2018, July

King Hamad sends Sheikh Isa Qasim abroad to get treatment and pays for it.

2018, November

Elections take place with a 67% turnout, and the first woman chairs the CoR.

2019, April

138 citizenships were revoked in a mass trial for a Hezbollah cell, while sixty nine were sentenced to life imprisonment.

2019, April

King reinstates citizenship for 551 inmates out of 985 who lost it after being accused of treason and being part of armed groups attempted failed coup.

2019, July

Three men executed. One non-national accused of murdering a   n Imam. The other two, Bahrainis charged with murdering a policeman during riots.

2020, November

Prime Minister, Prince Khalifa dies. Crown Prince, Shaikh Salman replaces him.

2020, September

Bahrain & UAE validate the Abraham Accords part of an Agreement with Israel, overseen by USA.

Introduction

While the whole world was riveted by the events in Tunisia, Egypt, Libya, and Syria, little attention was given to the effects of the pan-Arab unrest, best known as the Arab Spring, felt in Bahrain. On February 14, 2011, Bahrainis came out to demand reforms through a termed revolution. At the center of the revolution were longstanding grievances over the distribution of wealth and power, including calls for a fully elected Government, representative elected Council, and free elections. Like in uprisings of other Arab countries, it inspired a new generation of protestors from a wide range of backgrounds who did not feel represented by existing political associations.

In no time and without any introductions, the calls for reform became calls for overthrowing the Government and the royal family. The peaceful demonstrations transformed into anarchy and riots calling for a complete shutdown of the Government, presenting the royal family prominent members to court, and announcing Bahrain as an Islamic republic.

Eighteen members of the Council of Representatives, Shura Council members, and Ministers resigned their posts in protest of the way the state responded to such radical calls—all of whom were exclusively Shiites.

The protests eventually ended, but the series of events that unfolded prior, during, and afterward has been the subject of much controversy. At first, it seemed peaceful and cross-sectarian, but the situation became progressively more violent and more complex, heightening the Sunni-Shia split. Two narratives developed from these events; neither is wholly accurate and perhaps more importantly, neither holds a basis for a solution.

The strong political stances taken by both the Government and the mainstream opposition societies regarding the 2011 uprising in the Kingdom of Bahrain has generated significant tensions and the circulation of diverse narratives, not only on the events of the protests but on the Bahraini political system overall. The most marked division in the trajectories of the narratives by the Government and the mainstream political opposition lies within the response to the revolution in Bahrain during the Arab Spring.

It is crucial to understand Bahrain's unique position in the uprising as compared to other Arab nations and, therefore, the unique effects it had on the political scene in the Kingdom. In an age where information is readily available by various means to all, providing the right information becomes crucial—especially information that decision-makers rely on. Many statements were made internationally by formal and informal bodies on the events taking place during February and March of 2011 in the Kingdom of Bahrain and were retracted after the realization that they were made without the full knowledge of the intricate elements that shape the political landscape of the Kingdom.

Western media reporting on Bahrain has produced a one-dimensional version of a complicated situation, with little attempt to probe realistic political decisions to curb the stalemate that has been in place since 2011. It has characterized the situation as a Tunisian-like struggle of a people against a regime—a Shia underclass versus a Sunna elite—with a focus on the abuse of civilians by Government forces. Even though most opposition is Shia, and there have been serious abuses, the divide in Bahrain is between the Sunna and Shia communities, not between the people and the Government. There is a large Sunni movement that describes itself as opposition but is almost completely ignored in Western reporting, and the calls for reform that began in 2011 have a long history in Bahrain. One can argue that in the last couple of years, everything pertaining to the political realm is as contested as it is complicated.

This book was developed to establish a comprehensive reference to the political scene in the Kingdom of Bahrain with the objective of showcasing the elements involved in the political configuration of Bahrain. Ultimately, the goal is to provide an outlook of the political system, an understanding of the events that explain the political, sectarian tensions and grievances in the island, the socio-political history, political affiliations, and how they started, what led to the unrest in Bahrain, and the current tensions in the political landscape. The aim is to group all related information in one well-referenced publication to serve as a reference on the Bahraini matter in the political arena and provide a basis for a solution to the friction and possible areas of improvement that can contribute to the building of a superior political structure in the Kingdom of Bahrain.

Kingdom of Bahrain

Geography

History

Culture

Education

Economy

Government

Foreign Relations

Demographics

Ethnic Groups

Religion

Languages

History of the Flag

Flag prior to 1820

Flag used between 1820 and 1932

Flag used from 1932 to 1972

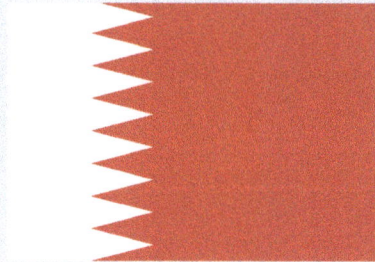

Flag used between 1972 and 2002

official flag since 2002

Royal flag since 2002

Coat of Arms

Royal Coat of Arms

Name:	Kingdom of Bahrain
Capital:	Manama
Official Language:	Arabic
King:	His Majesty King Hamad bin Isa al-Khalifa
Crown Prince:	Crown Prince & Prime Minister HRH
	Shaikh Salman bin Hamad bin Isa al-Khalifa
Independence Day:	August 15, 1971 (from the United Kingdom)
Government:	Constitutional Monarchy
Legislature:	The National Assembly is made of the
	Consultative Council and Council of Representatives
Location:	Arabian Gulf
Area Size:	779.95 Sq. Kilometers
Population:	Total: 1,501,611
Bahraini:	677,506 (45%)
Non-Bahraini:	823,610 (55%)
GDP (PPP):	Total -- $69,922 billion (2017 Estimates)
Per Capita:	$51,956
GDP (nominal):	Total -- $34,310
Per Capita:	$25,494 (2017) Estimates

The Kingdom of Bahrain is a small island and archipelago in the Arabian Gulf. It is located between the state of Qatar and the North-Eastern Coast of Kingdom of Saudi Arabia. The country has a total population of 1,501,611, with a total of 823,610 non-nationals.

Bahrain is the location of the ancient Dilmun civilization. It was renowned throughout the ancient world for its pearls up to the 19th century. The Portuguese occupied it in 1521. In 1602, Shah Abas I of the Safavid Dynasty chased out the Portuguese. The Bani Utbah clan conquered it in 1783, and the al-Khalifa Royal family have been ruling it since then.

In 1800, after a series of treaties, it became a British protectorate. It received its independence in 1971. From this period, it was an emirate until 2002, when it was declared a Kingdom.

Although oil is the mainstay of Bahrain's economy, it has tried to diversify. It has invested heavily in the banking and tourism sector. Thus, many financial institutions are located in the capital of Manama.

The country boasts a high Human Development Index, and the World Bank categorizes it as a high-income country.

Governorates

Capital Governorate

Population: 561,880
Size: 79 Km

Muharraq Governorate

Population: 268,626
Size: 67 Km

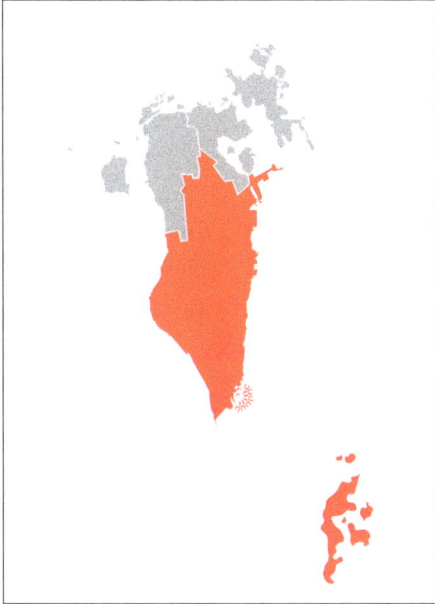

Southern Governorate

Population: 309,426
Size: 489 Km

Northern Governorate

Population: 363,159
Size: 146 Km

Geography

Bahrain originally had a land area of 665 km², but due to land reclamation, it has increased to its present size of 770 km². It is the third-smallest nation in Asia, behind the Maldives and Singapore.

It is an archipelago that is arid, flat and is located in the Arabian Gulf. The archipelago initially consisted of 33 islands, but due to aggressive land reclamation, since 2008, there are 88 islands in the archipelago today.

The country does not share a land border with any other country. However, it has a coastline of 16km.

The Kingdom has mild winters and long, hot summers. The seas around the country are shallow. As a result, they heat up quickly and result in high humidity. In summer, the temperature can reach up to 50° C. Rainfall is quite irregular, with the highest recorded maximum being 71.88 mm.

History

From Antiquity to Prophet Mohamed

In the earliest periods of antiquity, Bahrain was home to the Dilmun Civilization. It served as a trade center linking Mesopotamia with the Indus Valley. It was later ruled by the Assyrians and Babylonians from the sixth to the third century BC.

The Greeks referred to it as Tylos during the classical era. Under the rule of Alexander the Great, it became a part of the Hellenized world. In addition, it was the site of numerous Greek athletic contests..

Ardashir, the first ruler of the Sassanid Dynasty, defeated Sanatruq, the ruler of Bahrain in the third century AD, and incorporated it into the Sassanid Empire. Bahrain's pre-Islamic population consisted mainly of Christian Arabs, Jews, and Zoroastrians.

During the time of Prophet Muhammad, he had his first interaction with Bahrain when he led an attack against several tribes who were assembling there against him. The assembling tribes retreated when they saw that the Prophet was coming to attack them. According to traditional Islamic accounts, the Prophet sent al-Ala'a al-Hadrami as an envoy to Bahrain. The local ruler, Munzir Ibn-Sawa al-Tamini, responded positively by converting the entire area.

From the Middle Ages to the Arrival of the Bani Utbah Tribe

The Qarmatians, an Ismaili sect of Islam, seized Bahrain in 899 AD. In AD 976, the Abbasid Dynasty defeated the Qarmatians. They remained in Bahrain until 1076, when the Uyunid Dynasty defeated them and took control of Bahrain. In 1253, the Bedouin Usfurids defeated the Uyunids and, subsequently, controlled Eastern Arabia, which included Bahrain.

In 1330, Bahrain was made a tributary to the rulers of Hormuz. However, it was ruled locally by the Shiite Jarwanid Dynasty of Qatif. In the 15th century, it came under the control of the Jabrids, a Bedouin dynasty from the province of al-Ahsa'a in eastern Saudi Arabia.

In 1521, the Portuguese, allied with Hormuz, took control of Bahrain. They were expelled in 1602 by the Safavid Dynasty of Persia. The island remained under the control of Persians until the Bani Utbah conquered it in 1783. The al-Khalifa family was the head of the Bani Utbah tribe and, subsequently, became the rulers of Bahrain.

Colonial History

Early in the 19th century, regional and world powers tried to conquer Bahrain and threaten its sovereignty. To protect their position, the al-Khalifa family sought British protection. Even though they were recognized as Bahrain's rulers by the British in 1820, the Egyptian Government forced them to pay yearly tribute in 1830.

In 1860, Bahrain's al-Khalifas sought Persian and Ottoman protection due to fears of British conquest. This did nothing to prevent the British Government of India from overpowering Bahrain when the Persians refused to protect Bahrain. Bahrain was then placed under the British control and protection by Colonel Pelly's new treaty.

With the end of the Qatari-Bahraini war in 1868, the British signed another treaty with the al-Khalifas. This treaty prohibited the al-Khalifas from distributing territories except to Britain. They could also not enter into agreements with other foreign governments without first seeking British permission.

In 1892, the British established complete dominance over Bahrain due to civil unrest from the Bahraini people.

Bahraini merchants demanded a limit on British authority in 1911. They were arrested and exiled to India. Under a series of administrative reforms, the British replaced Shaikh Isa bin Ali with his son. Three years later, they made Charles Belgrave the de facto ruler of Bahrain. He served as an adviser to the ruler until 1957.

The Bahrain Petroleum Company discovered oil in 1931 in Bahrain. Production began the following year, and it led to the rapid modernization of the country.

In the 1950s, Bahrain was beset by sectarian clashes. This led the National Union Committee, a group formed by reformists, to demand an elected popular assembly. They also demanded the removal of Belgrave and organized several protests and general strikes. In 1965, there was a month-long uprising after hundreds of workers were sacked from the Bahrain Petroleum Company.

Independence to the new millennia

As independence from colonial Britain approached in 1971, the Shah of Iran claimed sovereignty over Bahrain. Despite this, he eventually gave in to a referendum for independence on August 15 by the United Nations.

Bahrain greatly benefited from the oil boom of the 1970s. It also benefited from the Lebanese civil wars of the 1970s and 1980s. This was because it became the Middle East's financial hub after many banks left Beirut during the wars, and settled in Bahrain.

Following the Iranian Revolution of 1979, led by an Iranian, some Bahraini Shia fundamentalist following the teachings of Ayatollah Khomeini attempted a failed coup in 1981 to export their revolution concept. Bahrain witnessed another uprising from 1994 to 2000. This uprising saw the alliance of leftists, liberals, and Islamists.

The uprising ended after King Hamad bin Isa al-Khalifa became Emir in 1999. He introduced several democratic reforms, including establishing an elected Council of representatives, giving women the right to vote and run for office, and releasing and pardoning exiled and political prisoners. This was carried out under the National Action Charter, which was widely accepted by a referendum, with 98.4% in favor, on February 14–15, 2001. As part of the implementation of the charter, the country became known as the Kingdom of Bahrain.

This political liberalization of Bahrain allowed it to sign a Free Trade Agreement with the United States in 2004.

During the Arab Spring of 2011, Bahrain's Shia started a revolution to oust the Sunni rulers. The Government initially allowed the protests, but subsequently, it had to put an end to them when the Shia refused to engage in earnest dialogue, especially after the protests became violent.

Culture

Islam is the dominant religion in Bahrain, and it reflects heavily on the local culture, though Bahrainis are known for their tolerance toward other religions. Marriages between Bahrainis and expatriates are common. In addition, Filipino-Bahrainis have integrated well into society. A living example is the Filipino child actress Mona Marbella Alawi.

The style of music in Bahrain is similar to what one would find in the region. Popular styles include the Khaliji and the Sawt. Ali Bahar played a central role in Bahraini musical culture. He is arguably one of the most popular singers in Bahrain, and he performed reggae and rock with his band *al-Ekhwa* `The Brothers`. Other classical names include Ahmed al-Jumairi, Khalid al-Sheikh, and the internationally acclaimed Maestro Waheed al-Khan.

The Bahrain Culture and Antiquities Authority (BACA) was established in 2015, with a mandate that includes overseeing the culture sector. The authority is headed by Shaikha Mai al-Khalifa, who played a major role in transforming the cultural scene. The authority took over the old houses and restored and transformed them into modern museums carrying the names of those who originally built them. Also, the authority launched the Spring of Culture festival, attracting families and art lovers from around the region, with names such as Fairouz and Andrea Bocelli attending.

Football is the most popular sport in the country. The national team has participated in the Arab Nations Cup, Asian Cup, and the FIFA World Cup Qualifiers. However, it has never been able to qualify for the World Cup, but won the GCC Cup for the first time in 2019. The country also has a Formula One racetrack and has hosted the Bahrain Grand Prix for the past 16 years.

Education

The year 1919 marked the beginning of the modern public school system in Bahrain when the al-Hidaya al-Khalifia School for Boys was established in Muharraq. In 1926, the Education Committee inaugurated the second public school for boys in Manama, and in 1928, the first public school for girls was opened in Muharraq.

Education in Bahrain is compulsory, and all school-age children attend either public or private schools. Children with disabilities attend specialized institutions. The Ministry of Education in Bahrain provides free education for all Bahraini and non-Bahraini students in public schools. Additionally, the Ministry provides free textbooks in every subject for all students in public schools at the beginning of each academic year.

Education in public schools is segregated: there are separate schools for boys and girls, with teaching and administrative staff of the same gender. However, in some instances, boys' public primary schools exist where the teaching and administrative staff are mixed. A choice of coeducation or segregation is available in private schools, while state universities are all coeducational.

In 2004, His Majesty King Hamad introduced a project that uses information and communication technology (ICT) to support primary and secondary education in Bahrain. This project is named King Hamad's Schools of the Future. The objective of this project is to link all schools within the Kingdom via the internet and introduce the concept of electronic education.

In addition to British intermediate schools, the island is served by the Bahrain School, a United States Department of Defense school that provides a K–12 curriculum, including the International Baccalaureate.

Private schools also exist that offer either the IB Diploma Programme or UK A levels. In 2007, St Christopher's School became the first school in Bahrain to offer a choice of IB or A levels for students. Numerous international educational institutions and schools have established links to Bahrain.

The Kingdom encourages institutions of higher learning, drawing on expatriate talent and the increasing pool of Bahraini nationals returning from abroad with advanced degrees. The University of Bahrain has been established for standard undergraduate and graduate study, and the College of Health Sciences, operating under the direction of the Ministry of Health, trains nurses, pharmacists, and paramedics. Both the Arabian Gulf University and Bahrain Medical University certify physicians.

The National Action Charter, passed in 2001, paved the way for the formation of private universities, and over thirteen currently operate in Bahrain. Asian institutes have also been established to provide quality education to Asian students. These include the Pakistan Urdu School and the Indian School, which provide for the needs of children whose families hail from the Indian Subcontinent and are residents of Bahrain.

Economy

Oil is a significant revenue earner for Bahrain. Despite this, the country is seriously diversifying away from the oil sector. It invests a lot in its financial sector and tourism to create an alternative for oil.

In 2006, a United Nations Economic and Social Commission for Western Asia report stated Bahrain was the fastest-growing economy in the Arab world. Additionally, based on the 2011 Index of Economic Freedom, Bahrain is the freest economy in the Arab world and the 12th freest in the world.

The Global Financial Centers Index listed Bahrain as the world's fastest-growing financial center in 2008. The financial sector has been able to grow at a rapid pace due to the stable demand for oil during periods under review.

Oil is Bahrain's top export, accounting for 11% of its GDP, including 60% of export receipts and about 70% of Government revenues. The second top export for Bahrain is aluminum, while finance and construction materials follow closely behind.

About 2.9% of the land in Bahrain is arable, and agriculture accounts for just 0.5% of its GDP. As a result, Bahrain depends heavily on imports for its food. Most of its meat comes from Australia, while it imports about 75% of its fruits.

In 2004, the free-trade agreement the country negotiated with the United States reduced trade barriers between both countries. However, due to the combination of the world financial crisis, the fall in oil prices, and unrest, the growth rate of its economy fell to 2.2% in 2012.

Following the oil price drop in 2016, the Kingdom faced some difficulties. This was felt through rapid inflation, the newly introduced VAT tax, and the pulling of support from many state-subsidized goods and services.

The 2030 Economic Vision

The 2030 Economic Vision, launched by King Hamad Bin Isa al-Khalifa in October 2008, embodied a comprehensive vision for the Kingdom of Bahrain that was aimed at creating a transparent approach to developing its economy while focusing on the main objective of improving the living standards of all Bahraini citizens.

The vision was launched after four years of elaborate discussions with a group of decision-makers in the public and private sectors, including Government institutions and concerned entities, in addition to several think tanks and international institutions. The Economic Vision 2030 focuses on crystallizing an integrated socio-economic Government, as well as the following three basic principles: competitiveness, integrity, and sustainability.

After the launch of the Economic Vision 2030, the Kingdom of Bahrain began an institutional economic reform program in line with its objectives. This led to the preparation of a national economic strategy that represents a roadmap to achieving the vision. This strategy is continuously revised to adapt to global changes and the Government's work program.

National Development Strategy

The Government developed a National Economic Strategy for the planning period of 2008–2014 to guide the direction of the economy and Government. It illustrated the links between Government policies, identified key initiatives to be implemented over the planning period, assigned responsibility for the initiatives, and outlined the actions necessary to achieve them.

Ever since the Economic Vision 2030 and the accompanying National Economic Strategy were adopted by the Kingdom, much progress has been achieved in reforming Bahrain's economy and increasing the effectiveness of Government institutions.

In light of experience and changing circumstances, the National Development Strategy presented the next step in Bahrain's journey toward the attainment of the vision, as it outlined the medium-term strategic direction of the country in the 2015–2018 planning period.

Tourism & Sustainable Growth

Represented by the Bahrain Tourism and Exhibitions Authority, Bahrain has always stressed the importance of shifting the tourism sector to be one of the main contributors to the economy. Bahrain implemented measures to increase the sector's contribution to GDP to reach 7% by 2018 in an aim to implement the Government's vision toward strengthening the economy in non-oil sectors and to highlight the Kingdom of Bahrain as a regional and global tourism hub.

The Kingdom has witnessed a significant improvement in the tourism sector in 2015–2016, demonstrated by the increase in the number of visitors to Bahrain, from 11.6 million visitors in 2015 to 12.3 million visitors in 2016, registering an annual growth rate of 6%. There was also an increase in the ratio of the number of hotel guests, which rose from 1.2 million to 1.3 million, an increase of 5%. The rise in these key indicators had a positive impact on the rate of tourist residency, which recorded an annual rise of 21.7%, from 2.3 days to 2.8 days. This directly impacted the rate of tourism's contribution to the annual non-oil GDP of the Kingdom by 37%, which contributed to the 4.6% non-oil GDP for 2015 increasing to a rate of 6.3% in 2016.

Women's Role in the Economy

The Economic Development Board expects an annual 5% increase in the contribution of women to the Bahraini economy, to 45.6% in 2020.

According to statistics from the Information and Government Authority, the number of Bahraini women joining both the private and public sectors reached 35.7% of the total workforce in 2015.

The education and health sectors continued to be favored by Bahraini women. However, the number of women working in financial services, commerce, and construction increased significantly. The relative growth in the number of working women is attributed to the rise in academic qualifications as the percentage of women earning academic certifications reached 60% of all graduates.

In the field of business and entrepreneurship, the percentage of commercial registrations owned by women has grown from 39% to almost 41%, an increase of 1.96% from 2010 to June 2014. Besides, the percentage of commercial registrations that have been active for more than five years has reached 56% of the total active commercial registration records.

The contribution of the various economic sectors in the gross domestic product (2015)	
Sector	Contribution Percentage
Agriculture and fishing	0.32%
Building and construction	7.39%
Commerce	4.61%
Financial projects	17.18%
Government services	14%
Hotels and restaurants	2.44%
Oil and natural gas	13.35%
Processing industries	17.34%
Real estate and business services	5.70%
Social and personal services	6.04%
Transport and telecommunications	7.52%
Water and electricity	1.41%

Government

Presently, Bahrain is a constitutional monarchy headed by King Hamad bin Isa al-Khalifa. The King has a broad range of executive powers. He heads the military, appoints the Prime Minister, appoints the upper house of the National Assembly, dissolves the lower house, and chairs the judicial Council.

The Prime Minister is the head of Government. The present Prime Minister is Shaikh Khalifa bin Salman al-Khalifa. He has been the Prime Minister since 1971.

The legislature of Bahrain is bicameral, with a Shura Council and a Council of Representatives.

The Shura Council has forty members who are appointed by the King every four years. The Council of Representatives also has forty members who are elected for four-year terms.

Laws passed by the Council of Representatives have to be approved by the Shura Council. The King then has to give his assent. If he doesn't, the law can only be passed by a two-thirds majority of both houses.

Foreign Relations

Bahrain plays a moderating role in regional politics. It adheres to the views of the Arab League on a two-state solution for the Israeli-Palestinian issue.

It is also one of the founding members of the Gulf Cooperation Council (GCC). It founded the GCC with five other states on May 26, 1981. It has carried out all GCC policies on economic and security cooperation. In 1994, it supported the GCC decision to drop all secondary and tertiary sanctions against the state of Israel.

The present Bahraini Foreign Minister is Abdullatif bin Rashid al-Zayani. He started his career as a Mathematics and Statistics Professor at the University of Maryland. Prior to this post he served as Secretary General of the Cooperation Council for the Arab Gulf States from 2011 until 2020 ..

In 2006, Bahrain got elected to head the UN's General Assembly. As an appreciation of this honor, the country appointed Haya bint Rashid al-Khalifa as the president of the assembly. She is the first Middle Eastern woman and the third woman to hold the position.

During the Arabian Gulf War of 1990 to 1991, Bahrain was a member of the coalition that acted to free the state of Kuwait. The coalition's air force operated from the Shaikh Isa Air Base, while its fleets operated from Manama. During this period, the capital was hit by Scud missiles fired from Iraq. At the break of hostilities, Bahraini students in Iraq and Kuwait went missing. It is suspected that they were victims of Saddam Hussein's secret police.

After the successful liberation of Kuwait, the United States of America and Bahrain strengthened their ties by signing a ten-year agreement in October 1991. The agreement allowed American forces to get access to Bahraini facilities. It also allowed America to relocate and store equipment for future crises. In 1995, America established the US Fifth Fleet in the Arabian Gulf and had its headquarters in Manama.

Bahrain took an active part in the coalition that fought to remove the Taliban and Al Qaeda fighters from Afghanistan in 2001. Due to this, George Bush recognized Bahrain as a major non-NATO ally.

However, in the runup to the US operation in Iraq, Bahrain offered asylum to Saddam Hussein as a way to reduce tension, much to the annoyance of Washington.

Bahrain's relationship with Iran is quite tense. This is due to Iran's role in the attempted 1981 coup by Shiite fundamentalists. There are also Bahraini suspicions of an Iranian role in the unrest of the 1990s. Also, occasional claims of sovereignty over Bahrain by Iranian officials exist. The US also accused Iran of sponsoring the 2011 protests in Bahrain.

Bahrain has had a long-standing dispute with Qatar over the Hawar Islands. Fortunately, this was resolved in a compromise decision by the International Court of Justice in 2001. Relations between Bahrain and Qatar had improved until 2017, when Bahrain, Saudi Arabia, and the Emirates took a stand against Qatar, accusing it of taking part in the unrest in Bahrain and supporting unrest in the region.

In 2011, Bahrain requested the help of Arab gulf states to put an end to the unrest that occurred.

The country has bilateral relationships with more than 190 countries all over the world. It has twenty five embassies to the Arab League, three consulates to the United Nations, and four permanent missions to the European Union. It also has thirty six embassies from different countries.

Bahrain and the United Nations

- Bahrain's first participation in the UN was in the 21st Session in 1966.

- Bahrain joined the UN on September 21, 1971.

- Bahrain chaired the Security Council in December 1998.

- Bahrain received non-permanent membership to the Security Council from 1998 to 1999.

- The UN endorsed Shaikha Haya Rashed al-Khalifa as a chairwoman of the 61st General Assembly (September 2006 - September 2007), making her the first Arab and Muslim woman to chair the assembly.

Demographics

Bahrain has a total population of 1,501,611 people, with 823,610 being non-nationals. Although the majority of the Bahraini population is Middle Eastern, a sizeable percentage of the population is from South Asia. In 2008, about 290,000 Indians lived in Bahrain. This makes them the single largest non-national group in the country.

Bahrain is the fourth most densely populated sovereign state in the world, with a population density of about 1,646 people per km2. The northern parts of the island are more densely populated than the southern parts. A lot of the Bahraini population is concentrated in the Northern Governorate of the country. The Northern Governorate has witnessed such large-scale urbanization that it is usually referred to by some as a single metropolitan area.

Ethnic Groups

Bahrain is also ethnically diverse. The Shia population is divided into Baharna and Ajam. Most of the Shia population is Baharna. The Shia Ajam are descended from Iran and are typically referred to as Persian Shias, while a small majority of Shia Bahrainis are Hasawis from al-Ahsa'a, the eastern province of Saudi Arabia.

The Sunni Bahrainis are also divided into two groups: Arabs and Huwala. The Sunni Arabs are the most influential group. They hold most governmental positions, and the royal family is Sunni Arabs. The Huwala are Iranian Sunnis. A small minority of Sunnis have Baloch origins. Bahrainis of African origin come mostly from East Africa and are concentrated in Riffa and on Muharraq Island.

Religious and Ethnic Groups in Bahrain

MUSLIMS

SUNNITES

The native Sunni population has been historically compartmentalized into the three groups listed below, with the Sunni Arabs forming the majority of the Bahraini population.

Sunni Bahrainis are mostly concentrated in areas such as Riffa, Busaiteen, Budaiya, Jasra, Zallaq, Askar, Jaw, al-Dour, West Eker, and Um al-Hassam, among others.

Arabs

Sunni Arabs are mostly descendants of tribes from central Arabia and are the most influential ethnic group in Bahrain. They hold the most Government positions, and the Bahraini monarchy is Sunni Arabs. Sunni Arabs have traditionally lived in areas such as Zallaq, Muharraq, Riffa, and the Hawar Islands.

Afro-Arabs

Most Bahrainis of African descent originate from East Africa and have traditionally lived on Muharraq Island and in Riffa.

Huwala

The Huwala are the descendants of Sunni Iranians who migrated to the Arab states of the Arabian Gulf during the 19th century or later. Many of them originally lived in al-Awadhiya and al-Hoora, both of which are now exclusively populated by foreigners of Filipino, Indian, and Bengali origins. However, they later resettled to Muharraq Island and Riffa.

SHIITES

Baharna

The Baharna claim they are the original pre-Islamic inhabitants of Bahrain. However, this is disputed by scholars. The Baharna are closely related to the Shia of Qatif and even speak a similar dialect. The Baharna live in Manama, in almost all the villages of the main island of Bahrain, several villages on the island of Muharraq in the north, and on the island of Sitra to the east. They speak similar dialects with slight variations between villages, although the villages of Sitra have dialects that differ considerably from those of the main island. Palm tree farming and fishing were the traditional economic activities of the Baharna.

There are also Shia Arabs concentrated in several neighborhoods in Muharraq city. They originally came from al-Hasa and are called *Hasawis*, and many of them were initially Sunnites. They are distinct from the Baharna from villages outside the city proper. As a result of their proximity to surrounding Sunni Arabs and Africans, they speak the Sunni dialect.

Ajam

The Shia Persians of Bahrain are a significant and influential ethnic minority whose ancestors arrived in Bahrain in the early 20th century as laborers, artisans, and merchants. There are large communities in Muharraq and Manama. Persians maintain a distinct culture and language but have long since assimilated into Bahraini culture. They tend to identify themselves more as Persian Bahrainis or Bahrainis than Iranians. Almost all are bilingual in Arabic and Persian, with school, work, and daily affairs conducted in Arabic and Persian usually relegated to the family domain. Almost all have possessed Bahraini citizenship since birth. In most cases, their parents, and in some cases their grandparents, are also holders of Bahraini citizenship.

JEWS

Bahraini Jews constitute one of the world's smallest Jewish communities. Today the community has a synagogue with thirty seven people and a small Jewish cemetery.

There are Talmudic references of a Jewish community in the geographic areas of present-day Bahrain as well as references in Arabic texts of a Jewish presence in Hajar (eastern coast of inland Arabia) dating back to the Prophet Mohammed's time.

CHRISTIANS

Native Christians that hold Bahraini citizenship are approximately 1,000.

The majority of Christians are originally from Iraq, Palestine, and Jordan, with a small minority having lived in Bahrain for many centuries; the majority have been living as Bahraini citizens for less than a century. There are also smaller numbers of native Christians who originally hail from Lebanon, Syria, and India.

The majority of Christian Bahraini citizens tend to be Orthodox Christians, with the largest church by membership being the Eastern Orthodox Church. They enjoy religious and social freedom. Bahrain has Christian members in the Bahraini Government. Bahrain is one of two GCC countries to have a native Christian population; the other country, Kuwait, also has a Christian population but in smaller numbers, with less than 400 Christian Kuwaiti citizens.

Eastern Orthodox Christians in Bahrain traditionally belong to the jurisdiction of the Eastern Orthodox Patriarchate of Antioch and all of the East. The Eastern Orthodox parish in Bahrain was organized in the year 2000 by Constantine Papastephanou of Baghdad and Kuwait, who also had ecclesiastical jurisdiction over the Eastern Orthodox in Bahrain and the United Arab Emirates.

Foreign citizens who live and work in Bahrain make up the majority of Christians in Bahrain. They include people from Europe, North and South America, Africa, Asia, and the

Middle East. They belong to various Catholic, Orthodox, and Protestant churches.

ASIANS

INDIANS

There were 197,273 Indian workers and 56,666 dependents as of 2014—the last population census conducted in the Kingdom and most of the public sector. Most of them are either Hindus or Christians, with a sizable Sikh and Muslim minority. There are multiple schools that were established in the country in the 20th century that offer the CBSE curriculum, the oldest of which is the Indian School, which was first established in 1950.

PAKISTANIS

In 2014, there were 39,765 Pakistani workers in Bahrain and 8,647 dependents, and a further 30,000 have been given citizenship. A 2011 estimate states that 10,000 of them serve in security forces. The vast majority of Pakistanis in Bahrain are Muslim.

BANGLADESHIS

Bangladesh recognized and established diplomatic ties with Bahrain in 1974, although Bangladeshi expatriates started arriving decades before that. In 2014, there were 92,193 working in Bahrain and 3,116 dependents.

SRI LANKANS

In 2014, there were 5,790 Sri Lankan workers in Bahrain and a further 1,632 dependents.

FILIPINOS

In 2014, there were 25,568 Filipino workers in Bahrain and a further 3,189 dependents.

OTHERS

EGYPTIANS

In 2014, there were 8,083 workers and 10,176 dependents living in Bahrain.

BRITISH

In 2014, there were 2,367 British workers in Bahrain and 1,710 dependents. However, the *Gulf News* states there were 9,000 permanent British residents in 2013 and that 240 were given citizenship.

Religion

Bahrain has a majority Muslim population, which means that Islam is the official religion of Bahrain. There are no official figures for the proportion of Shias and Sunnas in Bahrain. According to the 2010 census, about 866,888 people are Muslim.

There is a small native Christian community in Bahrain. However, a combination of expatriates and natives puts the number of Christians at 367,683 as of the 2010 census. There is also a relatively small Jewish community in Bahrain. In total, they number about thirty seven.

Due to the influx of migrant workers from South Asian countries like India, Sri Lanka, and the Philippines, the proportion of Muslims as a percentage of the population has steadily decreased. In 2001, Muslims made up about 81.2% of Bahrain's population. In 2010, this percentage dropped to 70.2%. In the 2001 census, about 9.8% of the population were Hindus and other religions. There are no corresponding figures for the 2010 census because it combined all non-Muslim religions in a single group.

Languages

The official language of Bahrain is Arabic. There is a Bahraini dialect of Arabic that differs significantly from standard Arabic. Arabic is essential in Bahrain. A person cannot become a member of Parliament if he is not fluent in Arabic.

A significant number of Bahrainis and non-Bahrainis speak Persian, the official language of Iran. Some others speak Urdu, the official Pakistani language. Other languages spoken in their corresponding immigrant communities include Malayalam, Nepali, Tamil, and Hindi.

However, all commercial institutions and road signs are bilingual, which means there is always an English and Arabic translation for them.

Constitution

On June 20, 1972, the Bahraini Emir, Shaikh Isa bin Salman al-Khalifa, issued a royal decree enjoining the creation of an assembly to draft the Constitution. The newly created Constitutional Assembly presented a draft consisting of 109 articles and five significant chapters: The State, Basic Principles of Society, General Rights and Duties, Branches of the Government, and General Rules and Procedures. The Emir promulgated the Constitution on December 6, 1973.

The Constitution was based on several pivotal principles specified in Articles 1, 2, and 33. First, it established Bahrain as *a sovereign independent Islamic Arab* state with democratic governance. Next, the Constitution stated that the rule of the Shaikh is hereditary. Furthermore, it proclaimed Islam the official religion of the state and that the Emir was the head of the state.

The establishment of the Constitution also envisioned the adaption of the formal structure of Government. Article 43 urged the establishment of the National Council, which was to be the sole legislative body. In the original Constitution, the National Council included only the elected Council of Representatives, which consisted of 40 members. Its first session took place on December 16, 1973. Members of the Council were directly elected by their respective constituents.

The original Bahraini Constitution aimed to introduce the concept of separation of powers. To some degree, it managed to do so by introducing independent legislative, executive, and judicial branches of Government. Nevertheless, all legislative, executive and judicial decisions were still strictly dependent on the approval of the Emir. Specifically, legislation only became law after being studied and ratified by the ruler. Additionally, although Article 101 of the Constitution established an autonomous judiciary independent of any outside influence, all judicial decisions were made in the name of the Emir.

Remarkably, the fundamental principles defined in the original Bahraini Constitution bared a number of similarities with those of the Qatari Constitution. Notably, the Bahraini Constitution, just like the Qatari Constitution, proclaimed the country a sovereign and independent Arab state. Similar to the Qatari Constitution, the Bahraini Constitution promulgated Islam to the status of the official religion and established Sharia law as the primary source of legislation, but not limited to it. Furthermore, the Bahraini Constitution also stated that the Emir is the head of state and that his power is hereditary.

However, due to the growing animosity between the National Council and the ruling family, the Emir officially abrogated it in 1975. Following the abrogation of the Constitution, the discontent among the Shia community erupted into violent clashes. After widespread protests, thousands of arrests, and even bombings in the capital, the Emir issued a decree to establish the Shura Council in 1992 in an effort to squelch the unrest. Composed of thirty members but later expanded to fourty , this new Council ultimately failed at placating the opposition. Meanwhile, violence was only gaining momentum.

Contemporary Constitution

After the demise of the Emir, Shaikh Isa bin Salman al-Khalifa, in 1999, his son Hamad bin Isa al-Khalifa came to power with the express intention of reform. In a referendum that was supported by 98.4% of votes, the National Action Charter—a revamp of the Constitution—was established in February 2001. The National Action Charter introduced the 40-member Council of Representatives (CoR), and the first elections were held in 2002. Together with the appointed Shura Council, the CoR comprised the National Assembly, in other words, the Bahraini Parliament.

However, the King issued the Amended Constitution on February 14, 2002, which later came to be known as the New Constitution. Notably, this new Constitution was derivative of the original Constitution of 1973 in many aspects. Before proceeding to a more detailed description of this Constitution's content, it is essential to delineate the four main points that it encompasses. First, the Constitution maintains Bahrain as a hereditary, constitutional monarchy, with the King as the official head of state.

Next, it stipulates the form of Government as a sovereign democracy and guarantees the freedoms of its citizens. Furthermore, the Constitution introduces the concept of separation of powers, though it places the King as the vanguard of all three branches. Additionally, it states that the National Assembly is bicameral: the lower house is directly elected by secret ballot, and the Upper House, which serves as an advisory body, is appointed solely by the King.

The King

As per the Constitution, the King exercises the powers of appointing and dismissing the Prime Minister and the Council of Ministers and has the right to put forth a law for a popular referendum. The King also serves as the Commander in Chief of the armed forces and holds power to appoint military, judicial, and civil officials, ambassadors, and the delegates of the Shura Council. Furthermore, the King's powers include ratifying amendments, proposing and vetoing legislation, as well as awarding honors and granting pardons. Since the Constitution establishes the position of the King as hereditary, the only legal mechanisms of removal provided by the Constitution are resignation or death.

The Executive

The Prime Minister and the Council of Ministers supervise the Government and the implementation of national policy, while the Prime Minister also oversees the activities of the Council of Ministers. The Constitution further states that both the Prime Minister and the Council of Ministers serve as advisers to the King. When it comes to the mechanisms of removal of the Prime Minister and the Council of Ministers, the Constitution provides more diverse options: removal can be achieved either through the King's order, by resignation, or

Government Structure as per the Constitution

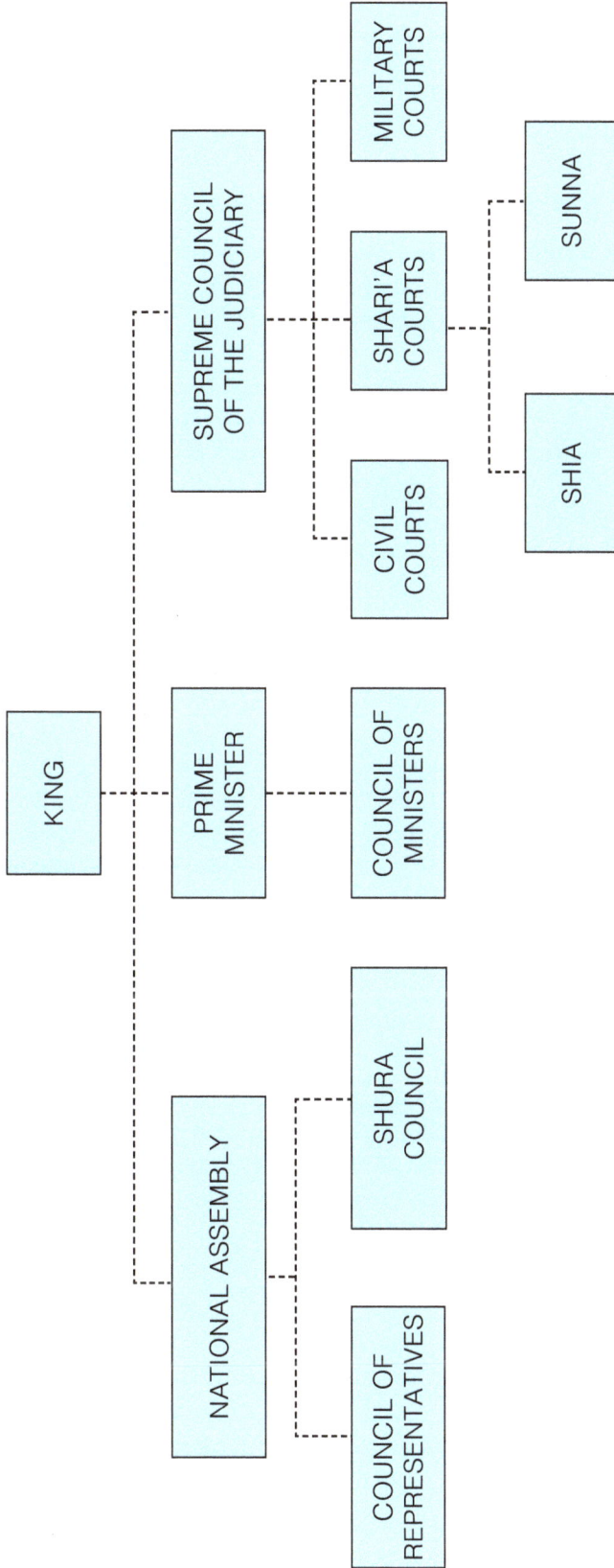

```
                              KING
                               |
         ┌─────────────────────┼─────────────────────┐
         |                     |                     |
  NATIONAL ASSEMBLY      PRIME MINISTER      SUPREME COUNCIL
                                             OF THE JUDICIARY
         |                     |                     |
    ┌────┴────┐                |          ┌──────────┼──────────┐
    |         |                |          |          |          |
  SHURA    COUNCIL OF     COUNCIL OF    CIVIL    SHARI'A    MILITARY
 COUNCIL   REPRESENTATIVES  MINISTERS   COURTS    COURTS     COURTS
                                                    |
                                              ┌─────┴─────┐
                                             SHIA       SUNNA
```

as a consequence of a vote of no confidence by the Council of Representatives. Concurrently, the Council of Ministers can be dissolved by the Prime Minister or in case of the Prime Minister's resignation.

The Legislative and the Parliament

The legislative branch of the Government, the National Assembly, is established through Chapter IV of Section 3 of the Constitution. The National Assembly is delegated with two chambers—the Council of Representatives and the Shura Council, first established in 1992 as an attempt to placate the community and prevent further clashes. It is composed of fourty members appointed by the King and serves as an advisory body to the King. Members of the Shura Council serve four-year terms and have the power to veto legislation. The Shura Council is formally limited to amending draft legislation and reviewing the annual budget in tandem with the CoR. The CoR is composed of fourty members who are directly elected by their constituents. Each representative has the power of interpellation and a vote of no confidence, which can be achieved through a two-thirds supermajority vote.

The Council of Representatives is further stratified into five permanent committees: The Legislative and Legal Affairs Committee; the Financial and Economic Affairs Committee; the Foreign, Defense, and National Security Affairs Committee; the Services Committee; and the Environment Committee. Composed of eight members, the Legislative and Legal Affairs Committee reviews draft laws and assists in compiling legislative texts. The Financial and Economic Affairs Committee is occupied with socioeconomic development and financial matters, including budget planning. The Foreign, Defense, and National Security Committee prioritizes the Kingdom's international outlook and is composed of seven members. The Services Committee also comprises seven members and is tasked with implementing educational and other social policies, such as labor and media affairs, cultural, health, and sports issues. The Committee on the Environment specializes in housing and postal, agricultural, infrastructure, and water matters.

The Judiciary

The Kingdom of Bahrain has a dual court system consisting of both Civil and Sharia courts. In Article 104, the Constitution stipulates that the judiciary is entirely independent and that *under no circumstances may the course of justice be interfered with.* According to the Constitution, Sharia—Islamic law based on the Qur'an, Hadith, and Sunna—is the principle source of law in the Kingdom of Bahrain (Art.2).

The civil branch of the judicial system is three-tiered, dealing with commercial, civil, and criminal cases as well as cases about the personal status of non-Muslims. The Courts of Minor Causes (also referred to as the Lower Courts or Courts of Execution) have jurisdiction over civil and commercial cases. The Middle Courts, on the other hand, deal with criminal cases. The High Court of Appeal, otherwise known as the Senior Civil Court, is the second level of the Bahraini judicial system, whereas the Court of Cassation is at the very top. The Court of Cassation is the final court of appeal for all matters of a civil, commercial, or criminal nature.

The Sharia court system handles cases related to the personal status of Muslims regardless of their status as Bahraini nationals. There are two levels within the Sharia side of the judicial system: the Senior Sharia Court and the High Sharia Court of Appeal. At each level, there are two distinct courts, one for Sunna Muslims and the other for Shia Muslims. In July of 2017, the personal status law (also known as the family law) was finally codified across both the Sunna and Shia Sharia courts, meaning standardized law will be applicable for citizens from both sects.

Bahrain additionally has a system of Military Courts whose jurisdiction is limited to offenses committed by members of the armed and security forces and those with national security offenses.

Governance of the Judiciary

The Supreme Council of the Judiciary (SCJ) was established in 2000 to supervise the judicial system. According to the 2002 Constitution, the King is the chair of the SCJ. The other members are judges from the Court of Cassation and the Highest Courts of Appeal.

National Safety Court

In March of 2011, a period of unrest and Martial Law, a special military court was created to try illegal protesters, rioters, their leaders, and self-acclaimed activists. This court, named the Court of National Safety, is presided over by two civil judges and one military judge, all appointed by the commander in chief of the Bahraini Defense Force. All cases are prosecuted by the public military prosecutor.

Constitutional Court

The Constitution also established a Constitutional Court, comprising a president and six members who are all appointed by royal order. This court is tasked with ensuring the constitutionality of all laws and statutes. The King may refer any draft legislation to this court to assess its compatibility with the Constitutional Court's decisions, which are binding on everyone, including all state authorities.

Constitution and the Civil Rights Provisions

The civil rights of citizens are emphasized in Chapter II of the Constitution. Freedom, equality, trust, and knowledge are thereby established as the backbone of Bahraini society. The rights of children and the elderly, as well as rights pertaining to gender equality, are protected by Articles 4 and 5 of the Constitution. Article 8 gives every citizen access to healthcare. Chapter III, Article 18 further solidifies citizens' rights and freedoms by maintaining that *People are equal in human dignity, and citizens are equal before the law in public rights and duties. There shall be no discrimination among them based on gender, origin, language, religion, or creed.*

Articles 19, 20, and 21 of the Constitution give citizens the right to justice. Specifically,

Article 19 ensures proper evidence collection and protection from unjustified arrests; additionally, it prohibits cruel treatment and torture. Meanwhile, Article 20 safeguards due process and the presumption of innocence as well as the right to counsel, and Article 21 establishes extradition procedures and prohibits extradition of political refugees.

Fundamental human freedoms and rights are also expressed in Articles 18 and 19 and are expanded on in Articles 22 to 29. In their respective order, freedom of religion is guaranteed by Articles 18 and 22; freedom of movement is ensured by Article 19; Article 22 establishes freedom of opinion, while Article 23 postulates freedom of expression; Article 24 maintains freedom of press; Articles 25 and 26 warrant privacy rights of citizens; and freedom of association, assembly, and petition are protected by Articles 27, 28, and 29 respectively. Evidently, the Constitution provides a comprehensive range of fundamental civil liberties and rights.

Another issue is the relatively low representation of women within the Bahraini Government and CoR. Unlike the constitutions of Afghanistan, post-Saddam Iraq, and Algeria, to name a few, the Bahraini Constitution does not stipulate any sort of electoral quota for female representation. An electoral quota is commonly instituted in countries where female representation is low, particularly due to residual societal or religious norms. Such a quota is an effective way of ensuring a minimum number of female representatives are appointed or elected but does not change the mindset of society. The Constitution ensures that equality between the two genders is in place, and the King took that into consideration by increasing the number of appointed women either in the Shura Council or as Ministers, which set an excellent example to the masses. This resulted in the election of six women (including the speaker of the house) in 2018, compared to no females in 2002.

Challenging Areas

According to the Constitution, the process of adopting a law requires approval by the Council of Representatives, the Shura Council and, subsequently, ratification by the King. Importantly, this mechanism presupposes that the Shura Council possesses legislative powers. Such delegation of powers served as a catalyst for discontent among the opposition. Arguing that the National Action Charter did not envision legislative powers for the Shura Council, the opposition considered this amendment illegitimate, even though they did not do the proper legislative due diligence prior to encouraging their followers to vote in approval. Consequently, the opposition boycotted the first elections in 2002 under the new Constitution, which could have been their proper political tool to alter it. The Shura Council, as its members are appointed by the King, was also denounced by the opposition as a safeguard against the elected Council of Representatives and, thus, a way to dilute popular opinion.

The committee, initially created for drafting the National Action Charter and composed of 46 members, drew inspiration from the constitutional models of Singapore, Egypt, UK, and Kuwait. The National Action Charter made Parliament bicameral, where the first chamber is directly elected and the second chamber is appointed by the King and serves an advisory function. However, the amendments to the Constitution of 2002 gave the Shura Council legislative capacity by requiring approval to pass a law and giving its president a vote in the event of a deadlock. Accordingly, this system only alienated the opposition and resulted in their ensuing boycott of parliamentary elections and political life.

Amendments to the Constitution

In an attempt to settle the unrest of the Arab Spring, King Hamad bin Isa al-Khalifa announced a national reconciliation dialogue. Aimed at bridging the enmity between the components of the Bahraini society and the Government, this dialogue introduced constitutional reforms. Equivocal to a degree, the brochure of the Bahraini Council of Representatives from 2016 states the following about the outcomes of the dialogue: *One of the primary issues that were agreed upon at the dialogue is holding an expanded series of amendments to the Constitution of the Kingdom to enrich the political experience and the constitutional institutions of the state.*

Constitutional Amendments

1. Citizenship And Nationality

Bahraini nationality shall be determined by law. A person inherently enjoying his Bahraini nationality cannot be stripped of his nationality except in case of treason, and such other cases as prescribed by law. (Art. 17)

A Constitutional Court shall be established and shall comprise a President and six members, all of whom are appointed by a Royal Order for a period specified by the law. The court's area of competence is to watch over the constitutionality of laws and statutes.

2. Jurisdiction And Access

The law shall state the regulations that ensure that the members of the Court are not liable to dismissal, and specifies the procedures that are followed before the Court. The law shall guarantee the right of the Government, Consultative Council, the Chamber of Deputies and notable individuals and others to challenge before the Court the constitutionality of laws and statutes. ...

The King may refer to the Court any draft laws before they are adopted to determine the extent of their agreement with the Constitution. ... (Art. 106)

3. Education

a. The State sponsors the sciences, humanities and the arts, and encourages scientific research. The State also guarantees educational and cultural services to its citizens. Education is compulsory and free in the early stages as specified and provided by law. The necessary plan to combat illiteracy is laid down by law.

b. The law regulates care for religious and national instruction in the various stages and forms of education, and at all stages is concerned to develop the citizen's personality and his pride in his Arabism. (Art. 7)

4. Employment Rights And Protection

a. Work is the duty of every citizen, is required by personal dignity and is dictated by the public good. Every citizen has the right to work and to choose the type of work within the bounds of public order and decency.

b. The State guarantees the provision of job opportunities for its citizens and the fairness of work conditions.

c. Compulsory work cannot be imposed on any person except in the cases specified by law for national exigency and for a fair consideration, or pursuant to a judicial ruling.

d. The law regulates the relationship between employees and employers on an economic basis while observing social justice (Art. 13)

5. Equality And Non-Discrimination

Justice is the basis of Government. Cooperation and mutual respect provide a firm bond between citizens. Freedom, equality, security, trust, knowledge, social solidarity and equality of opportunity for citizens are pillars of society guaranteed by the State. (Art. 4)

6. Equality And Non-Discrimination

b. The State guarantees reconciling the duties of women towards the family with their work in society, and their equality with men in political, social, cultural, and economic spheres without breaching the provisions of Islamic canon law (Shari'a). ... (Art. 5)

7. Equality And Non-Discrimination

People are equal in human dignity, and citizens are equal before the law in public rights and duties. There shall be no discrimination among them on the basis of sex, origin, language, religion or creed. (Art. 18)

8. Obligations Of The State

b. The King safeguards the legitimacy of the Government and the supremacy of the Constitution and the law and cares for the rights and freedoms of individuals and organizations. … (Art. 33)

9. Limitations And/Or Derogations

The public rights and freedoms stated in this Constitution may only be regulated or limited by or in accordance with the law, and such regulation or limitation may not prejudice the essence of the right or freedom. (Art. 31)

10. Limitations And/Or Derogations

It is impermissible to suspend any provision of this Constitution except during the proclamation of martial law, and within the limits prescribed by the law. It is not permissible under any circumstances to suspend the convening of the Consultative Council or the Chamber of Deputies during that period or to infringe upon the immunity of their members, or during the proclamation of a state of national safety. (Art. 123)

11. Marriage And Family Life

a. The family is the basis of society, deriving its strength from religion, morality, and love of the homeland. The law preserves its lawful entity, strengthens its bonds and values, under its aegis extends protection to mothers and children, tends the young and protects them from exploitation and safeguards them against moral, bodily and spiritual neglect. The State cares in particular for the physical, moral and intellectual development of the young.

b. The State guarantees reconciling the duties of women towards the family with their work in society, and their equality with men in political, social, cultural, and economic spheres without breaching the provisions of Islamic canon law (Shari'a).

c. The State guarantees the requisite social security for its citizens in old age, sickness, disability, orphanhood, widowhood or unemployment, and also provides them with social insurance and healthcare services. It strives to safeguard them against ignorance, fear and poverty.

d. Inheritance is a guaranteed right governed by the Islamic Shari'a. (Art. 5)

12. Participation In Public Life And Institutions

e. Citizens, both men, and women are entitled to participate in public affairs and may enjoy political rights, including the right to vote and to stand for elections, in accordance with this Constitution and the conditions and principles laid down by law. No citizen can be deprived of the right to vote or to nominate oneself for elections except by law. … (Art. 1)

13. Participation In Public Life And nstitutions

b. The State guarantees reconciling the duties of women towards the family with their work in society, and their equality with men in political, social, cultural, and economic spheres without breaching the provisions of Islamic canon law (Shari'a). … (Art. 5)

14. Participation In Public Life And Institutions

b. Citizens are equal in the assumption of public posts in accordance with the conditions specified by law. (Art. 16)

15. Government

d. The King appoints and dismisses the Prime Minister by Royal Order, and appoints and dismisses Ministers by Royal Decree as proposed by the Prime Minister. ... (Art. 33)

16. Government

The Council of Ministers shall consist of the Prime Minister and a number of Ministers. (Art. 44)

17. Government

a. The incumbent of a Ministry must be a Bahraini, aged not less than 30 years by the Gregorian Calendar and must enjoy full political and civil rights. Unless otherwise provided, the provisions pertaining to Ministers apply also to the Prime Minister. ... (Art. 45)

18. Head Of State

b. The regime of the Kingdom of Bahrain is that of a hereditary constitutional monarchy, which has been handed down by the late Shaikh Isa bin Salman al-Khalifa to his eldest son Shaikh Hamad bin Isa al-Khalifa, the King. Thenceforward it will pass to his eldest son, one generation after another, unless the King in his lifetime appoints a son other than his eldest son as successor, in accordance with the provisions of the Decree on inheritance stated in the following clause.

c. All provisions governing inheritance are regulated by a special Royal Decree that will

have a constitutional character, and which can only be amended under the provisions of Article 120 of the Constitution. ... (Art. 1)

19. Head Of State

a. The King is Head of State, and its nominal representative and his person are inviolate. He is the loyal protector of the religion and the homeland, and the symbol of national unity. ... (Art. 33)

20. Legislature

The National Assembly consists of two Chambers: The Consultative Council and the Chamber of Deputies. (Art. 51)

21. Legislature

The Consultative Council consists of forty members appointed by Royal Decree, in accordance with the procedures, conditions, and the method defined by Royal Decree. (Art. 52)

22. Legislature

A member of the Consultative Council must be a citizen of Bahrain, and for naturalized citizens at least ten years must have elapsed since acquiring their citizenship. He must not be a citizen of another country, with the exception of citizens of the member state the Cooperation Council of the Arab States of the Gulf, on the condition that his Bahraini citizenship be his original citizenship. He must enjoy full civil and political rights, and must be enrolled in an electoral register. His age must not be less than 35 years by the Gregorian calendar on the date of appointment, and he must have the requisite experience or have performed a valuable service to the nation. (Art. 53)

23. Legislature

The Chamber of Deputies comprises forty members elected by a direct, secret general ballot in accordance with the provisions of the law. (Art. 56)

24. Legislature

A member of the Chamber of Deputies must meet the following requirements:

a. He must be a citizen of Bahrain, and for naturalized citizens at least ten years must have elapsed since acquiring their citizenship. He must not be a citizen of another country, with the exception of citizens of the member states of the Cooperation Council of the Arab States of the Gulf, on the condition that his Bahraini citizenship is original citizenship. He must enjoy full civil and political rights and must be enrolled in the in an electoral register.

b. On the day of his election, he must be not less than thirty years of age by the Gregorian Calendar.

c. He must read and write Arabic fluently. … (Art. 57)

25. Political Rights And Association

e. Citizens, both men, and women are entitled to participate in public affairs and may enjoy political rights, including the right to vote and to stand for elections, in accordance with this Constitution and the conditions and principles laid down by law. No citizen can be deprived of the right to vote or to nominate oneself for elections except by law. … (Art. 1)

26. Political Rights And Association

b. The State guarantees reconciling the duties of women towards the family with their work in society, and their equality with men in political, social, cultural, and economic spheres without breaching the provisions of Islamic canon law (Shari'a). … (Art. 5)

27. Political Rights And Association

The freedom to form associations and unions on national principles, for lawful objectives and by peaceful means is guaranteed under the rules and conditions laid down by law, provided that the fundamentals of the religion and public order are not infringed. No one can be forced to join any association or union or to continue as a member. (Art. 27)

28. Property, Inheritance And Land Tenure

d. Inheritance is a guaranteed right governed by the Islamic Shari'a. (Art. 5)

29. Property, Inheritance And Land Tenure

c. Private ownership is protected. …

g. The State shall make the necessary arrangements to ensure the exploitation of land suitable for productive farming, and shall strive to raise the standards of farmers. The law lays down how small farmers are to be helped and how they can own their land. … (Art. 9)

30. Protection From Violence

a. The family is the basis of society, deriving its strength from religion, morality, and love of the homeland. The law preserves its lawful entity, strengthens its bonds and values, under its aegis extends protection to mothers and children, tends the young and protects them from exploitation and safeguards them against moral, bodily and spiritual neglect. ... (Art. 5)

31. Protection From Violence

c. Compulsory work cannot be imposed on any person except in the cases specified by law for national exigency and for a fair consideration, or pursuant to a judicial ruling.

... (Art. 13)

32. Protection From Violence

d. No person shall be subjected to physical or mental torture, or inducement, or undignified treatment, and the penalty for so doing shall be specified by law. Any statement or confession proved to have been made under torture, inducement, or such treatment, or the threat thereof, shall be null and void. (Art. 19)

33. Public Institutions And Services

c. The State guarantees the requisite social security for its citizens in old age, sickness, disability, orphanhood, widowhood or unemployment, and also provides them with social insurance and healthcare services. It strives to safeguard them against ignorance, fear and poverty.... (Art. 5)

34. Status Of International Law

a. The application of this Constitution does not breach the treaties and agreements which Bahrain has concluded with states and international organizations.

b. Exceptionally to the provisions of the second clause of Article 38 of this Constitution,

all laws, laws by Decrees, Decrees, statutes, orders, edicts and circulars that have been issued and are in force prior to the first meeting convened by the National Assembly remain proper and valid, unless amended or rescinded in accordance with the regulations prescribed in this Constitution. (Art. 121)"

35. Religious Law

In the name of God on high, and with His Blessing, and with His help, we Hamad bin Isa al-Khalifa, Sovereign of the Kingdom of Bahrain, in line with our determination, certainty, faith, and awareness of our national, pan-Arab and international Responsibilities; and in acknowledgment of our obligations to God, our obligations to the homeland and the citizens, and our commitment to fundamental principles and our responsibility to Mankind. ...

This amendment has taken account of all the lofty values and the great human principles enshrined in the National Action Charter. These values and principles confirm that the people of Bahrain surge ahead in their triumphant march towards a bright future, God willing, a future in which the efforts of all parties and individuals unite, and the authorities in their new garb devote themselves to achieve the hopes and aspirations under his tolerant rule, declaring their adherence to Islam as a faith, a code of laws and a way of life, with their affiliation to the great Arab nation, and their association with the Gulf Cooperation Council now and in the future, and their striving for everything that will achieve justice, good and peace for the whole of Mankind.

The amendments to the Constitution proceed from the premise that the noble people of Bahrain believe that Islam brings salvation in this world and the next, and that Islam means neither inertness nor fanaticism but explicitly states that wisdom is the goal of the believer wherever he finds it he should take it, and that the Qur'an has been remiss in nothing.

In order to achieve this goal, it is essential that we listen and look to the whole of the human heritage in both East and West, adopting that which we consider to be beneficial and suitable and consistent with our religion, values and traditions and is appropriate to our circumstances, in the conviction that social and human systems are not inflexible tools and instruments which can be moved unchanged from place to place, but are messages conveyed to the mind, spirit and conscience of man and are influenced by his reactions and their circumstances of his society.

Thus these constitutional amendments are representative of the advanced cultural thought of our beloved nation. They base our political system on a constitutional monarchy founded on counsel [shura], which in Islam is the highest model for governance, and on the people's participation in the exercise of power, which is the foundation of modern political thought. ...

(Preamble)

36. Religious Law

a. The Kingdom of Bahrain is fully sovereign, independent Islamic Arab State ... (Art. 1)

37. Religious Law

The religion of the State is Islam. The Islamic Shari'a is a principal source for legislation. ... (Art. 2)

38. Religious Law

b. The State guarantees reconciling the duties of women towards the family with their work in society, and their equality with men in political, social, cultural, and economic spheres without breaching the provisions of Islamic canon law (Shari'a). ...

d. Inheritance is a guaranteed right governed by the Islamic Shari'a. (Art. 5)

Status of the Constitution

b. The King safeguards the legitimacy of the Government and the supremacy of the Constitution and the law, and cares for the rights and freedoms of individuals and organizations. ... (Art. 33)

39. Status of the Constitution

a. The application of this Constitution does not breach the treaties and agreements which Bahrain has concluded with states and international organizations.

b. Exceptionally to the provisions of the second clause of Article 38 of this Constitution, all laws, laws by Decrees, Decrees, statutes, orders, edicts and circulars that have been issued and are in force prior to the first meeting convened by the National Assembly remain proper and valid, unless amended or rescinded in accordance with the regulations prescribed in this Constitution. (Art. 121)

40. Military Judiciary 2017

b. A law to reposition military judiciary and outlines its jurisdiction in Defense Force, National Guard and Public Security. ... (Art. 105)

Ruling Family

HRH King Hamad bin Isa al-Khalifa
HRH Prince Salman bin Hamad al-Khalifa
Ruling Family Council

Bahrain became a constitutional monarchy after King Hamad bin Isa al-Khalifa initiated wide-ranging political reforms. His reforms were in line with the National Action Charter, a package of political changes endorsed by the people of Bahrain. In a popular referendum, 98.4 percent of the population voted in favor of creating a constitutional monarchy in Bahrain.

Prior to 2002's popular referendum, the al-Khalifa family has ruled Bahrain since the 17th century. They first arrived in the Gulf coast region after migrating with other tribesmen from what's known today as Kuwait. Together, the al-Khalifa family and the other tribesmen formed a group called the al-Utub, and consequently, they became known as the Banu-Utuba. The Banu-Utuba went to the Qatar Peninsula and made their first occupation of Bahrain in 1700. The founder of the current al-Khalifa family, Shaikh Khalifa bin Mohammed, left Kuwait after the death of his son Shaikh Mohammed bin Khalifa. The al-Khalifas then settled in present-day Qatar until Shaikh Nasser bin Mathkoor, the governor of Bahrain, attacked the al-Khalifas' territory in 1783. Shaikh Khalifa's brother, Shaikh Ahmed, was in charge of defending Zubara while his brother was on his pilgrimage to Mecca. Shaikh Ahmed's forces succeeded in defending his territory and had his forces seize Awal, the old name of Bahrain. Ultimately, Shaikh Ahmed (also known as Ahmed al-Fateh) became the first al-Khalifa ruler of the Bahrain islands because his brother passed away while in Mecca.

King Hamad's great-great-grandfather Shaikh Isa bin Ali al-Khalifa was one of the longest-reigning monarchs of the Gulf region. His reign lasted sixty three years. In 1923, he was forced to abdicate his power by the British political advisor. Isa bin Ali's successor, Hamad bin Isa, was considered only a vice-ruler until Isa's death in 1932. Hamad bin Isa then ruled Bahrain from 1932–1942. Under his rule, he regularly invited prominent noblemen and political figures from the United Kingdom and elsewhere to dine at the Emiri Palace. Hamad was succeeded by Salman bin Hamad al-Khalifa. Salman's son Isa bin Salman succeeded him and ruled Bahrain from 1961–1999.

HRH King Hamad bin Isa al-Khalifa

After succeeding his father, King Hamad served as Bahrain's second Emir. He began his primary education at the age of six, in addition to reciting the Holy Quran and studying the principles of Islam and the Arabic language. In 1964, after completing his primary education with honors, he was proclaimed Crown Prince on June 27. He went to Leys public school in Cambridge for his secondary schooling and then joined the Mons Officer Cadet School at Aldershot in Hampshire, England. When he returned to Bahrain, he played an active role in preparing the outline of the Bahrain Defense Force (BDF). He was appointed the head of the Defense Directorate and became a member of the State Council in 1970. The following year, he became Minister of Defense. He has been involved in various fields of Bahrain's development, including culture, sports, military, technology, and health sciences.

When King Hamad ascended the throne, his duties included appointing and dismissing the Prime Minister and his Ministers, commanding the army, chairing the Higher Judicial Council, appointing Parliament's upper half, and dissolving its lower half. Under the King's reign, he appointed several Shi'ite individuals into positions in the Government.

HRH Prince Salman bin Hamad al-Khalifa

The eldest son of His Majesty King Hamad bin Isa al-Khalifa and Her Royal Highness Princess Sabeeka bint Ibrahim al-Khalifa is Crown Prince, Deputy Supreme Commander, and Prime Minister Salman bin Hamad al-Khalifa. He received his primary education in Bahrain and subsequently, attended the American University in Washington, DC, graduating with a BA in public administration. He went on to pursue postgraduate studies at the University of Cambridge, where he earned a Master's in Philosophy and History.

His Royal Highness was sworn in as Crown Prince of the State of Bahrain on March 9, 1999, following his father's accession to the throne as Emir of Bahrain, and he assumed the post of Commander in Chief of the Bahrain Defense Force on March 22 the same year. Prior to his appointment as Crown Prince, His Royal Highness Prince Salman served as Undersecretary of Defense from 1995 to 1999 and as vice-chairman and then Chairman of the Bahrain Centre for Studies and Research. On March 3, 2002, he was appointed the Chairman of the Bahrain Economic Development Board (EDB), which is responsible for formulating and overseeing the Kingdom's economic development strategy and attracting foreign direct investment into Bahrain. In January 2008, His Majesty King Hamad appointed His Royal Highness Prince Salman to the post of deputy supreme commander of the armed forces.

In March 2013, His Royal Highness was appointed by His Majesty the King as first deputy Prime Minister. In this capacity, he played a crucial role in promoting development within the Kingdom, as well as supporting the development of significant economic, education, and health services.

In November 2020 he was decreed as Prime Minister succeeding Prince Khalifa bin Salman al-Khalifa.

Ruling Family Council

The al-Khalifa's family Council was based on the provision of Article 21 No. 12 of the Emiri Decree. The Council is responsible for looking after the affairs of minors, deciding upon all personal status matters involving a member of the family, and handling financial affairs for all members of the family.

Decisions in relation to the al-Khalifa family are legislated through the Ruling Family Council. The Council deals with internal family disputes, particularly those relating to the appropriation of land and the acquisition and sale of real estate and other relevant property. Al-Khalifa family members are not allowed to assign such matters to an external court of law.

The law does not require a specific number of members for the court; however, the Ruling Family Council is currently made up of several members who are appointed by order of the King. The Council must include members of the ruling family, but there is the possibility for the inclusion of external professionals.

Bahrain Rulers 1783-2021	
Ruler	Year
Ahmed al-Fateh	1783–1796
Abdulla bin Ahmed al-Khalifa	1796–1843
Salman bin Ahmed al-Khalifa	1796–1825
Khalifa bin Salman al-Khalifa	1825–1834
Mohamed bin Khalifa al-Khalifa	1834–1869
Mohamed bin Abdulla al-Khalifa	1869
Isa bin Ali al-Khalifa	1869–1932
Hamad bin Isa al-Khalifa	1932–1942
Salman bin Hamad al-Khalifa	1942–1961
(Independence 1971)	
Isa bin Salman al-Khalifa	1961–1999
Hamad bin Isa al-Khalifa	1999–Current

Government

Cabinet

The Kingdom of Bahrain has been a Constitutional Monarchy since 2002 when King Hamad held a national referendum. Before King Hamad's ascension to the throne, Bahrain was a British protectorate and maintained close ties with the United Kingdom until its independence in 1971. Two years after Bahrain's independence, the nation adopted its first Constitution, which provided a partially elected National Assembly. When King Hamad succeeded his father as the Emir of Bahrain in 1999, he began to institute reforms for political development and democratization. King Hamad's reforms split the political authority between the King and the bicameral National Assembly. Bahrain's Government is based on the separation of powers, the rule of law, respect for human rights, and freedom of association. However, the King is the designated head of state and commander in chief of the armed forces. He is given the power to appoint Cabinet Ministers, judges, and members of the upper house.

The next political leader under King Hamad is his eldest son, Prime Minister Salman bin Hamad al-Khalifa. Bahrain's Prime Minister is the head of the Government. He is tasked with supervising the performance of the Council of Ministers, the implementation of the Council's decisions, and the coordination between the various ministries. Prince Salman is the Commander in Chief of the Bahrain Defense Force. Prior to his appointment as Prime Minister, Prince Salman has been directly involved in aligning the Government's reform program with the delivery principles and aspirations of the 2001 National Action Charter. Some of the current priorities he is undertaking include strengthening existing institutions, enhancing accountability, and ensuring rights and justice with a focus on improved quality of life and economic growth.

Cabinet

HRH Prince Salman bin Hamad al-Khalifa
The Crown Prince, Deputy Supreme Commander, and First Deputy Prime Minister

H.H. Shaikh Mohamed bin Mubarak al-Khalifa
Deputy Prime Minister

H.H. Shaikh Ali bin Khalifa al-Khalifa
Deputy Prime Minister

H.E. Jawad bin Salem al-Arrayed
Deputy Prime Minister

H.E. Shaikh Khalid bin Abdulla al-Khalifa
Deputy Prime Minister

H.E. Mohamed bin Ebrahim al-Mutawa
Minister of Cabinet

Lt- General Shaikh Rashid bin Abdulla al-Khalifa
Minister of Interior

H.E. Shaikh Khalid bin Ahmed bin Mohamed al-Khalifa
Minister of Foreign Affairs

H.E. Shaikh Salman bin Khalifa al-Khalifa
Minister of Finance and National Economy

H.E. Dr. Majid bin Ali al-Nuaimi
Minister of Education

H.E. Wael al-Mubarak
Minister of Electricity and Water Affairs

H.E. Shaikh Khalid bin Ali bin Abdulla al-Khalifa
Minister of Justice, Islamic Affairs and Endowment

H.E. Essam bin Abdulla Khalaf
Minister of Works, Municipalities and Urban Planning

H.E. Jameel bin Mohamed Ali Humaidan
Minister of Labor & Social Development

H.E. Kamal bin Ahmed Mohamed
Minister of Transportation and Telecommunications

H.E. Bassem bin Yacoub al-Hamar
Minister of Housing

H.E. Ghanim bin Fadhel al-Buainain
Minister for Shura Council and House of Representatives Affairs.

H.E. Faeqa bint Saeed al-Saleh
Minister of Health

H.E. Aymen Tawfiq al-Moayyed
Minister of Youth and Sports Affairs

Major-General Abdulla al-Nuaimi
Minister of Defense Affairs

H.E. Zayed bin Rashid al-Zayani
Minister of Industry, Commerce & Tourism

H.E. Ali bin Mohamed al-Rumaihi
Minister of Information Affairs

H.E. Shaikh Mohamed bin Khalifa al-Khalifa
Minister of Oil

Cabinet Communal Breakdown

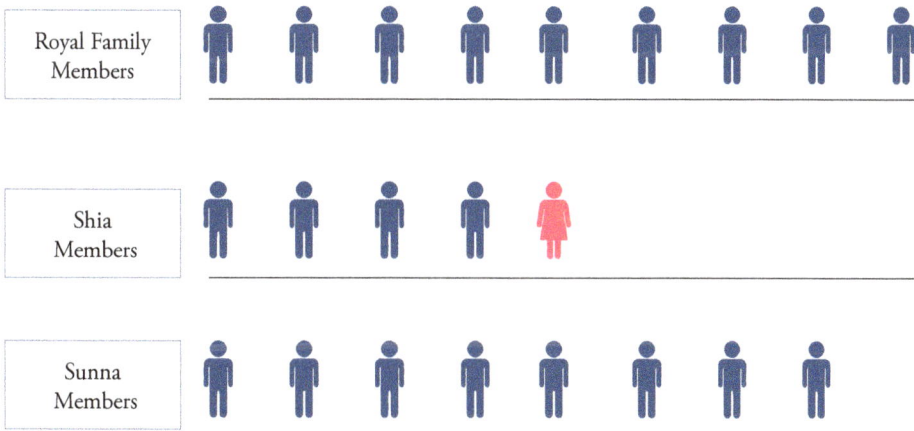

Al-Majalis al-Baladiyah
Municipal Councils

Mandate
Improvement

Bahrain's Municipal Councils were first established in 1919. The first Municipality consisted of eight members, who were elected annually. Under Shaikh Mohammed bin Isa al-Khalifa, the number of Municipality members increased from the original eight to twenty to keep up with the increasing population. At this point in the Municipality's history, Bahrain's economy was growing, which led people to urge the Government to hold an election for the Council. In 1949, the Municipality membership increased to twenty four. Now the Ministry has twenty eight members, of which fourteen members represent the state Ministries, and the other fourteen represent the citizens. The Municipalities are administered from Manama under a central Municipal Council, whose members are appointed by Shaikh Salman bin Hamad.

Currently, there are four governorates in Bahrain, though, in the past, there have been five Governorates. The four governorates are the Capital, Muharraq, Northern, and Southern, while in 2014, the Central Governorate was dissolved. The decision to disestablish the fifth Municipality followed the National Dialogue, which outlined the following five key components: redefining electoral districts; revised appointment process for Shura Council members and measures to ensure Council of Representatives can question actions of Ministers, including the Prime Minister; new rights of approval for Council of Representatives on cabinet appointments; further judicial reform, including strengthening constitutional independence of the judiciary; and new codes of conduct for Security Forces.

Mandate

Today the Ministry of Municipalities Affairs and Urban Planning is tasked with providing extensive services with direct bearing on every home, commercial outlet, and facility that touches every citizen, expat, resident, and employer. Some of the Municipalities' duties include cleaning roads, renting buildings to tenants and shops, expanding roads, opening markets & slaughterhouses, and purifying water.

The Ministry's work also includes coordinating development plans with Bahrain's National Strategic Master Plan. Bahrain is working on updating its development strategies to be in line with the UN's sustainable development goals. In 2016, the Ministry provided the necessary areas to meet the citizens' various development needs, categorically decent housing. Besides, the Councils are essential for their participation in studying urban planning projects to include the needs of their communities within the nation's development process.

Recent developments with the Ministry of Municipalities Affairs and Urban Planning include fruitful cooperation with the legislative and executive branches of Bahrain's Government. The Prime Minister was informed about directives to add more parking lots to old neighborhoods

1927 Municipal Council Members

for the health and education facilities in those areas. Other initiatives from the Municipalities and Urban Planning Ministry include ensuring the health, security, and safety of workers and paying attention to the cleanliness of beaches and harbors.

Within each Municipality, a specific number of city blocks are grouped to form an area. Those areas form a constituency in the country's electorate. Each constituency elects its MP and Municipal Council.

Improvement

Though the Governorates are meant to serve Bahrain's population, the Municipalities could be improved to ensure that the Ministry's work is as practical as it can be. When it comes to Municipal elections, the system remains inequitable. Seat allocation is adjusted to reflect the population distribution, but there are some areas that are more sparsely populated while receiving a disproportionate number of seats. The process of winning a seat also varies. For specific seats, a candidate only requires a few hundred votes, while other governorates require thousands of votes to win a seat. If the Government were to create a uniform voting system where every citizen believes their vote matters, it would help enhance Bahrain's democracy.

Municipal Elections Analysis

2002 Municipal Elected Members

2006 Municipal Elected Members

2010 Municipal Elected Members

2014 Municipal Elected Members

2014 Municipal Appointed Members

2018 Municipal Elected Members

2018 Municipal Appointed Members

History of Candidates Running for Municipal Seats, 2002 - 2014

Male and Female Candidates Running for Municipal Seats, 2002 - 2014

Male and Female Candidates Running for Municipal Seats,
2002 - 2014, Muharraq Governorate

Male and Female Candidates Running for Municipal Seats,
2002 - 2014, Central Governorate

Male and Female Candidates Running for Municipal Seats,
2002 - 2014, Northern Governorate

Male and Female Candidates Running for Municipal Seats,
2002 - 2014, Capital Governorate

Male and Female Candidates Running for Municipal Seats,
2002 - 2014, Southern Governorate

#	Governerate	Constituency	Elected Member	Vote	Percentage
1	Capital	1	Abdulaziz al-Khaja		51.54%
2	Capital	2	Majeed Milad		76.19%
3	Capital	3	Sadiq Rahma		54.20%
4	Capital	4	Mohamed Abdulla		68.40%
5	Capital	5	Tariq Mohamed		75.97%
6	Capital	6	Jaffar al-Qaidoom		52.10%
7	Capital	7	Yousef Hashem		56.89%
8	Capital	8	Shamlan al-Shamlan		60.71%
9	Capital	9	Jameel Khadhem		64.67%
10	Capital	10	Murtada Bader		69.70%
11	Muharraq	1	Khalifa Ali		51.48%
12	Muharraq	2	Salah al-Jowder		51.27%
13	Muharraq	3	Abdulmajeed Abdulrahman	Votes Not Available	70.95%
14	Muharraq	4	Ebrahim al-Doy		77.50%
15	Muharraq	5	Hasan Yousef		56.30%
16	Muharraq	6	Isa al-Majid		50.76%
17	Muharraq	7	Ali al-Muqla		60.49%
18	Muharraq	8	Mohamed al-Wazzan		59.53%
19	Muharraq	9	Sameer Khadem		67.22%
20	Muharraq	10	Mubarak al-Junaid		70.12%
21	Northern	1	Majeed al-Sayed Ali		74.96%
22	Northern	2	Juma'a al-Aswad		88.42%
23	Northern	3	Hashem Khadhem		78.10%
24	Northern	4	Alawi Saeed		56.19%
25	Northern	5	Omran Hussein		54.55%
26	Northern	6	Mubarak al-Dowseri		53.77%

2002 Municipal Elected Members*

#	Governerate	Constituency	Elected Member	Vote	Percentage
27	Northern	7	Mohamed al-Fardan		56.40%
28	Northern	8	Mohamed Ali		55.31%
29	Northern	9	Jawad Fairouz		68.30%
30	Northern	10	Emir Salman		90.30%
31	Central	1	Abbas Mahfoudh		52.90%
32	Central	2	Abdulla al-A'ali		83.24%
33	Central	3	Yousef Buzaid		58.02%
34	Central	4	Isa al-Qadi		52.08%
35	Central	5	Ebrahim Ismail		67.90%
36	Central	6	Ebrahim Ahmed	Votes Not Available	58.44%
37	Central	7	Redha Humaidan		63.00%
38	Central	8	Abdulrahman al-Hasan		63.09%
39	Central	9	Walid Hejres		55.18%
40	Central	10	Ebrahim Fakhro		56.13%
41	Southern	1	Khalid al-Buainaiyn		62.19%
42	Southern	2	Khalid al-Ghanem		64.40%
43	Southern	3	Ali al-Muhannadi		62.65%
44	Southern	4	Abdulrahman Bubshait		50.90%
45	Southern	5	Khalid al-Bufalah		100.00%
46	Southern	6	Adel Hussein		69.70%
47	Southern	7	Khalid al-Buainaiyn		58.24%
48	Southern	8	Hamad al-Fadalah		60.00%
49	Southern	9	Yousef al-Dowseri		62.58%
50	Southern	10	Mubarak al-Dowseri		50.90%

*As per Royal Decree No.3/2002 concerning the Municipal Elections system on 13th Feb, each district consistes of 10 freely elected seats wining by majority of votes (51% or more).

2006 Municipal Elected Members

#	Governerate	Constituency	Elected Member	Vote	Percentage
1	Capital	1	Tariq al-Sheikh	1476	53.27%
2	Capital	2	Majeed Milad	2625	60.26%
3	Capital	3	Sadiq Rahma	2300	70.40%
4	Capital	4	Hameed Ali	4585	94.30%
5	Capital	5	Fadhel Abbas	1349	52.45%
6	Capital	6	Khamis al-Rumaihi	1318	59.42%
7	Capital	7	Abdulmajeed al-Seba'a	1931	54.84%
8	Capital	8	Sadiq al-Basri	2543	62.91%
9	Muharraq	1	Mohamed al-Mutawa	1169	58.45%
10	Muharraq	2	Yousef al-Rayes	1884	55.20%
11	Muharraq	3	Abdulnaser al-Mahmeed	1998	76.94%
12	Muharraq	4	Mohamed Hamada	4341	60.59%
13	Muharraq	5	Ahmed al-Awadhi	1907	51.43%
14	Muharraq	6	Mohamed Abbas	2507	51.70%
15	Muharraq	7	Ali al-Muqla	4931	61.40%
16	Muharraq	8	Sameer Khadem	3162	71.98%
17	Northern	1	Ahmed al-Alawi	8295	79.79%
18	Northern	2	Amin Hasan	6393	95.29%
19	Northern	3	Abdulghani Abdulaziz	5879	78.27%
20	Northern	4	Mubarak al-Dowseri	1119	52.73%
21	Northern	5	Yousef Hussein	4767	87.20%
22	Northern	6	Khalid al-Kaa'bi	4248	67.85%
23	Northern	7	Yousif Rabie	4924	68.57%
24	Northern	8	Ali Abdulla	4617	51.41%
25	Northern	9	Ali Mansour	7002	78.11%

#	Governerate	Constituency	Elected Member	Vote	Percentage
			2006 Municipal Elected Members		
26	Central	1	Abbas Hasan	6480	70.30%
27	Central	2	Adel al-Sitry	6863	83.98%
28	Central	3	Adnan al-Malki	3200	63.83%
29	Central	4	Isa al-Qadhi	3962	63.93%
30	Central	5	Radhi Aman	3846	57.52%
31	Central	6	Sadiq Rabie	4511	66.81%
32	Central	7	Abdulrahman al-Hasan	3350	65.20%
33	Central	8	Walid Hejres	6090	82.23%
34	Central	9	Abdulrazzq Hattab	2596	69.69%
35	Southern	1	Theyab al-Noaimi	1466	64.80%
36	Southern	2	Ali al-Mohannadi	1597	69.01%
37	Southern	3	Mohsen Ali	1132	52.48%
38	Southern	4	Yousef al-Dowseri	442	52.49%
39	Southern	5	Nasser al-Mansori	446	55.27%
40	Southern	6	Mubarak al-Dowseri	100	62.50%

2010 Municipal Elected Members

#	Governerate	Constituency	Elected Member	Vote	Percentage
1	Capital	1	Ghazi al-Dowseri	1282	56.13%
2	Capital	2	Majeed Milad	1888	53.20%
3	Capital	3	Sadiq Rahma	1771	81.00%
4	Capital	4	Mohamed Mansour	3238	87.70%
5	Capital	5	Hussein Gargour	1633	68.00%
6	Capital	6	Adnan al-Noaimi	712	56.02%
7	Capital	7	Fadhel Isa	1469	52.50%
8	Capital	8	Sadiq al-Basri	2467	79.30%
9	Muharraq	1	Mohamed al-Motawa'a	2660	66.24%
10	Muharraq	2	Fatima Salman	1492	52.59%
11	Muharraq	3	Abdulnasseral-Mahmeed	1610	56.70%
12	Muharraq	4	Khalid Bu-Unq	4261	69.17%
13	Muharraq	5	Ghazi al-Murbati	1375	60.02%
14	Muharraq	6	Mohamed Abbas	4037	78.50%
15	Muharraq	7	Ali al-Muqla	3001	52.94%
16	Muharraq	8	Ramzi al-Galaleef	2442	54.19%
17	Northern	1	Ahmed Adnan	7158	85.40%
18	Northern	2	Hussein Mansour	n/a	100.00%
19	Northern	3	Abdulghani Abdulaziz	5460	79.00%
20	Northern	4	Jassim al-Dowseri	1578	61.30%
21	Northern	5	Nader Hussein	4664	82.30%
22	Northern	6	Khalid al-Ka'abi	3260	51.24%
23	Northern	7	Jaafar Sha'aban	5281	64.40%
24	Northern	8	Ali Abdulla Hasan	5766	55.30%
25	Northern	9	Jassim Mahdi	8641	91.90%

			2010 Municipal Elected Members		
#	Governerate	Constituency	Elected Member	Vote	Percentage
26	Central	1	Hussein al-Oraibi	3494	61.56%
27	Central	2	Adil al-Sitry	7025	91.30%
28	Central	3	Khalid Yousef	2268	55.22%
29	Central	4	Ghazi al-Hamar	3921	59.40%
30	Central	5	Abdulredha al-Mohsen	3068	51.30%
31	Central	6	Sadiq Rabie	4886	90.80%
32	Central	7	Ahmed al-Ansari	2868	53.40%
33	Central	8	Yousif al-Sabbagh	4163	55.41%
34	Central	9	Abdulrazzq Hattab	3268	73.90%
35	Southern	1	Mohamed Mousa	2063	62.21%
36	Southern	2	Ali al-Mohannadi	1393	63.70%
37	Southern	3	Mohsen Ali	1644	59.78%
38	Southern	4	Bader al-Dowseri	599	53.10%
39	Southern	5	Nasser al-Mansori	393	50.40%
40	Southern	6	Isa al-Dowseri	n/a	100.00%

2014 Municipal Elected Members*

#	Governerate	Constituency	Elected Member	Vote	Percentage
1	Muharraq	1	Yousif al-Rayes	3266	56.26%
2	Muharraq	2	Mohamed al-Sinan	3545	66.80%
3	Muharraq	3	Najim al-Sinan	3200	65.88%
4	Muharraq	4	Ghazi al-Murbati	3157	53.70%
5	Muharraq	5	Mohamed Herz	3034	55.63%
6	Muharraq	6	Ali al-Nasouh	321	54.87%
7	Muharraq	7	Subah al-Dowseri	4264	51.42%
8	Muharraq	8	Yousif al-Thawadi	3652	57.26%
9	Northern	1	Ali al-Shuwaikh	n/a	100.00%
10	Northern	2	Fatima Abbas	239	64.59%
11	Northern	3	Abdulla al-Dowseri	2294	61.80%
12	Northern	4	Hamad al-Dowseri	769	51.99%
13	Northern	5	Ahmed al-Kooheji	585	58.79%
14	Northern	6	Abdulla Ashour	660	55.46%
15	Northern	7	Budoor bin Rajab	708	55.46%
16	Northern	8	Mohamed bu-Alshouk	2746	52.56%
17	Northern	9	Khalid Qambar	1947	54.78%
18	Northern	10	Taha al-Junaid	4376	64.74%
19	Northern	11	Mohamed Buhamoud	2774	71.42%
20	Northern	12	Hussein al-Khayyat	1229	58.25%
21	Southern	1	Abdulla Mubarak	2557	53.38%
22	Southern	2	Mohamed al-Khal	2595	55.24%
23	Southern	3	Ahmed al-Ansari	3085	53.01%
24	Southern	4	Yousif al-Sabbagh	3072	53.58%
25	Southern	5	Mohamed Mousa	4331	60.51%
26	Southern	6	Najib al-Kuwari	3148	53.90%

#	Governerate	Constituency	Elected Member	Vote	Percentage
			2014 Municipal Elected Members*		
27	Southern	7	Abdullatif Mohamed	2819	59.22%
28	Southern	8	Bader al-Tamimi	2679	71.12%
29	Southern	9	Bader al-Dowseri	2144	60.34%
30	Southern	10	Isa al-Dowseri	927	91.42%

#	Governerate	Member	Position
		2014 Municipal Appointed Members**	
1	Capital	Mohamed al-Khuzaie	Chairman
2	Capital	Mazen al-Omran	Vice-Chairman
3	Capital	Ahmed bin Hindi	
4	Capital	Eman al-Qahtani	
5	Capital	Deema al-Haddad	
6	Capital	Saleh Taradeh	
7	Capital	Abdulwahed al-Nakkal	
8	Capital	Aziza Kamal	
9	Capital	Lamees al-Baharna	
10	Capital	Majdi al-Nasheet	
11	Capital	Maram al-Sharbati	
12	Capital	Maha al-Shehab	
13	Capital	Waheeb al-Nasser	

*In 2014 the Capital Municipality came by Royal appointment instead of elections.
**The number of appointed members in the capital is not fixed.

#	Governerate	Constituency	Elected Member	Vote	Percentage
			2018 Municipal Council Elected Members		
11	Muharraq	1	Waheed al-Mannaie	4165	54.05%
12	Muharraq	2	Hasan Farouq	2981	50.27%
13	Muharraq	3	Basem al-Mujadmi	3292	63.59%
14	Muharraq	4	Ghazi al-Murbati	3170	61.78%
15	Muharraq	5	Saleh Buhaza'a	4762	57.78%
16	Muharraq	6	Fadhel al-Oud	1905	72.02%
17	Muharraq	7	Ahmed al-Muqahwi	7099	69.08%
18	Muharraq	8	Abdulaziz al-Ka'abi	5037	51.52%
19	Northern	1	Shubbar al-Wedaie	857	58.74%
20	Northern	2	Badriya Ebrahim	n/a	100.00%
21	Northern	3	Mohamed al-Dowseri	2241	58.41%
22	Northern	4	Faisal Shabeeb	2287	52.93%
23	Northern	5	Ahmed al-Kooheji	1393	50.20%
24	Northern	6	Hussein al-A'ali	1427	56.31%
25	Northern	7	Zeina Jassim	1448	52.37%
26	Northern	8	Yassein Zainal	3316	50.90%
27	Northern	9	Abdulla Mubarak	3291	58.80%
28	Northern	10	Mohamed al-Dhahen	5808	68.07%
29	Northern	11	Ahmed al-Mannaie	3723	59.30%
30	Northern	12	Zeinab al-Derazi	2767	60.10%
31	Southern	1	Eman al-Qallaf	2632	53.12%
32	Southern	2	Mallalah Shaheen	3013	59.31%
33	Southern	3	Abdulla Ebrahim	2988	50.50%
34	Southern	4	Omar Abdulrahman	4659	60.48%
35	Southern	5	Abdullatif Mohamed	3682	51.84%
36	Southern	6	Khalid Janahi	3677	60.41%

2018 Municipal Council Elected Members

#	Governerate	Constituency	Elected Member	Vote	Percentage
37	Southern	7	Abdulla Bubshait	3705	54.51%
38	Southern	8	Bader al-Tamimi	4642	75.14%
39	Southern	9	Talal al-Bashir	2096	53.83%
40	Southern	10	Hezam al-Dowseri	539	83.31%

2018 Municipal Appointed Members*

#	Governerate	Member	Position
1	Capital	Saleh Taradeh	Chairman
2	Capital	Aziza Kamal	Vice-Chairman
3	Capital	Khulood Al-Qattan	
4	Capital	Lulwa al-Mutlaq	
5	Capital	Mubarak al-Noaimi	
6	Capital	Mohamed al-Abbas	
7	Capital	Abdulwahed al-Nakkal	
8	Capital	Maha al-Shehab	
9	Capital	Huda Sultan	

*The number of appointed members in the capital is not fixed.

Male Vs. Female Candidates
running for Municipal Councils 2002 - 2014

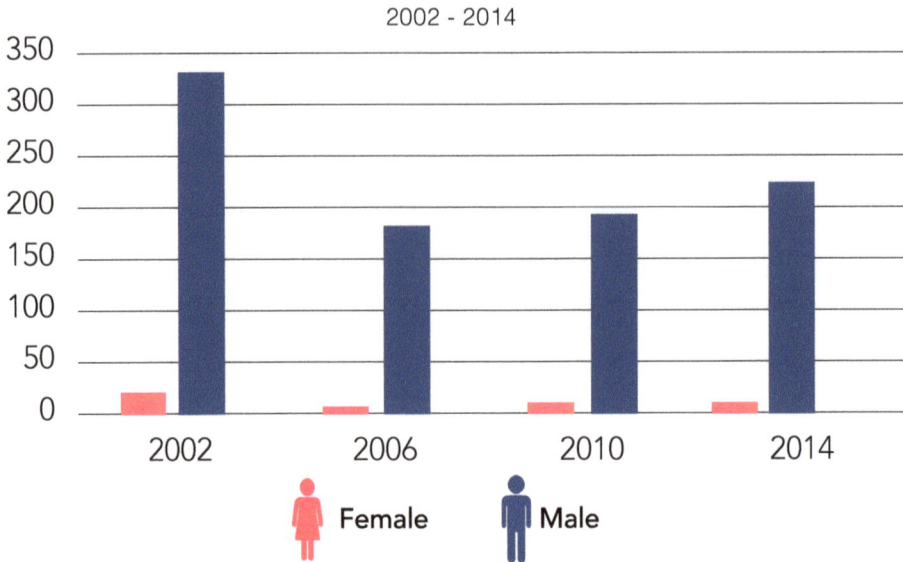

2002 - 2014

	2002	2006	2010	2014
Female				
Male				

Female   Male

Male and Female Candidates
Running for Municipal Seats

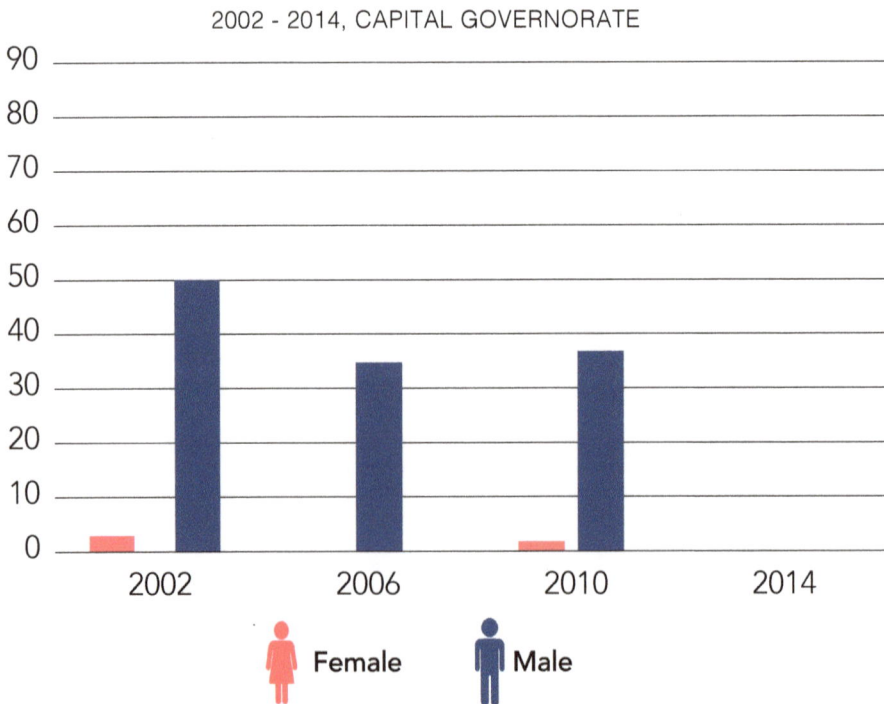

2002 - 2014, CAPITAL GOVERNORATE

	2002	2006	2010	2014
Female				
Male				

Female   Male

Male and Female Candidates
Running for Municipal Seats

2002 - 2014, MUHARRAQ GOVERNORATE

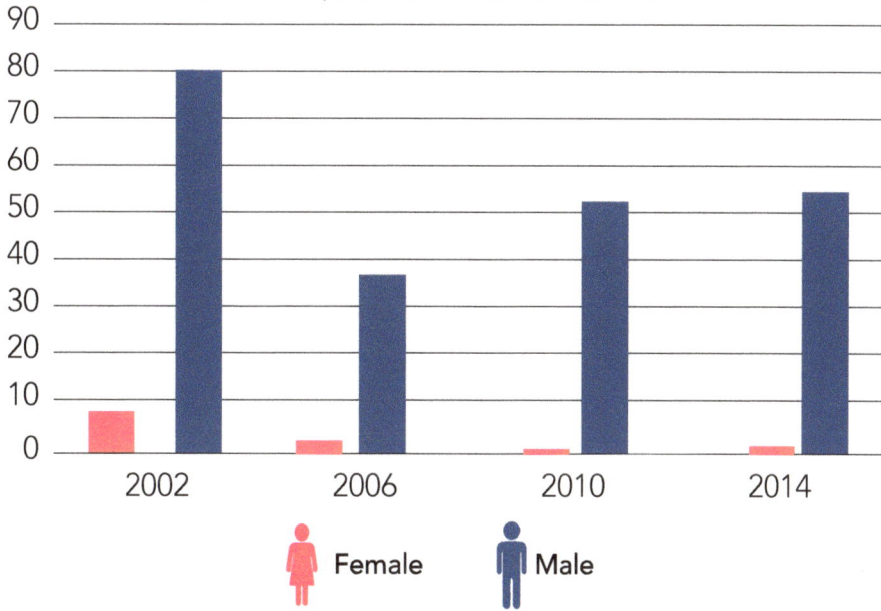

Male and Female Candidates
Running for Municipal Seats

2002 - 2014, CENTRAL GOVERNORATE

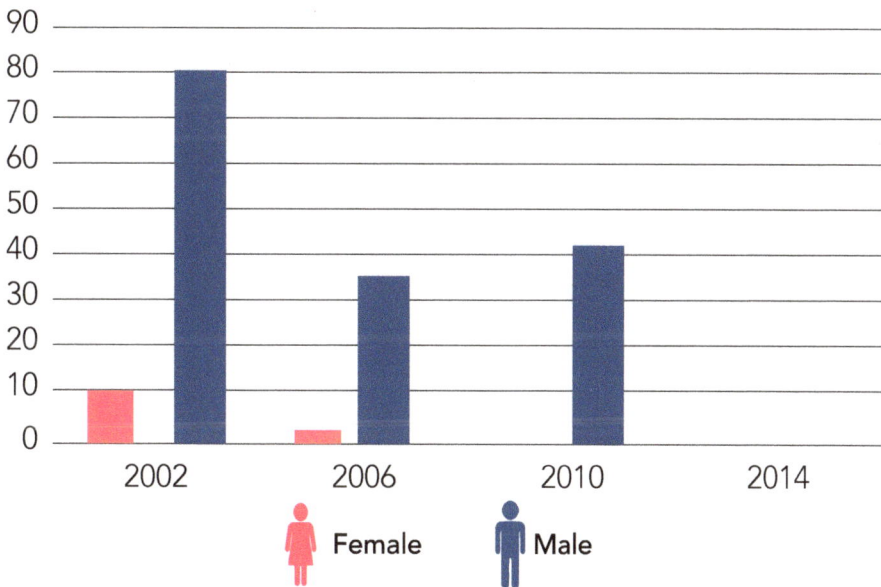

Male and Female Candidates Running for Municipal Seats

2002 - 2014, NORTHERN GOVERNORATE

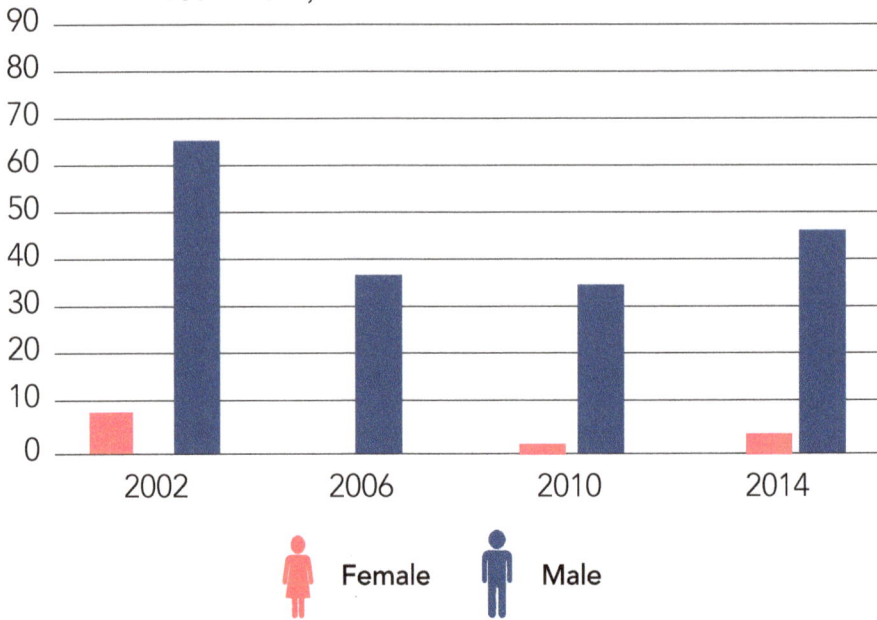

Female   Male

Male and Female Candidates Running for Municipal Seats

2002 - 2014, SOUTHREN GOVERNORATE

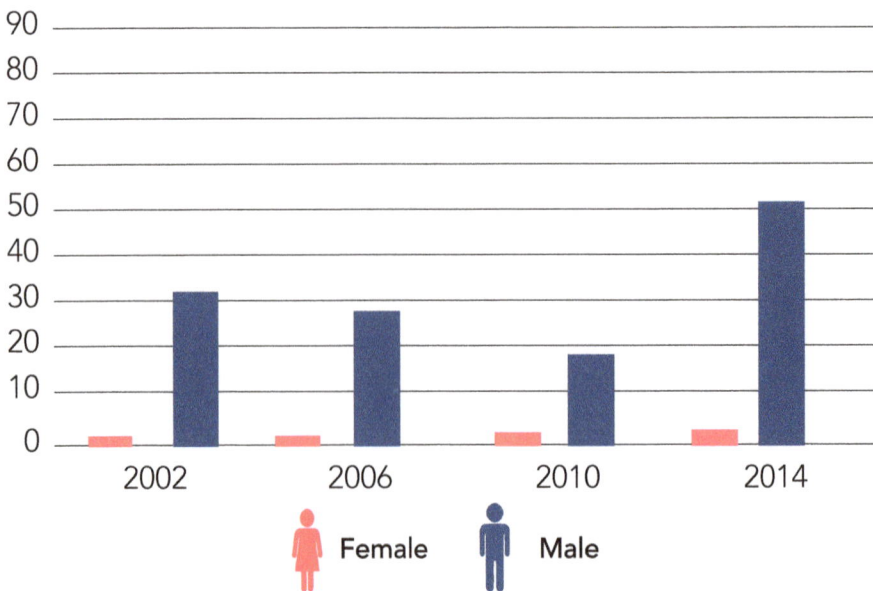

Female   Male

Al-Majlis al-Watani
National Assembly

The Relationship between both chambers
of the National Assembly
Procedure in Government Legislation

National Assembly

(2002–PRESENT)

80 MEMBERS

40 MEMBERS
COUNCIL OF REPRESENTATIVES

(THE LOWER HOUSE)

40 MEMBERS
CONSULTATIVE COUNCIL

(THE UPPER HOUSE)

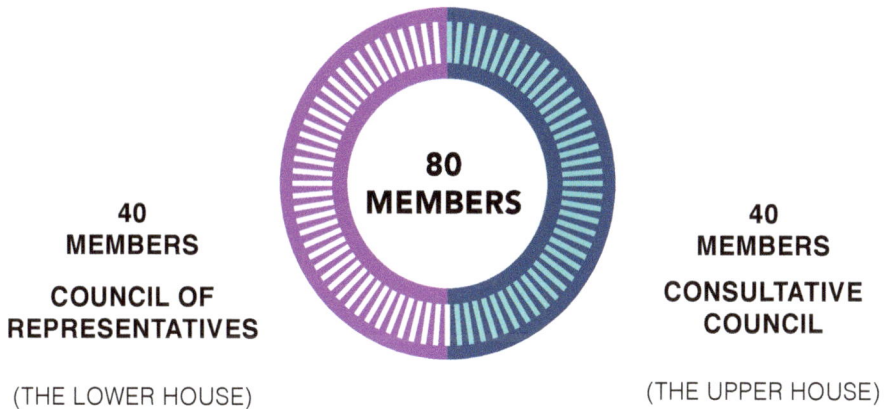

The National Assembly is the name of both Chambers of the Bahraini National Council when the upper and the lower house have a joint session, as laid out in the Constitution of 2002.

It has eighty seats from the fourty elected members of Majlis al-Nuwab, known as the Council of Representatives (the Lower House), and the fourty royally appointed members of Majlis al-Shura, known as the Consultative Council (the Upper House).

It is chaired by the Speaker of the Council of Representatives, or by the Speaker of the Consultative Council if the former is absent. This practice was reversed as decreed by the King in the 2012 dialogue that followed the unrest.

Under the 1973 Constitution (Article 43), the National Assembly was a single-chamber Parliament consisting of thirty members elected by universal suffrage. However, the Emir at the time, Shaikh Isa bin Salman al-Khalifa, decreed that women would not be considered part of universal suffrage and were not allowed to vote in the 1973 parliamentary elections.

The Relationship between both chambers of the National Assembly

All laws, except for royal decrees, must be passed by both chambers of the National Assembly. The powers and roles of the two houses are set out in the 2002 National Charter and were somewhat revised in 2012. The Parliamentary codes set out in greater detail how the procedural business of Parliament is carried out. The procedures themselves have been modified on several occasions.

Procedure in Government Legislation

New laws and modifications to existing laws may be drafted by Government departments and then submit to the Council of Representatives for approval. The bill will then be delegated to the relevant Council committees. These can provide recommendations to the Council of Representatives to either accept or reject the draft or accept it with modifications. The bill will then be debated and voted on by the entire Council of Representatives, which will often accept the recommendations of the specialist committee. However, the Council sometimes sends the bills back to the committee for further drafting and consultation.

Once the Council of Representatives has voted on the draft, it is passed to the Shura Council for debate. Complications can arise when the two houses of Parliament disagree over proposed amendments or have significantly differing views on the legislation. If both Councils disagree over any bill twice, the National Assembly convenes, chaired by the speaker of the Council of Representatives, to discuss the disputed items only. The bill is passed only by the majority of votes of attendees. In case of rejection, the bill cannot be submitted again to the National Assembly in the same legislative session. The result is that the draft is circulated between the various committees as compromise drafts are debated and approved, and in some cases, legislation can be held up indefinitely. In all cases, the speaker of the Council of Representatives shall refer all bills passed by both chambers to the Prime Minister, who submits them to the King.

The Government and the Parliamentary Authority Office can agree to mark a piece of legislation as urgent, prioritizing it for debate at the committee level and so that it will be addressed in the first available open parliamentary session for approval. Inevitably, there are different understandings of what constitutes urgent legislation. For example, in April 2015, MPs blocked several bills marked as urgent, claiming they did not merit the label and this obstructed other business. Council of Representatives itself can also decide to initiate the drafting of legislation. In some cases, it is encouraged to take the task by the Government. The drafting is undertaken by the relevant specialized committee, which seeks external advice from Government departments, experts, and legal specialists on legislation they are drafting or reviewing.

Similar processes apply for the occasional amendments to the Constitution, for example, those made in 2012. However, the conditions for the Constitution's amendment are stricter, requiring a two-thirds majority vote.

Majlis al-Shura
Shura Council

Shura Council's Role and Achievement

The National Assembly was created in June 1972 and dissolved on August 26, 1975. The legislative powers in Bahrain were controlled by the Council of Ministers until the Consultative Council was established in 1992, and consisted of 40 appointed members with the power to propose draft laws. However, on February 14, 2002, the Constitution was amended, and one of the changes ordered the establishment of a legislative committee composed of two, rather than one, councils. The Consultative Council also referred to as the *Majlis al-Shura* or Shura Council, is the name given to the upper house of the National Assembly, the main legislative body in the Kingdom of Bahrain. It also reinstituted the elected Council of Representatives, *Majlis al-Nuwab*, the lower house of the National Assembly with the power to propose and ratify draft laws. They both constitute the National Assembly of Bahrain `Parliament,` and each of the Councils is composed of fourty members.

Members of the Shura Council are appointed by the King. They must be Bahraini nationals and must be over the age of thirty five upon appointment. The term of appointment is four years, and a representative whose membership has reached its term may be reappointed. If for any reason, a seat in the Consultative Council becomes vacant before the end of the term, the King shall appoint a successor for the remaining period of the predecessor. Members may submit their resignation to the president of the Council, who, in turn, refers it to the King. The membership ends only upon approval of the King on such resignation. The King appoints the president of the Consultative Council for a term similar to that of the Council of Representatives, while the members of the Shura Council itself are in charge of the election of two vice-presidents for each session. The Consultative Council holds its meetings during the term of the National Assembly. If the assembly is dissolved, the Council puts an end to its sessions.

Commission Members

COMPARATIVE COMPOSITION OF THE
SHURA COUNCILS

2006	2010	2014	2018
19 Shiite	19 Shiite	19 Shiite	19 Shiite
19 Sunnite	19 Sunnite	19 Sunnite	19 Sunnite
1 Christian	1 Christian	1 Christian	1 Christian
1 Jew	1 Jew	1 Jew	1 Jew

Shura Council's Role and Achievement

Occasionally, the question as to why a small nation like the Kingdom of Bahrain requires a two-chamber assembly is raised. Since the establishment of the National Assembly by King Hamad through the 2002 National Action Charter, elements of the opposition have sought to abolish the Upper House, arguing that the country's legislative power should be solely in the hands of elected members in the Council of Representatives. However, many examples demonstrate that the appointment of the Shura Council plays a vital role in the protection and consolidation of the Kingdom's reformist and tolerant social model. A few significant proposals from Shura members include the unified Family Law, which will ensure that both Shia & Sunna women and families have equal rights before the law; legislation passed for the prevention of serving clerics from participating in politics; and proposed amendments to the law for protecting victims of rape.

The role of the Shura Council for the functioning of the Government and in the implementation of a superior model of governance in the Kingdom of Bahrain based on a progressive vision and reforms is outlined in the factors below:

1. Safeguarding the Constitution

One of the Shura Council's most important roles is ensuring the compatibility of legislation with the progressive and reformist vision of Bahrain's Constitution. The National Action Charter prohibits discrimination on the grounds of gender, religion, or nationality and enshrines the rights and freedoms of all components of society. As a result, the Shura Council is empowered to amend or block any legislation that they deem to be out of line with the spirit of the Constitution.

In addition, by being appointed by the King, Shura members are also accountable to him in demonstrating dedicated performance and a commitment to his vision of reform while supporting the democratization process in the context of consolidating Bahrain as a constitutional monarchy.

2. Prevents a 'tyranny of the majority'

Having two chambers of Parliament ensures a system of mixed Government and that the necessary checks and balances are in place so that the democratic system is protected. It safeguards against the scenario of a particular party winning a substantial majority and using this mandate to force through anti-democratic legislation and oppress vulnerable minorities that are not represented in the CoR.

3. Appointments sanctioned by the King ensure diversity in the legislative process

As elections depend heavily on the public mood, a particular society or agenda is usually favored. By appointing the members of a second chamber, which happens in many countries, it ensures a representative diversity of deputies from all social classes, religious faiths, range of professions, and the full spectrum of political affiliations. Furthermore, it ensures that those who are often disfavored in elections are represented, e.g., women, minorities, the disabled, progressives, and civil society activists.

This allows for technical expertise and gives minority communities a role in the legislative process. For example, a Bahraini Christian woman, Alice Samaan, and a Bahraini Jewish man have been appointed as members. Furthermore, after the widespread disappointment that no women were elected to the lower house in the 2002 general election, four women were appointed to the Consultative Council. Currently, out of the fourty members of the Council, nine are women, constituting 22.5%. Two of these have been appointed to the Cabinet Nada Haffadh, the first Bahraini woman to become a cabinet Minister in 2004 as Minster of Health, and Fatima al-Baloushi, appointed to the Cabinet as Social Affairs Minister, who also previously served on the Council.

Furthermore, the appointment of Shura members ensures a high proportion of technocrats with a diversity of the required skills needed for the legislative process. Since a high number of appointments are successful former members of the CoR and experienced legislators, the legislative experience is conserved and consolidated, and the Shura Council is often more rigorous in scrutinizing legislation and ensuring that laws are well written, which fulfills the purpose of establishing such a Council.

4. The Shura Council defends the rights of women and minorities

Since mid-2015, the Women and Families Committee in the elected chamber has been dominated by Islamist members who have blocked pro-women legislations, such as the amendments to the UN's CEDAW legislation on women's rights. On the other hand, the Shura Council has supported these laws as well as other laws concerning domestic violence in 2015, with Shura members emphasizing the right of consent for women.

Moreover, Bahrain's Shura Council has always contained a much higher proportion of female deputies while also appointing representatives of minority groups.

5. Counters less progressive agendas

The Shura Council has frequently acted as a check on socially retrogressive legislation, which would limit the rights and freedoms of people of all religions and would make Bahrain a less desirable destination for tourism, such as the banning of pork and alcohol and a bill to compel the Government to only permit Islamic banking institutions to operate in the Kingdom.

Between 2006 and 2011, the majority of elected MPs were from either Shia or Sunna religious-political societies. The implication is that Islamists had an automatic veto on all legislation, and socially progressive laws had little chance of success. In this case, the Shura Council would lobby in favor of significant legislation that would protect Bahrain's cultural diversity from those with an ideological agenda.

Frequently, the Shura Council has been the source of far-sighted proposals for guaranteeing the rights and freedoms of all Bahrainis. Recent examples include the aforementioned amendments to the domestic violence law, the ban on serving clerics participating in politics, or separation of church and state, and the unified family law, among other essential proposals.

6. Resists populist pressures

The elected Council of Representatives is prone to proposing measures that they believe to be popular but that are unaffordable or impractical; such as wage increases, new community centers, sports facilities, bonuses and pensions to public sector workers, and new public sector institutions. At a time when the Government is trying to cut its expenditures due to the budget being walloped by decreased oil revenues. The Shura Council, as it is less influenced by popular and short-term pressures, has tended to be more supportive of measures that may not be popular but that are necessary for Bahrain's long-term economic growth and fiscal stability.

7. Giving voices to moderates and liberals from smaller constituencies

The division of electoral districts across Bahrain bare the result that only a small number of constituencies are amenable to liberal, progressive, and female candidates, particularly in Zayed Town and Isa Town. Meanwhile, areas like Muharraq, central Manama, Riffa, the south and Shia-majority constituencies in the north tend to be very conservative and often vote for Islamic politicians. It is a paradox, considering most of Bahrain tends to be liberal, tolerant, and open. However, the royal family, leading figures in the Government and the Constitution itself, tend to follow liberal and reformist worldviews. Thus, an appointed chamber in the National Assembly would provide a balance in views and, ultimately, in the legislative power of the Kingdom.

Majlis al-Nuwab
Council of Representatives

Elections Analysis

Originally established through Article 43 of the 1973 Bahraini Constitution, the CoR was the sole legislative body of the Bahraini Parliament—the National Assembly. As per the Constitution, the Assembly consisted of fourty two members. While thirty of the assembly's members were to be elected through a direct vote by their respective constituents, 12 held the status of ex-officio Ministers and were appointed by the Emir. With the 78.4% total electoral turnout of registered voters, newly appointed Ministers formed the new Government in December 1973 and conducted the first session of the National Assembly on December 16, 1973. However, as the relationships between the royal family and the National Assembly grew increasingly tense, Shaikh Isa bin Salman al-Khalifa dissolved the National Assembly by a royal decree in 1975.

The 2001 National Action Charter reintroduced the Bahraini National Assembly. Under the new Constitution, the National Assembly includes both the Shura Council and the Council of Representatives. In contrast to its format under the original Constitution, the new CoR is a fourty members legislative body of the Bahraini Parliament. Notably, all members of the CoR are directly elected in a two-round election, and a run-off electoral round is conducted if no absolute majority is achieved. The first elections for the contemporary CoR were held in 2002.

According to the Constitution, candidates to the Council must be listed in their constituent districts and should be at least thirty years of age. In addition, candidates must have Bahraini citizenship and be fluent in Arabic, both written and spoken. However, specific articles of the Constitution also impose restrictions on candidates. Specifically, persons with a criminal record and a prison sentence exceeding the length of six months may not participate as electoral candidates in the ten years following the day of conviction. Moreover, persons already holding ministerial and judicial offices are also ineligible to participate as candidates.

From the first elections in 2002 to the 2014 elections, an independent representative, Khalifa al-Dhahrani, served as speaker of the Council. Since the 2014 elections, the Speaker of the Council has been Ahmed al-Mulla, also an independent representative, followed by Fawzia Zainal, the first woman to be elected as a speaker. Speaker, who supervises the Council and facilitates cooperation with other legislative bodies. Notably, the first female representative was elected to the CoR in 2006, marking a historic development for women in the Kingdom.

Since then, the number of women represented in the Council rose to four, bringing the proportion of women in the Council to 10%. Despite the drop to nine female candidates in the 2010 elections, the number of female candidates participating in the parliamentary elections in Bahrain rose from eight in the 2002 elections to twenty two in the 2014 elections to a new high of fourty in 2018. However, the Kingdom still has no electoral quota to encourage the participation of women in parliamentary elections.

Being the main legislative body in the Bahraini political system, the Council has extensive legislative powers. The three main functions of the Council include amending the Constitution, proposing laws, and rejecting or accepting law decrees. Amending the Constitution is an onerous task: not only should amendments be submitted to the speaker of the Council by at least fifteen members of the CoR and fifteen members of the Shura Council, but also by the King. Proposing laws is a more temperate process. As per the Constitution, each member of the Council has the right to submit a law proposal to the speaker of the Council. However, the number of signees should not exceed five representatives and should comply with all constitutional provisions. The right to approve and reject law decrees is shared by the CoR and the Shura Council.

Other legislative powers of the CoR include approving international treaties and agreements, overseeing the work of the Government, submitting proposals to the executive, requesting parliamentary questions and interpellation, casting votes of no confidence, submitting the declaration of inability to work with the Prime Minister, and submitting inquiries. Approval of international agreements and treaties is essential in assuring their compliance with the Constitution. Meanwhile, oversight powers serve to check the work of the executive branch. The powers of interpellation and the vote of no confidence are vital tools to preclude malfeasance by officials. Inquiries are usually submitted to investigate a specific issue while requesting parliamentary questions is a tool used to obtain additional information about a specific matter. Simultaneously, the function to submit proposals to the executive enables the Council to submit formal proposals about issues outside of their legislative powers.

Structurally, the CoR includes the Bureau of the Council, the Reply to the Royal Speech Committee, five permanent committees, standing select committees, and various case-specific committees. The Bureau of the Council is chaired by the speaker of the Council, who is assisted by two deputy speakers as well as chairpersons of the five standing committees. The current speaker of the Council is Her Excellency Fawzia Zainal, a first-time-serving independent member. The four other standing committees include the Financial and Economic Affairs Committee, the Foreign, Defense, and National Security Affairs Committee, the Services Committee, and the Environment Committee.

The Legislative and Legal Affairs Committee is tasked with reviewing draft laws and cooperating with other committees in compiling legislature. The Legislative and Legal Affairs Committee consists of eight members. The priority of the Financial and Economic Affairs Committee is to address socioeconomic development issues and financial matters of other ministries, including annual budget planning. The Foreign, Defense, and National Security Committee is composed of seven members. This committee works on developing the Kingdom's foreign policies. The Services Committee also comprises seven members and specializes in the implementation of educational and social policies, including labor, media, cultural, health, and sports affairs. Consisting of seven members, the Committee on the Environment specializes in infrastructural matters, as well as agricultural and water issues.

The Reply to the Royal Speech Committee oversees the review of royal speeches and presents a reply to the CoR and, after the Council's approval, to the King. The members of the Reply to the Royal Speech Committee are subject to approval by the CoR after a formal nomination by the Bureau of the Council. Meanwhile, standing select committees usually, are introduced to examine special issues as ascribed by the Council. Standing select committees must be established after a formal request by at least five members of the Council, and the size of such committees should not exceed five members.

Depending on the nature of a specific issue, the CoR may also introduce ad hoc, joint, inquiry, and temporary committees. Current temporary committees include the Committee to Review the Government Action Plan. Ad hoc committees deal with preparing reviews, recommendations, and solution strategies for specific issues on the agenda. Inquiry committees are typically tasked with investigating discrepancies within the Council. Joint committees are established in instances when a discussed matter intersects jurisdictions of more than one standing committee. The CoR also includes the Inter-Parliamentary Group. Composed of both the CoR and the Shura Council, the Inter-Parliamentary Group has an executive committee, which is chaired by the speaker of the Council and consists of eight members, all of whom are approved by both legislative chambers. The primary purpose of the Inter-Parliamentary Group is to participate in international and domestic parliamentary conferences.

Legislative Elections Analysis

Council of Representatives Performance Analysis

2002 CoR Elected Members

Party	Total Elected Members	Male	Female
Independent	23	23	0
Political Societies	17	17	0

Party Mix   Male/Female Mix

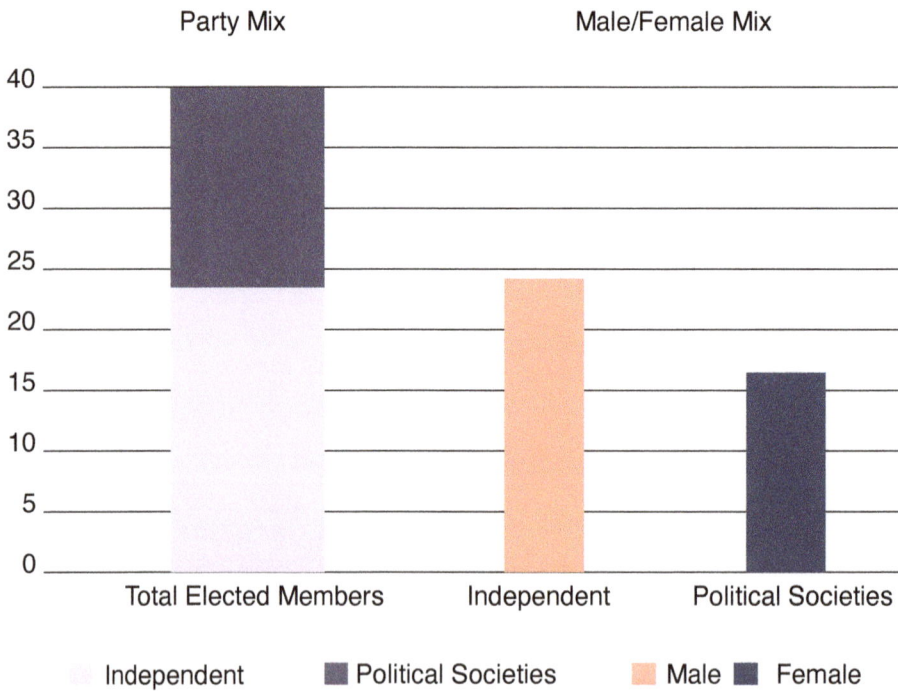

Independent   ■ Political Societies   ■ Male   ■ Female

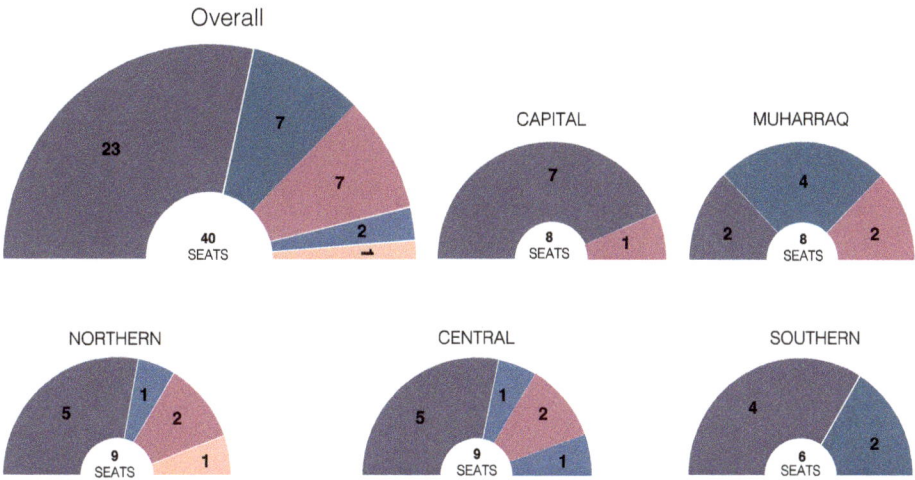

Overall

23 7 7 2
40 SEATS

CAPITAL
7 1
8 SEATS

MUHARRAQ
2 4 2
8 SEATS

NORTHERN
5 1 2 1
9 SEATS

CENTRAL
5 1 2 1
9 SEATS

SOUTHERN
4 2
6 SEATS

■ Independent

■ al-Asalah

■ al-Menbar

■ Progressive Tribune

■ Islamic league

#	Governerate	Constituency	Elected Member	Bloc	Vote	Percentage	Position
1	Capital	1	Saadi Ali	al-Menbar	1968	56%	
2	Capital	2	Isa bin Rajab	Independent	1131	55.55%	
3	Capital	3	Ebrahim Y. Abdulla	Independent	n/a	100%	
4	Capital	4	Abdulhadi Marhoun	Independent	717	70%	First Deputy
5	Capital	5	Hasan Bukhammas	Independent	742	73.61	
6	Capital	6	Ahmed Bahzad	Independent	1906	86.99%	
7	Capital	7	Yousif al-Hermi	Independent	1527	59.81%	
8	Capital	8	Abdulla al-A'ali	Independent	704	60.27%	
9	Muharraq	1	Isa al-Motawa'a	al-Asalah	1165	50.43%	
10	Muharraq	2	Abdulaziz al-Meer	al-Menbar	1926	58.63%	
11	Muharraq	3	Ali Ahmed	al-Menbar	1989	67.08%	
12	Muharraq	4	Isa abu al-Fat'h	al-Asalah	3066	56.98%	
13	Muharraq	5	Adil al-Ma'awdeh	al-Asalah	252	65.77%	Second Deputy
14	Muharraq	6	Ali al-Samaheji	Independent	570	59.69%	
15	Muharraq	7	Othman al-Rayes	Independent	3010	53.43%	
16	Muharraq	8	Ghanem al-Buaynain	al-Asalah	1990	53.75%	
17	Northern	1	Mohamed al-Khayat	Islamic League	2299	61.60%	
18	Northern	2	Jassim al-Mowali	Independent	1029	68.69%	
19	Northern	3	Sameer al-Shuwaikh	Independent	1128	58.02	
20	Northern	4	Abdulaziz al-Mousa	Independent	913	50.03%	
21	Northern	5	Abbas Ebrahim	Independent	680	67.53%	

#	Governerate	Constituency	Elected Member	Bloc	Vote	Percentage	Position
				2002 CoR Elected Members			
22	Northern	6	Mohamed Khalid	al-Menbar	4129	82.80%	
23	Northern	7	Yousif Zainal	Progressive Tribune	1405	58.01%	
24	Northern	8	Ahmed Hajji	al-Menbar	2485	53.06%	
25	Northern	9	Jassim Abdula'al	Independent	1358	59.28%	
26	Central	1	Farid Ghazi	Independent	1920	60.23%	
27	Central	2	Abdulnabi Salman	Progressive Tribune	1327	54.93%	
28	Central	3	Jihad Bukamal	Independent	4230	87.85%	
29	Central	4	Salah Ali Ahmed	al-Menbar	NO DATA AVAILABLE		
30	Central	5	Ahmed H. Abbas	Independent	1091	66.97%	
31	Central	6	Mohamed al-Abbas	Independent	573	50.18%	
32	Central	7	Ali Mattar	al-Asalah	2669	59.28%	
33	Central	8	Abdullatif al-Sheikh	al-Menbar	4003	69.27%	
34	Central	9	Khalifa al-Dhahrani	Independent	4237	90.15%	Speaker
35	Southern	1	Jassim al-Saiedi	Independent	1673	54.57%	
36	Southern	2	Hamad al-Muhannadi	al-Asalah	1214	65.06%	
37	Southern	3	Sami al-Beheri	al-Asalah	932	54.47%	
38	Southern	4	Abdulla K al-Dowseri	Independent	699	67.54%	
39	Southern	5	Mohamed al-Ka'abi	Independent	327	55.33%	
40	Southern	6	Mohamed F. al-Dowseri	Independent	n/a	100%	

2006 CoR Elected Members

Party	Total Elected Members	Male	Female
Independent	9	8	1
Political Societies	31	31	0

Party Mix   Male/Female Mix

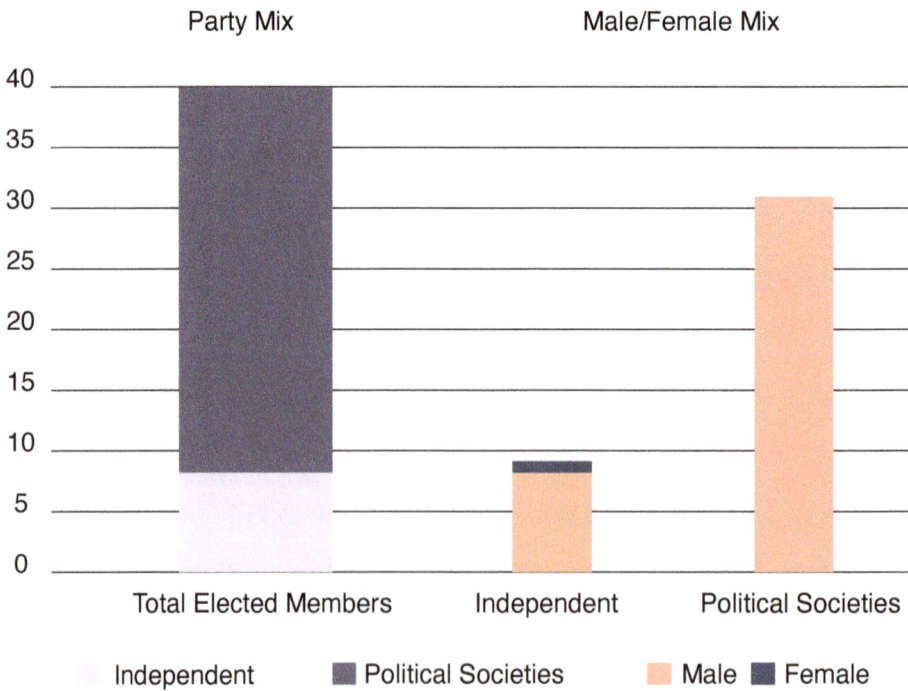

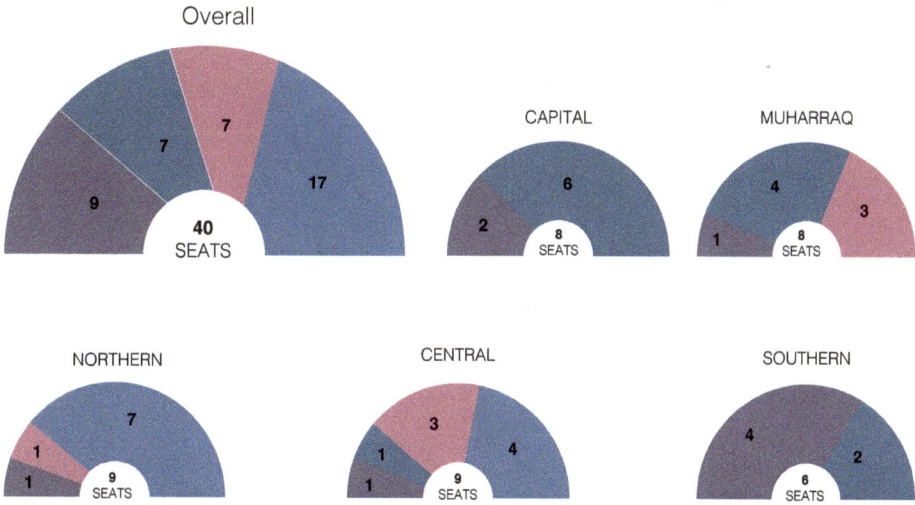

Overall

7 7 17

9

40
SEATS

CAPITAL

6

2

8
SEATS

MUHARRAQ

4 3

1

8
SEATS

NORTHERN

7

1

1

9
SEATS

CENTRAL

3 4

1

1

9
SEATS

SOUTHERN

4 2

6
SEATS

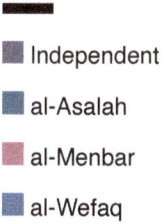

■ Independent

■ al-Asalah

■ al-Menbar

■ al-Wefaq

#	Governerate	Constituency	Elected Member	Bloc	Vote	Percentage	Position
			2006 CoR Elected Members				
1	Capital	1	Adil al-Asoomi	Independent	2383	68.62%	
2	Capital	2	Khalil al-Marzouq	al- Wefaq	2536	54.16%	First Deputy
3	Capital	3	Jassim al-Moamen	al- Wefaq	2022	58%	
4	Capital	4	Abduljalil Khalil	al- Wefaq	4548	89.26%	
5	Capital	5	Mohamed Y al-Meza'al	al- Wefaq	1426	53.95%	
6	Capital	6	Abdulrahman Bumjaid	Independent	1324	55.65%	
7	Capital	7	Abdulaziz Abdul	al- Wefaq	2502	63.89%	
8	Capital	8	Jamil Khadhim	al- Wefaq	2958	70.96%	
9	Muharraq	1	Adil al-Ma'awdeh	al-Asalah	1700	63.48%	
10	Muharraq	2	Ebrahim Busandal	al-Asalah	2511	70.63%	
11	Muharraq	3	Ali Ahmed	al-Menbar	1875	55.59%	
12	Muharraq	4	Isa abu al-Fat'h	al-Asalah	3890	52.75%	
13	Muharraq	5	Sami Qamber	al-Menbar	1811	55.05%	
14	Muharraq	6	Hamza Kadhim	Independent	4507	90.28%	
15	Muharraq	7	Nasser al-Fadhalla	al-Menbar	4983	60.00%	
16	Muharraq	8	Ghanem al-Buaynain	al-Asalah	3065	66.51%	Second Deputy
17	Northern	1	Ali Salman	al-Wefaq	9157	83.73%	
18	Northern	2	Makki Hilal	al-Wefaq	3997	57.97%	
19	Northern	3	Abdulhussain al-Mutaghawi	al-Wefaq	6507	81.72%	
20	Northern	4	Hasan S al-Dowseri	Independent	1236	56.75%	
21	Northern	5	Mohamed Jameel al-Jamri	al-Wefaq	4613	79.93%	
22	Northern	6	Mohamed Khalid	al-Menbar	4970	53.79%	

#	Governerate	Constituency	Elected Member	Bloc	Vote	Percentage	Position
			2006 CoR Elected Members				
23	Northern	7	Jassim H Ghuloom	al-Wefaq	5058	65.28%	
24	Northern	8	Jawad Fairouz	al-Wefaq	5418	57.44%	
25	Northern	9	Hasan A Juma	al-Wefaq	7278	77.38%	
26	Central	1	Jalal Fairouz	al-Wefaq	7203	77.17%	
27	Central	2	Abdulla al-A'ali	al-Wefaq	5779	67.07%	
28	Central	3	Ebrahim al-Ha'adi	al-Menbar	3214	62.31%	
29	Central	4	Salah Ali	al-Menbar	4066	53.64%	
30	Central	5	Abdali Hasan	al-Wefaq	4384	62.31%	
31	Central	6	Haider Hasan	al-Wefaq	6476	91.87%	
32	Central	7	Abdulhalim Murad	al-Asalah	2915	51.78%	
33	Central	8	Abdullatif al-Sheikh	al-Menbar	4344	56.40%	
34	Central	9	Khalifa al-Dhahrani	Independent	3890	70.34%	Speaker
35	Southern	1	Jassim al-Saiedi	Independent	2757	70.90%	
36	Southern	2	Hamad al-Muhannadi	al-Asalah	1276	53.80%	
37	Southern	3	Sami al-Beheri	al-Asalah	1166	53.44%	
38	Southern	4	Abdulla K al-Dowseri	Independent	656	62.90%	
39	Southern	5	Khamis al-Romaihi	Independent	423	52.29%	
40	Southern	6	Latifa al-Quoud	Independent	n/a	100.00%	

2010 CoR Elected Members

Party	Total Elected Members	Male	Female
Independent	14	13	1
Political Societies	26	26	0

Party Mix

Male/Female Mix

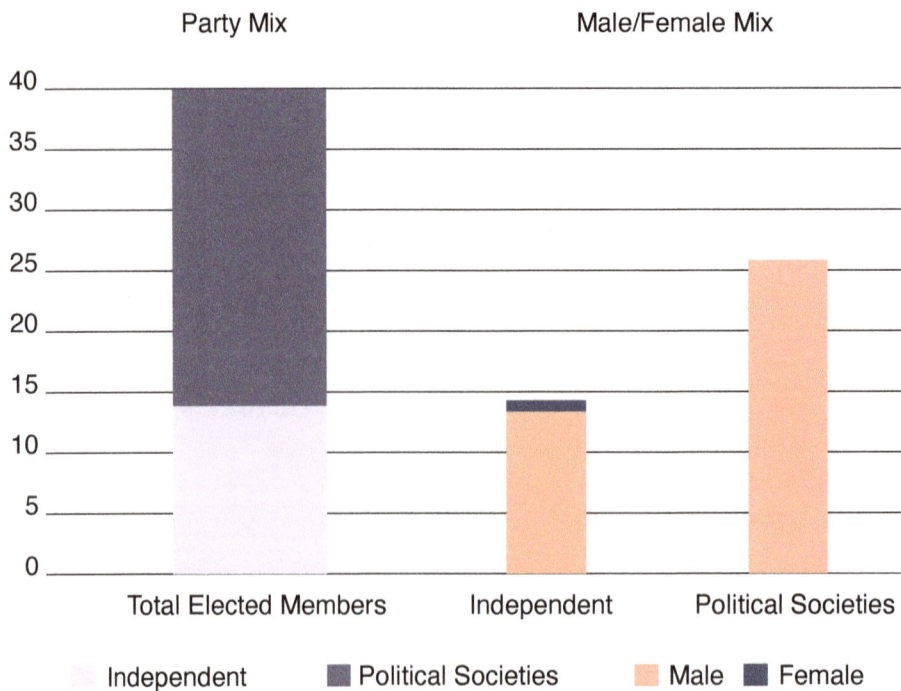

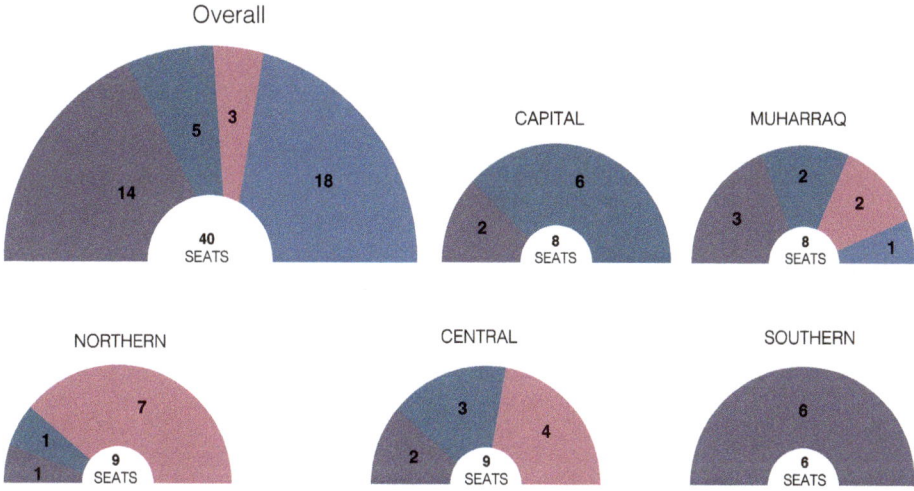

Overall

40
SEATS

CAPITAL

8
SEATS

MUHARRAQ

8
SEATS

NORTHERN

9
SEATS

CENTRAL

9
SEATS

SOUTHERN

6
SEATS

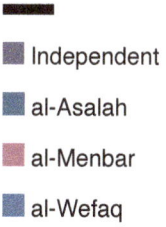

Independent

al-Asalah

al-Menbar

al-Wefaq

2010 CoR Elected Members

#	Governerate	Constituency	Elected Member	Bloc	Vote	Percentage	Position
1	Capital	1	Adil al-Asoomi	Independent	1878	65.30%	
2	Capital	2	Khalil al-Marzouq	al-Wefaq	2141	58.40%	First Deputy
3	Capital	3	Hadi al-Mosawi	al-Wefaq	1926	85.60%	
4	Capital	4	Abduljalil Khalil	al-Wefaq	n/a	100.00%	
5	Capital	5	Mohamed Y al-Meza'al	al-Wefaq	1667	67.20%	
6	Capital	6	Abdulrahman Bumjaid	Independent	1144	56.90%	
7	Capital	7	Abdulmajeed al-Sebea	al-Wefaq	1842	63.50%	
8	Capital	8	Jamil Khadhim	al-Wefaq	2818	86.20%	
9	Muharraq	1	Adil al-Ma'awdeh	al- Asalah	n/a	100.00%	
10	Muharraq	2	Abdulhameed al-Meer	al-Menbar	1737	58.60%	
11	Muharraq	3	Ali Ahmed	al-Menbar	1675	55.03%	
12	Muharraq	4	Mahmoud al-Mahmoud	Independent	3418	52.85%	
13	Muharraq	5	Isa al-Kooheji	Independent	1891	57.60%	
14	Muharraq	6	Ali al-Asheeri	al-Wefaq	4422	83.80%	
15	Muharraq	7	Otham al-Rayes	Independent	4562	55.70%	
16	Muharraq	8	Ghanem al-Buaynain	al-Asalah	2774	59.49%	
17	Northern	1	Mattar Mattar	al-Wefaq	7689	85.70%	
18	Northern	2	Ali al-Aswad	al-Wefaq	6577	87.70%	
19	Northern	3	Abdulhussain al-Mutaghawi	al-Wefaq	6523	90.00%	
20	Northern	4	Hasan S al-Dowseri	Independent	1545	57.80%	
21	Northern	5	Majeed Shubbar	al-Wefaq	5132	86.80%	
22	Northern	6	Mohamed al-Ammadi	al-Menbar	3777	56.82%	

#	Governerate	Constituency	Elected Member	Bloc	Vote	Percentage	Position
				2010 CoR Elected Members			
23	Northern	7	Jassim H Ghuloom	al-Wefaq	5107	59.00%	
24	Northern	8	Jawad Fairouz	al-Wefaq	5954	55.00%	
25	Northern	9	Hasan Sultan	al-Wefaq	8814	89.40%	
26	Central	1	Salman Salem	al-Wefaq	6175	67.50%	
27	Central	2	Abdulla al-A'ali	al-Wefaq	7252	89.00%	
28	Central	3	Adnan al-Malki	al-Asalah	2533	59.36%	
29	Central	4	Isa al-Qadi	Independent	3905	55.99%	
30	Central	5	Abdali Hasan	al-Wefaq	3501	56.70%	
31	Central	6	Hasan Marzouq	al-Wefaq	5308	92.00%	
32	Central	7	Abdulhalim Murad	al-Asalah	3178	55.90%	Second Deputy
33	Central	8	Ali Zayed	al-Asalah	3888	50.20%	
34	Central	9	Khalifa al-Dhahrani	Independent	3586	77.40%	Speaker
35	Southern	1	Jassim al-Saiedi	Independent	2538	62.70%	
36	Southern	2	Abdulla bin Huwail	Independent	1194	52.40%	
37	Southern	3	Ahmed al-Mulla	Independent	2012	71.99%	
38	Southern	4	Abdulla K al-Dowseri	Independent	n/a	100.00%	
39	Southern	5	Khamis al-Romaihi	Independent	n/a	100.00%	
40	Southern	6	Latifa al-Quoud	Independent	n/a	100.00%	

2011 CoR Bi-Election Elected Members

Party	Total Elected Members	Male	Female
Independent	16	13	3
Political Societies	2	2	0

Party Mix   Male/Female Mix

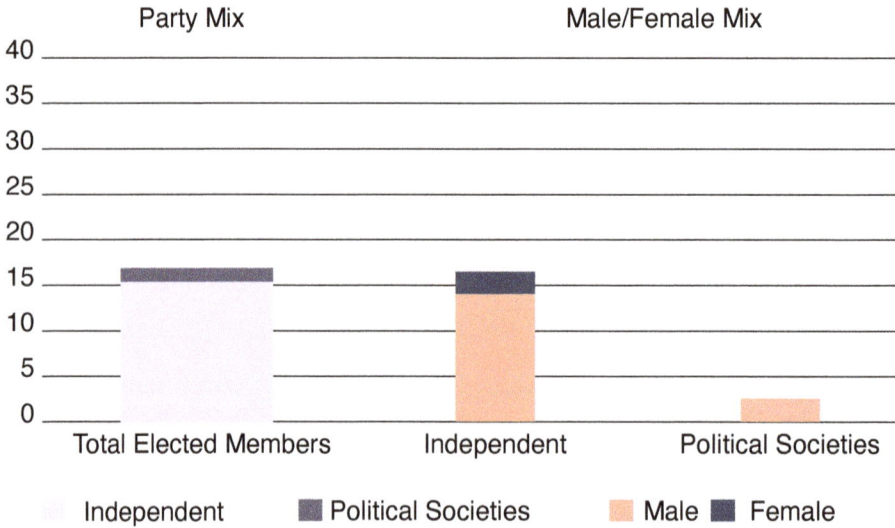

CAPITAL

MUHARRAQ

NORTHERN

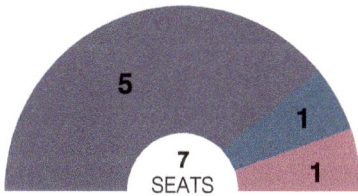

CENTRAL

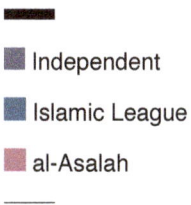

Independent

Islamic League

al-Asalah

#	Governerate	Constituency	Elected Member	Bloc	Vote	Percentage	Position
			2011 CoR Bi-Election Elected Members				
1	Capital	2	Ahmed Qarata	Independepnt	791	53.30%	
2	Capital	3	Ebtisam Hejris	Independepnt	366	54.00%	
3	Capital	4	Ali Shamtoot	Independepnt	148	56.50%	
4	Capital	5	Hasan bu Khammas	Independepnt	499	71.80%	
5	Capital	7	Abdulhakim al-Shemmari	Independepnt	1121	60.40%	
6	Capital	8	Jamal Saleh	Independepnt	430	69.40%	
7	Muharraq	6	Abbas al-Madhi	Independepnt	n/a	100.00%	
8	Northern	1	Ali al-Uttaish	Islamic League	831	65.30%	
9	Northern	2	Sawsan Taqawi	Independepnt	n/a	100.00%	
10	Northern	3	Ali al-Durazi	Independepnt	n/a	100.00%	
11	Northern	5	Salman al-Sheikh	Independepnt	460	53.40%	
12	Northern	7	Khalid al-Malood	al-Asalah	2018	57.10%	
13	Northern	8	Mohamed bu Qais	Independepnt	2999	55.30%	
14	Northern	9	Khalid Abdula'al	Independepnt	335	51.20%	
15	Central	1	Sumaya al-Jowder	Independepnt	1725	51.00%	
16	Central	2	Ahmed al-Sa'ati	Independepnt	595	57.40%	
17	Central	5	Osama Muhanna	Independepnt	443	51.50%	
18	Central	6	Jawad Hussein	Independepnt	n/a	100.00%	

2012 CoR Bi-Election Elected Members							
#	Governerate	Constituency	Elected Member	Bloc	Vote	Percentage	Position
1	Muharraq	8	Sameer al-Khadem	Independent	1739	52.81%	

2014 CoR Elected Members

Party	Total Elected Members	Male	Female
Independent	33	30	3
Political Societies	7	7	0

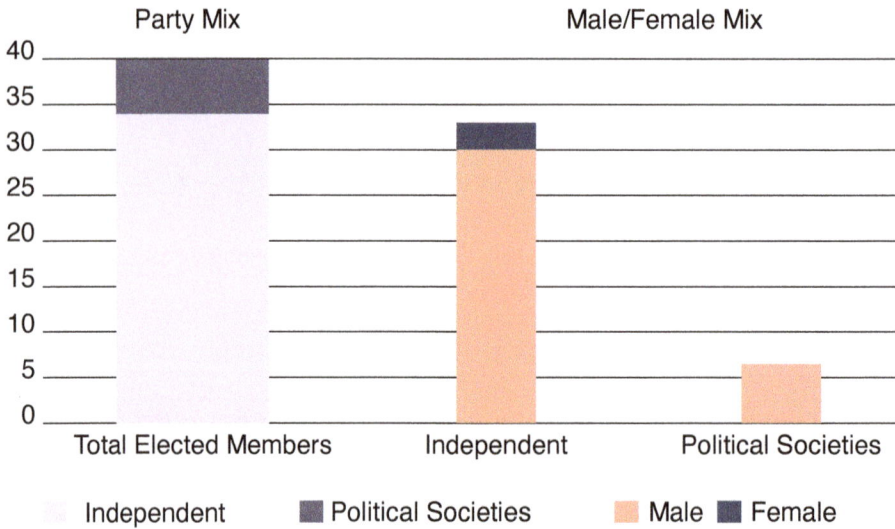

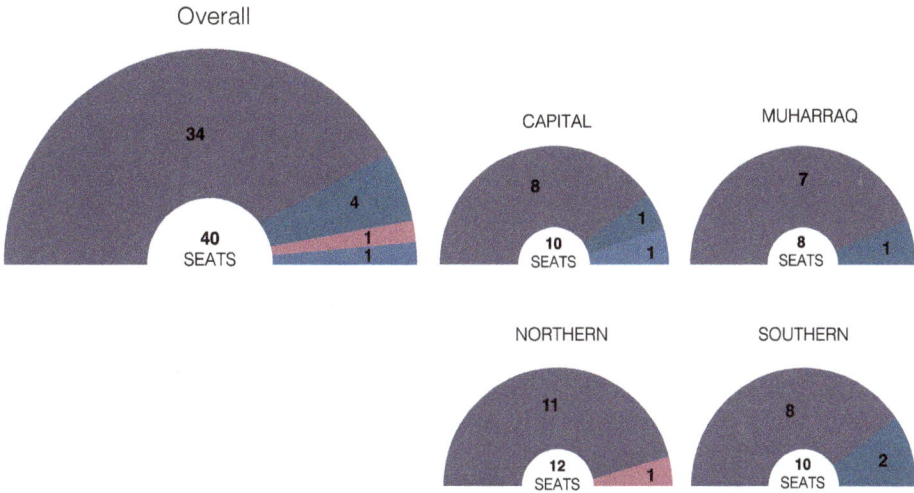

Overall

34

40
SEATS

4
1
1

CAPITAL

8

10
SEATS

1

1

MUHARRAQ

7

8
SEATS

1

NORTHERN

11

12
SEATS

1

SOUTHERN

8

10
SEATS

2

Independent

al-Asalah

al-Menbar

Islamic league

#	Governerate	Constituency	Elected Member	Bloc	Vote	Percentage	Position
				2014 CoR Elected Members			
1	Capital	1	Adil al-Asoomi	Independent	2265	54.50%	
2	Capital	2	Ahmed Qarata	Independent	1224	60.30%	
3	Capital	3	Adil Hameed J	Independent	394	65.02%	
4	Capital	4	Abdulrahman Bumjaid	Independent	2052	59.55%	
5	Capital	5	Nasser al-Qaseer	Independent	1047	55.60%	
6	Capital	6	Ali al-Uttaish	Islamic League	1280	69.30%	
7	Capital	7	Usama al-Khaja	Independent	2094	60.40%	
8	Capital	8	Majeed al-Asfoor	Independent	n/a	100.00%	
9	Capital	9	Mohamed Milad	Independent	500	62.27%	
10	Capital	10	Nabil al-Balushi	al-Asalah	2151	55.97%	
11	Muharraq	1	Ali bu Farsan	Independent	3182	54.18%	
12	Muharraq	2	Ebrahim al-Hammadi	Independent	2761	51.41%	
13	Muharraq	3	Jamal bu Hasan	Independent	2568	52.31%	
14	Muharraq	4	Isa al-Kooheji	Independent	3022	50.82%	
15	Muharraq	5	Mohamed al-Jowdar	Independent	3358	61.20%	
16	Muharraq	6	Abbas al-Madhi	Independent	308	52.92%	
17	Muharraq	7	Ali al-Muqla	al-Asalah	4057	50.55%	
18	Muharraq	8	Abdulrahman bu Ali	Independent	4197	55.66%	
19	Northern	1	Fatima al-Asfoor	Independent	276	51.11%	
20	Northern	2	Jalal Khadhem	Independent	247	66.76%	

2014 CoR Elected Members

#	Governerate	Constituency	Elected Member	Bloc	Vote	Percentage	Position
21	Northern	3	Hamad al-Dowseri	Independent	1984	58.56%	
22	Northern	4	Ghazi al-Rahma	Independent	853	55.82%	
23	Northern	5	Ali al-Aradhi	Independent	534	53.35%	First Deputy
24	Northern	6	Roua al-Hayki	Independent	762	61.30%	
25	Northern	7	Majed al-Majed	Independent	489	55.51%	
26	Northern	8	Isa Turki	Independent	3101	58.48%	
27	Northern	9	Abdulhameed Mohamed	Independent	1977	56.12%	
28	Northern	10	Mohamed al-Ammadi	al-Menbar	4551	66.67%	
29	Northern	11	Jamal Dawood	Independent	3097	61.67%	
30	Northern	12	Jameela al-Sammak	Independent	1158	71.26%	
31	Southern	1	Khalid al-Shaer	Independent	3281	67.79%	
32	Southern	2	Mohamed al-Ahmed	Independent	3163	66.30%	
33	Southern	3	Abdulhalim Murad	al-Asalah	3716	63.40%	Second Deputy
34	Southern	4	Mohamed al-Marafie	Independent	2938	50.79%	
35	Southern	5	Khalifa al-Ghanem	Independent	3505	52.14%	
36	Southern	6	Anas bu Hindi	al-Asalah	3676	62.79%	
37	Southern	7	Abdulla bin Huwail	Independent	3540	59.28%	
38	Southern	8	Dheyab al-Noaimi	Independent	2787	57.65%	
39	Southern	9	Mohsin al-Bakri	Independent	2144	60.34%	
40	Southern	10	Ahmed al-Mulla	Independent	834	80.27%	Speaker

2018 CoR Elected Members

Party	Total Elected Members	Male	Female
Independent	34	28	6
Political Societies	6	6	0

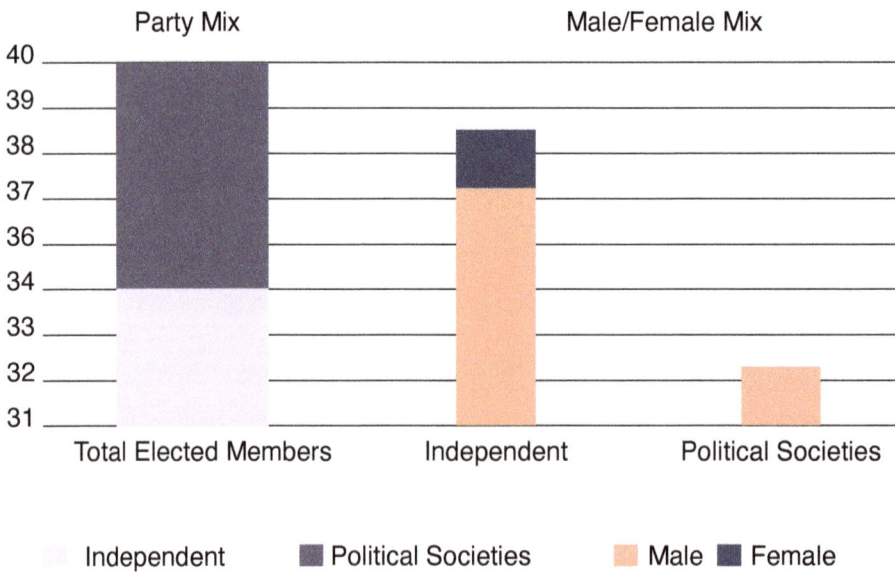

Party Mix   Male/Female Mix

Total Elected Members   Independent   Political Societies

Independent   ■ Political Societies   Male ■ Female

Overall

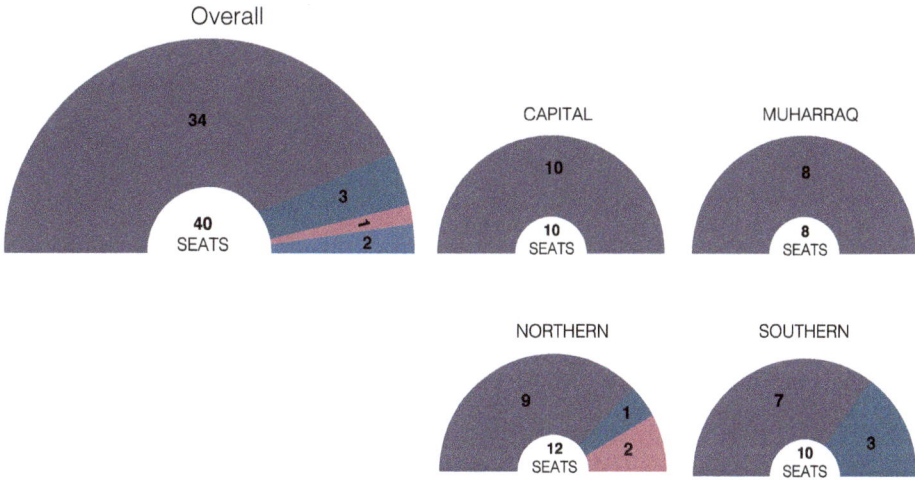

34

40
SEATS

3

1

2

CAPITAL

10

10
SEATS

MUHARRAQ

8

8
SEATS

NORTHERN

9

1

12
SEATS

2

SOUTHERN

7

10
SEATS

3

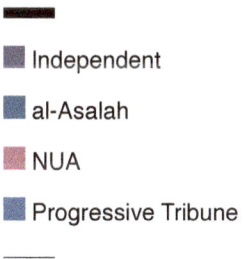

Independent

al-Asalah

NUA

Progressive Tribune

#	Governerate	Constituency	Elected Member	Bloc	Vote	Percentage	Position
1	Capital	1	Adil al-Asoomi	Independent	3182	75.21%	
2	Capital	2	Sawsan Kamal	Independent	1894	70.62%	
3	Capital	3	Mamdouh al-Saleh	Independent	906	52.19%	
4	Capital	4	Ammar al-Banai	Independent	2490	66.31%	
5	Capital	5	Ahmed Saloum	Independent	1891	69.17%	
6	Capital	6	Masouma Abdulrahim	Independent	2137	54.20%	
7	Capital	7	Zainab Abdulamir	Independent	3029	56.29%	
8	Capital	8	Fadhel al-Sawwad	Independent	1085	62.94%	
9	Capital	9	Ammar Abbas	Independent	1769	74.20%	
10	Capital	10	Ali Ishaqi	Independent	3279	55.93%	
11	Muharraq	1	Hamad al-Kooheji	Independent	4171	53.86%	
12	Muharraq	2	Ebrahim al-Nefaie	Independent	2932	53.28%	
13	Muharraq	3	Mohamed Isa	Independent	3096	58.64%	
14	Muharraq	4	Isa al-Kooheji	Independent	3531	57.41%	
15	Muharraq	5	Khalid Bu-Unq	Independent	4917	59.49%	
16	Muharraq	6	Hisham al-Asheeri	Independent	1556	59.12%	
17	Muharraq	7	Ammar Qamber	Independent	7317	71.31%	
18	Muharraq	8	Yousif al-Thawadi	Independent	5246	58.44%	
19	Northern	1	Kaltham al-Hayki	Independent	838	58.77%	
20	Northern	2	Fatima Abbas	Independent	686	51.58%	

2018 CoR Elected Members

#	Governerate	Constituency	Elected Member	Bloc	Vote	Percentage	Position
21	Northern	3	Abdulla al-Dowseri	Independent	2409	61.34%	
22	Northern	4	Ghazi al-Rahma	Independent	2456	55.59%	
23	Northern	5	Falah Hashim	Progressive Tribune	1417	51.79%	
24	Northern	6	Abdulnabi Salman	Progressive Tribune	2662	56.20%	First Deputy
25	Northern	7	Ahmed al-Demstani	Independent	1508	52.11%	
26	Northern	8	Abdulla al-Thawadi	NUA	4166	63.90%	
27	Northern	9	Yousif Zainal	Independent	3186	56.28%	
28	Northern	10	Basem al-Malki	Independent	4938	57.25%	
29	Northern	11	Mohamed bu Hamoud	Independent	3731	59.61%	
30	Northern	12	Mahmoud al-Bahrani	Independent	2590	56.49%	
31	Southern	1	Ahmed al-Amer	Independent	2871	56.92%	
32	Southern	2	Isa al-Qadhi	Independent	3312	64.46%	
33	Southern	3	Ahmed al-Ansari	al-Asalah	3784	54.90%	
34	Southern	4	Ali Zayed	al- Asalah	4312	56.01%	Second Deputy
35	Southern	5	Fawzeya Zainal	Independent	4570	53.47%	Speaker
36	Southern	6	Abdulrazzaq Hattab	al-Asalah	3711	58.82%	
37	Southern	7	Ali al-Noaimi	Independent	3267	52.82%	
38	Southern	8	Mohamed al-Sisi	Independent	3984	63.26%	
39	Southern	9	Bader al-Dowseri	Independent	2288	57.13%	
40	Southern	10	Isa al-Dowseri	Independent	539	83.31%	

Election Voting History

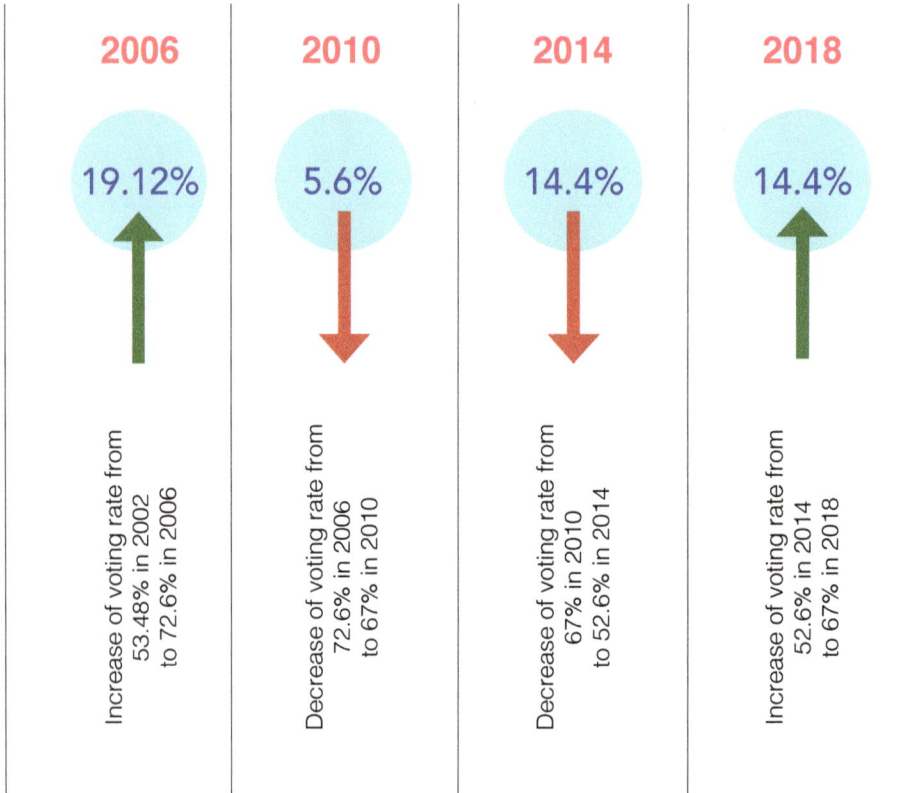

2006	2010	2014	2018
19.12%	5.6%	14.4%	14.4%
Increase of voting rate from 53.48% in 2002 to 72.6% in 2006	Decrease of voting rate from 72.6% in 2006 to 67% in 2010	Decrease of voting rate from 67% in 2010 to 52.6% in 2014	Increase of voting rate from 52.6% in 2014 to 67% in 2018

Silent Segment

27.4%

Rate of non-participant voters from 2002 to 2018 election

Boycott

19.12%

Highest voting boycott rate on record

Governorates Constituencies Distribution

40 CONSTITUENCIES DISTRIBUTED OVER FOUR GOVERNATES

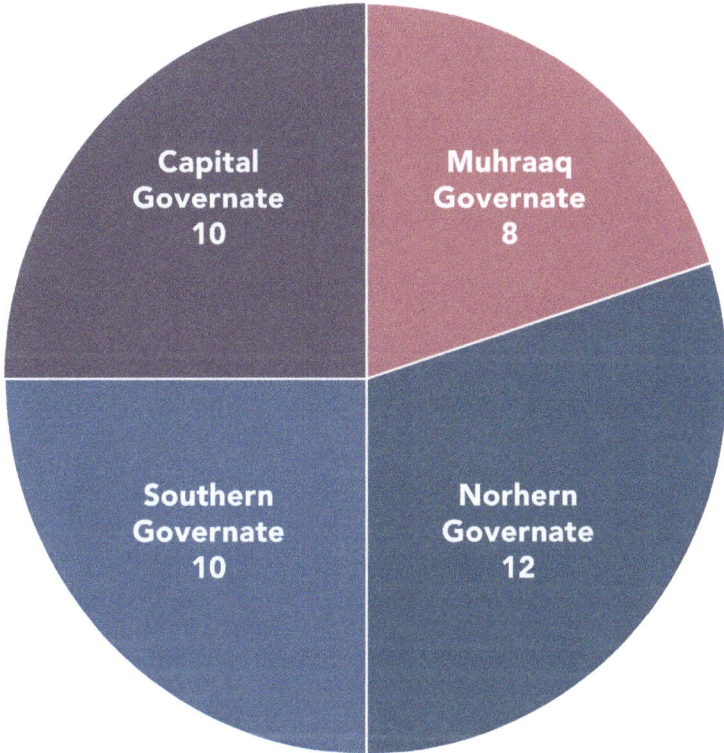

Capital Governate 10 — Muhraaq Governate 8 — Southern Governate 10 — Norhern Governate 12

- Capital Governate
- Northern Governate
- Muharraq Governate
- Southern Governate

Male VS. Female Candidates

Total Candidates	2002	2066	2010	2014	2018
	185	224	134	288	292
Female Candidates	8	17	7	22	40
Male Candidates	177	207	127	266	252

Women Vs. Men at the Council of Representatives

2002 - 2018

Year	Political Societies		Independent	
	Female Members	Male Members	Female Members	Male Members
2002	0	17	0	23
2006	0	31	1	9
2010	0	26	1	14
2011 (Bi-Elections)	0	2	3	16
2014	0	7	3	33
2018	0	7	6	34

Legislative Elections Voting History

2002- 2018

	2002	2006	2010	2014	2018
Votes in %	53.48	72.6	67	52.6	67

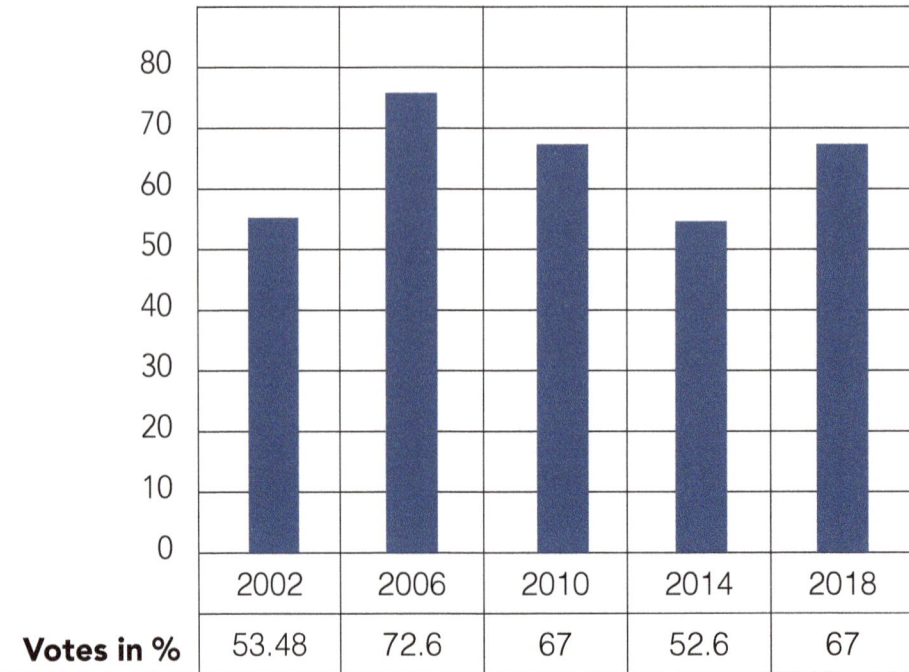

Council of Representatives Voting Participation

Male VS. Female, 2002 - 2014

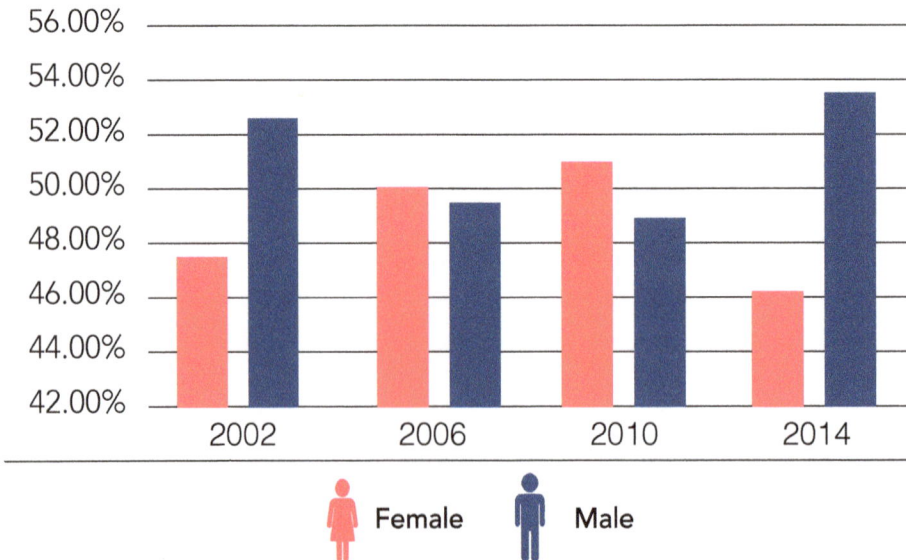

Female   Male

Male and Female Candidates
Running for Council of Representatives

2002 - 2018

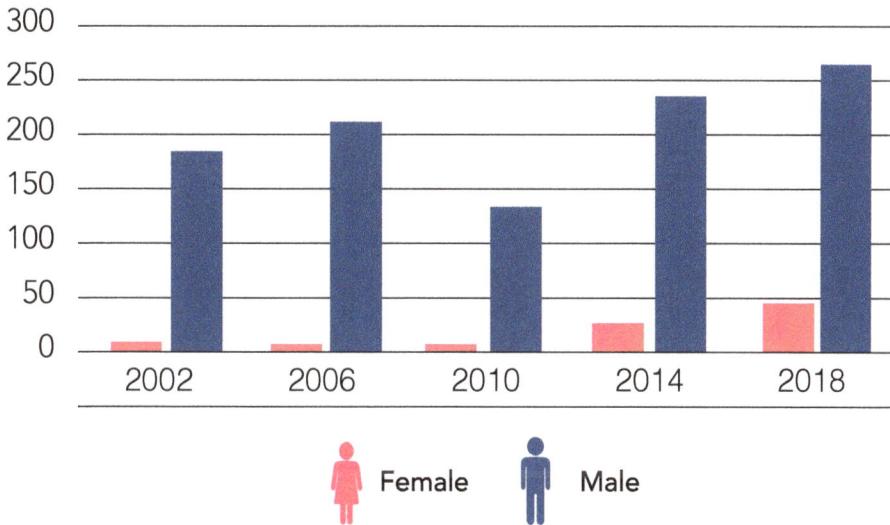

Male and Female Candidates
Running for Council of Representatives

2002 - 2014, Muharaq Governorate

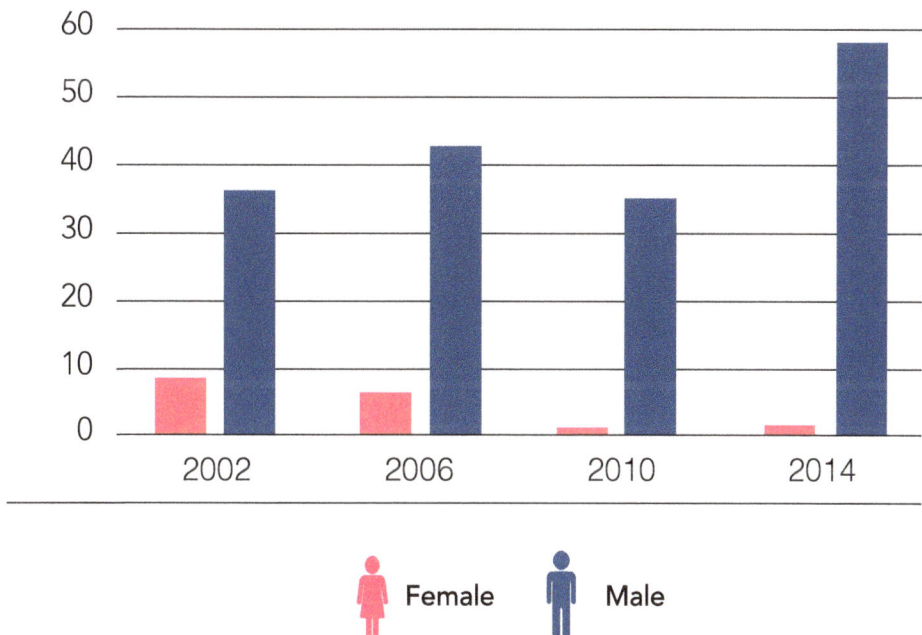

Male Vs Female History of Candidates Running for Council of Representatives

2002 - 2014, Central Governorate

Central Governorate was eliminated prior to 2014 elections.

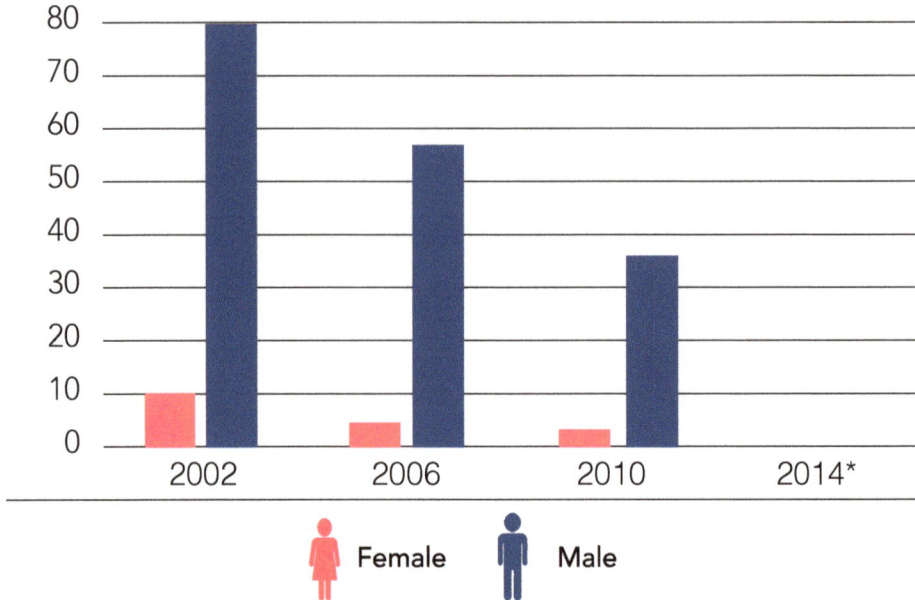

Female   Male

Male Vs Female History of Candidates Running for Council of Representatives

2002 - 2014, Northern Governorate

Central Governorate was eliminated prior to 2014 elections.

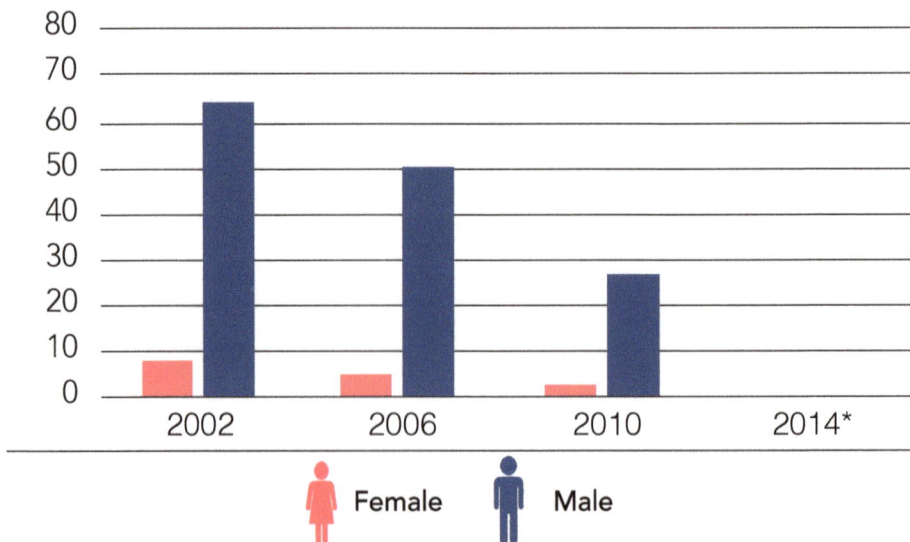

Female   Male

Male Vs Female History of Candidates Running for Council of Representatives

2002 - 2014, Capital Governorate

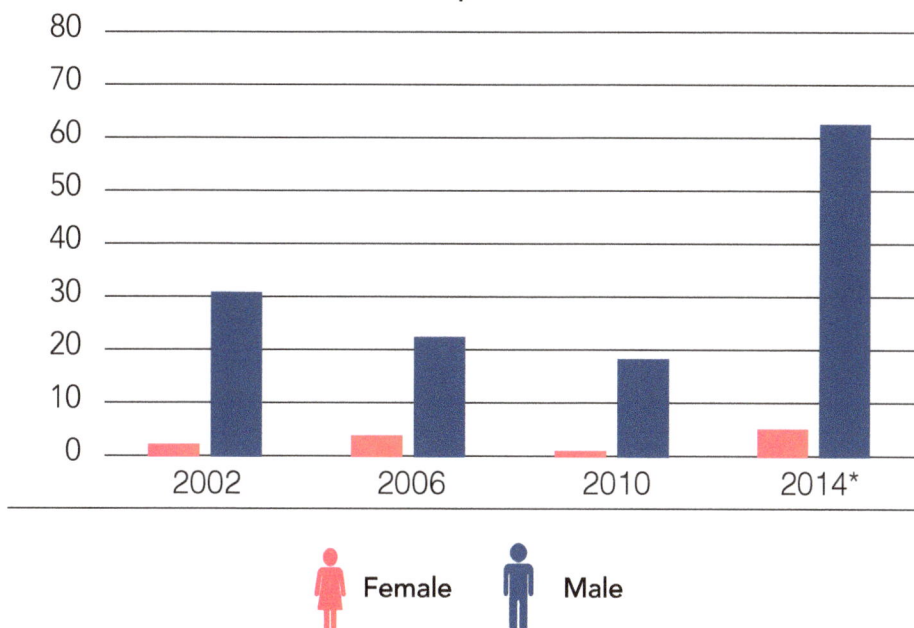

Male Vs Female History of Candidates Running for Council of Representatives

2002 - 2014, Southern Governorate

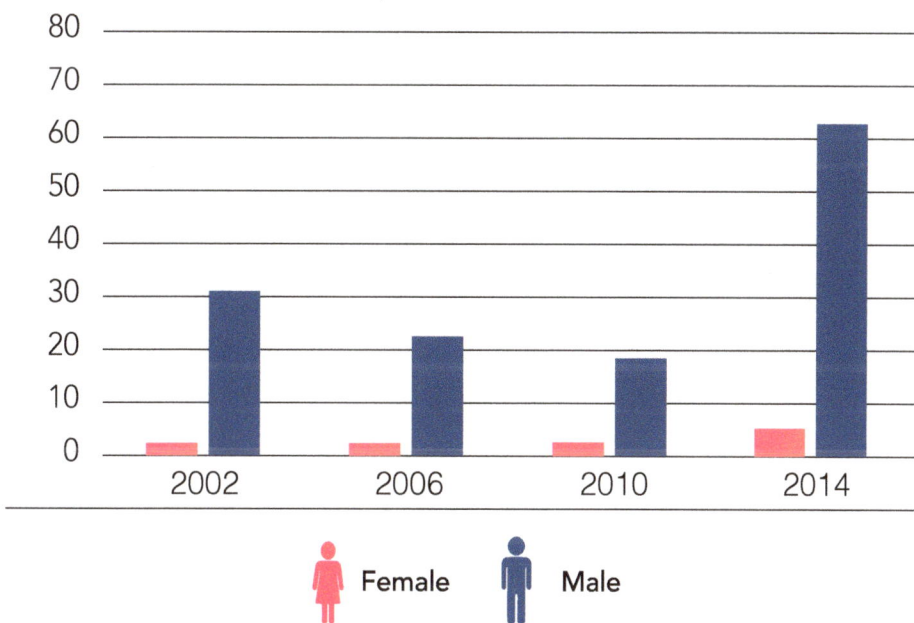

Proposed Legislations 2002 - 2018

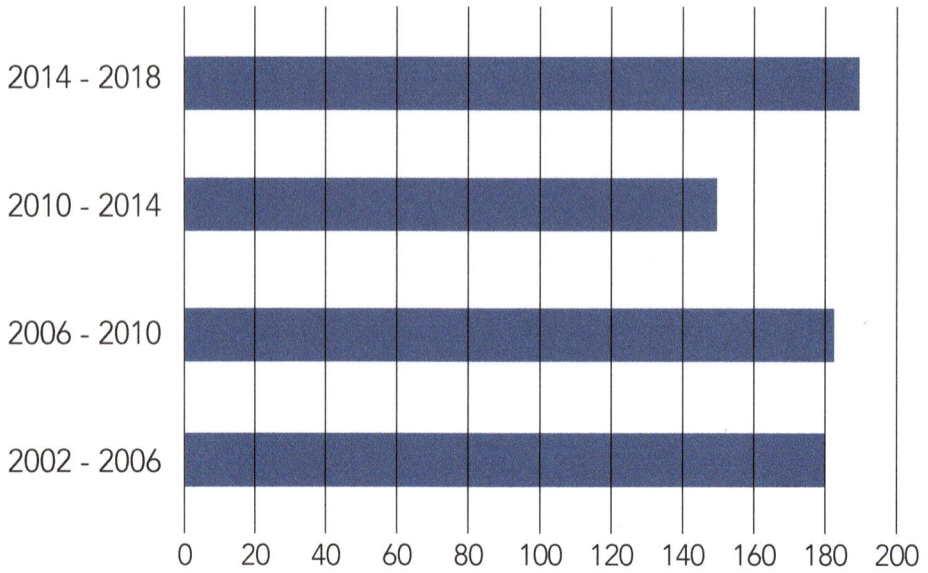

Proposed Legislations 2002 - 2018

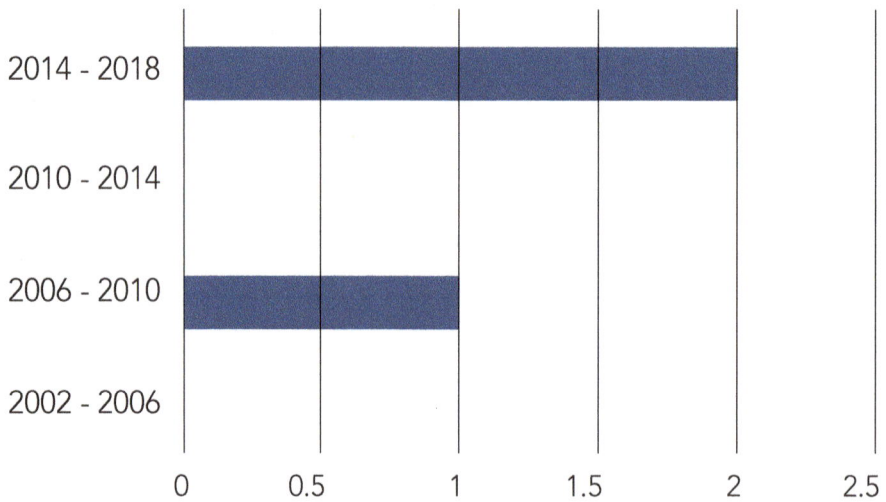

Proposed Legislations 2002 - 2018

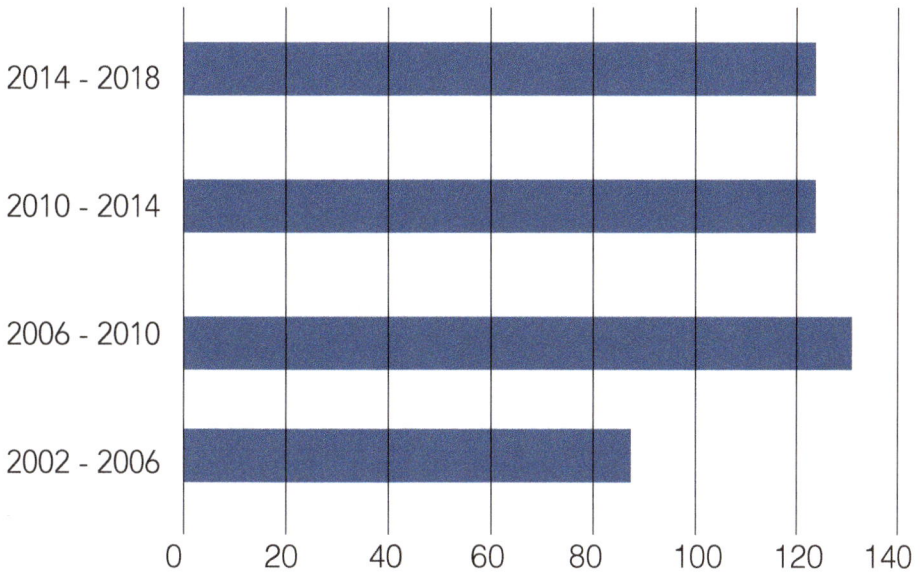

Hearings History 2002 - 2018

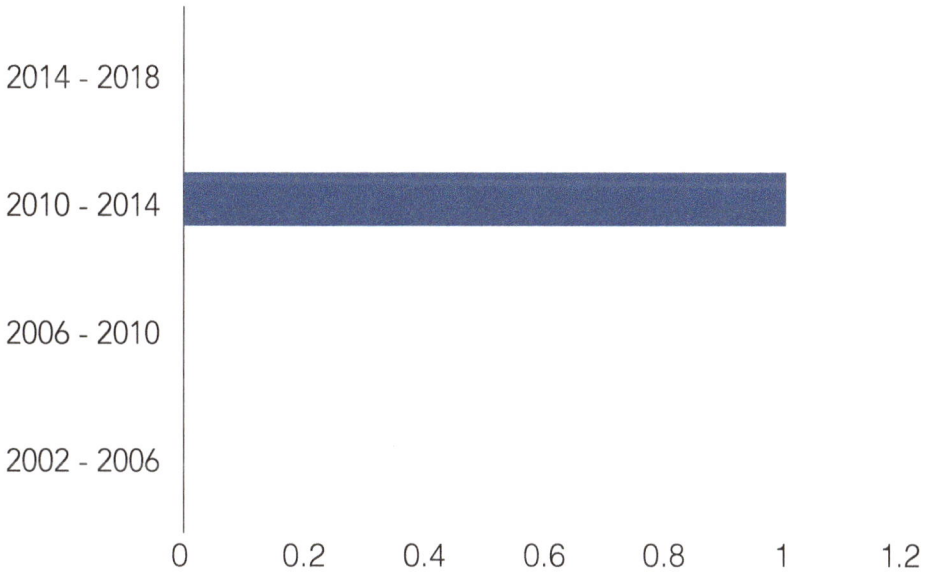

Petitionary Motions 2002 - 2018

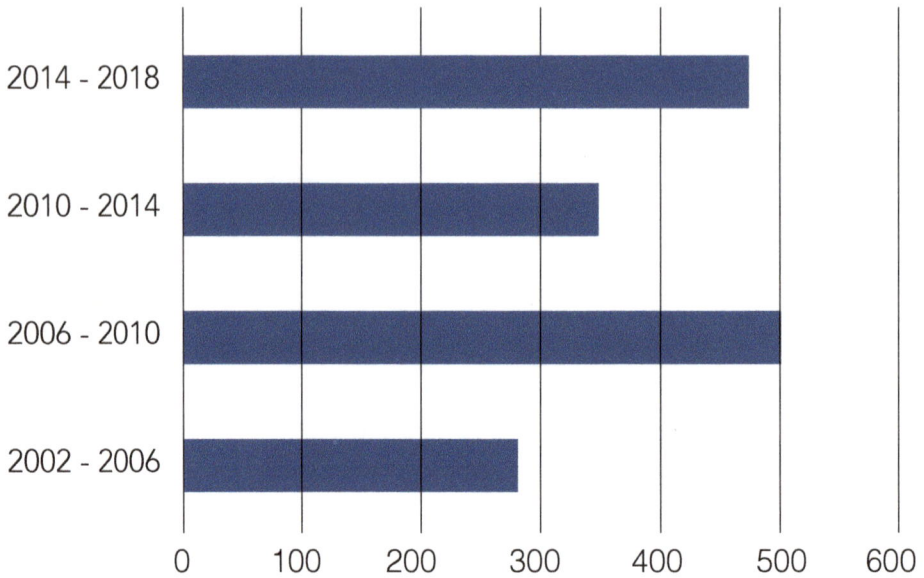

Period	Value
2014 - 2018	~475
2010 - 2014	~350
2006 - 2010	~500
2002 - 2006	~285

(Horizontal axis: 0, 100, 200, 300, 400, 500, 600)

Royal Decree History 2002 - 2018

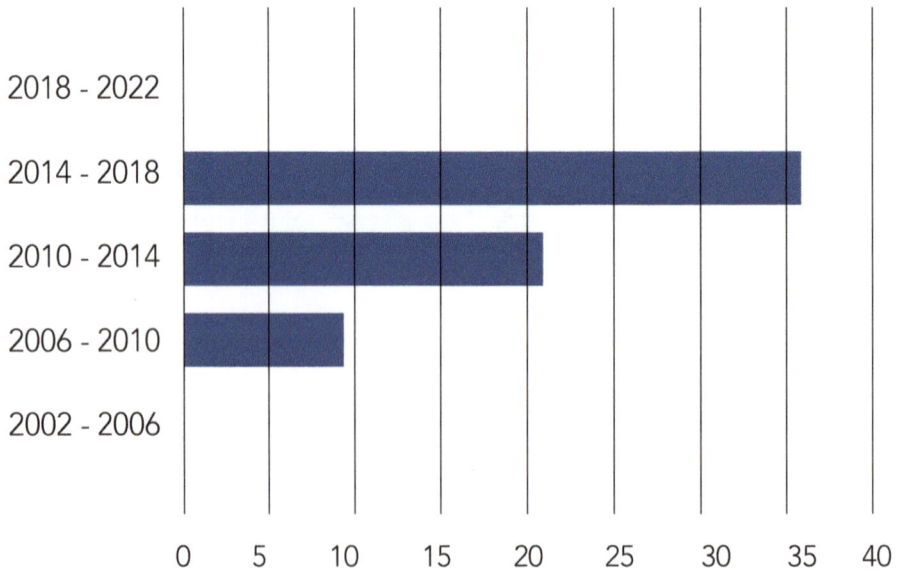

Period	Value
2018 - 2022	0
2014 - 2018	~35
2010 - 2014	~21
2006 - 2010	~10
2002 - 2006	0

(Horizontal axis: 0, 5, 10, 15, 20, 25, 30, 35, 40)

Council of RepresentativesProposed Legislations & Motions per Term 2002 - 2018

Focal	First Term	Second Term	Third Term	Fourth Term
Political	77	98	83	64
Finance & Economy	265	560	515	415
Foreign Affairs, Defense & National Security	45	140	127	78
General Services	272	636	837	578
Public Facilities & Environment	97	196	117	134
Youth & Sports	17	86	59	46
Women & Children	42	63	65	64
Total	**815**	**1779**	**1803**	**1379**

Council of Representatives Permanent Committees Comparison 2002 - 2018

Legislative Term	Legislative & Legal		Finance & Economy		Foreign Affairs, Defense & National Security		General Services		Public Facilities & Environment		Total	
	Meetings	Reports	Meetings	Reports	Meetings	Reports	Meetings	Reports	Meetings	Reports	Meetings	Reports
First Term	120	494	160	148	109	95	144	235	128	129	661	1101
Second Term	98	583	155	169	69	134	125	470	129	273	576	1629
Third Term	107	589	133	208	88	173	110	409	115	349	553	1728
Fourth Term	125	555	124	167	103	150	134	357	129	301	615	1530
Total	450	2221	572	692	369	552	513	1471	501	1052	2405	5988

Council of Representatives per Term Committees Analysis, Discussed Subjects 2002 - 2018

Committee	First Term				Second Term				Third Term				Fourth Term				Total
	Royal Decree	Proposed Legislation	Law Suggestio	Motion	Royal Decree	Proposed Legislation	Law Suggestio	Motion	Royal Decree	Proposed Legislation	Law Suggestio	Motion	Royal Decree	Proposed Legislation	Law Suggestio	Motion	
Legislative & Legal	0	42	56	42	2	44	69	44	15	91	22	58	11	45	67	42	650
Finance & Economy	0	40	32	42	3	65	36	92	14	107	12	54	11	65	26	35	634
Foreign Affairs, Defense & National Security	0	72	23	61	0	36	40	78	8	82	20	69	5	44	31	45	614
General Services	0	56	53	135	0	89	112	388	7	102	48	262	4	71	64	182	1573
Public Facilities & Environment	0	28	9	96	3	29	25	237	3	88	8	274	4	55	28	171	1058
Total	0	238	173	376	8	263	282	839	47	470	110	717	35	280	216	475	4529

Council of Representatives
Special Committees Analysis 2002 - 2018

Legislative Term	Palestine		Human Rights		Youth & Sports		Women & Children		Total	
	Meetings	Reports	Meetings	Reports	Meetings	Reports	Meetings	Reports	Meetings	Reports
First Term	No Data Available									
Second Term										
Third Term	7	1	21	3	11	47	3	11	42	62
Fourth Term	19	1	43	2	27	45	50	22	139	70
Total	**26**	**2**	**64**	**5**	**38**	**92**	**53**	**33**	**181**	**132**

Council of Representatives Investigation Committees & Their Prospective Reports per Term 2002 - 2018

Legislative Term	Formed Committees	Reports
First Term	4	4
Second Term	12	18
Third Term	10	13
Fourth Term	9	8

Council of Representatives Announcements per Term 2002 - 2018

Legislative Term	Term
First Term	36
Second Term	38
Third Term	92
Fourth Term	98
Total	264

Political Affiliations

Politics as we know it came onto the Bahraini scene only after the introduction of organized education, which paved the way for ideology carriers to introduce it to students who were not familiar with anything outside their own humble experience.

The Sunnite political movement started with the establishment of the Islamic Club in 1910 in al-Fadhel, Manama, a neighborhood known for giving birth to most of the Sunnite civic leaders. This was followed by the establishment of the Islamic Forum in 1928 and the al-Islah Society in 1941. The wave started in the form of clubs and social associations in response to the missionaries who came to the island through the American Mission Hospital to spread the Christian faith through charitable activities. These movements soon became political, participating in protests and or even taking sides in political debates, and they became more organized by colonial Britain.

Bahrain was ahead of its peers in the Gulf, having the first organized schooling system in 1919, that was followed by cultural clubs that bore the nationalist ideology influenced by the Syrian, Egyptian Iraqi, Kuwaiti, and Palestinian educational professionals who were hired to help start the educational system in Bahrain. In 1919, the Literary Club was established in Muharraq by Abdulla al-Zayed, Ahmed Fakhro, and Qasim al-Shirawi. The club played a significant role in encouraging nationalists to commit violence against the colonial British existence, not only in Bahrain but in the entire region. It hosted prominent names such as Amin al-Raihani, Abdulaziz al-Tha'alibi, and Sheikh Mohamed al-Shankeeti and was shut down in the late '20s for the role it played politically.

Shiites came to the organized political scene in 1968 through the formation of the al-Dawa'a Party. The party was established by Bahraini college students who had graduated from Iraqi universities and held revolutionary Islamic ideologies, with the help of Islamic clergy students from al-Najaf. They reached their peak right after the Islamic revolution of Iran took place, gaining moral support along with funding and training, and they called for replacing the ruling family with a radical Shiite regime, a replica of the Iranian Revolution.

Political Associations

A political party is formed by a group of persons organized to acquire and exercise political power. Political parties originated in their modern form in Europe and the United States in the 19th century, along with the electoral and parliamentary systems, whose development reflects the evolution of parties. The term party has since come to be applied to all organized groups seeking political power, whether by democratic elections or by revolution.

A fundamental distinction can be made between the conventional political parties and the political societies in the Kingdom of Bahrain. It is known throughout the world that a political party not only contributes toward civic development of the laws but forms and ousts Governments should they acquire enough seats in their respective legislative bodies.

Political societies can perform all the above, but they cannot form a Government, as the Constitution explicitly states that forming a Government is the sole responsibility of the appointed Prime Minister. However, it also gave the power to Parliament to investigate, interrogate, and even sack a Minister, or even choose not to cooperate with the Prime Minister if they presented a valid case and gathered the required votes.

Political Societies Law

As per the Constitution, second clause, Political Societies Law, No. 26, 2005, political societies are organized groups that are established through the law with a public manifesto of a group of people with similar political beliefs and goals who openly participate in democratic life to achieve legal, economic, and social aspirations that are in the best interest of the Kingdom and its citizens. The fourth clause of the same law strictly mentions some basic guidelines that shape the political framework in the Kingdom. It provides societies with the total freedom to practice within the legally depicted outline.

Political Trends

There are arguably four main political trends in Bahrain:

Secular left-wing

The left-wing groups have the lengthiest pedigree, going back to union activity and independence demands in the 1950s. Three existing societies -left-wing, nationalist, and Baathist- have their roots in this period. The 2002 Constitution legalized and formalized political societies. However, in subsequent rounds of elections, these organizations failed to achieve the success they enjoyed in previous decades. These societies joined the opposition's boycott of the political process in 2011. As the unrest took a sectarian turn, Sunnis, moderates, and the middle class abandoned these societies in large numbers, leaving unanswered questions over their continued relevance.

Secular Liberal

The weakest of these four trends are nationalist and liberal societies. A few societies, like the National Action Charter Society, received considerable support when they first emerged in 2002, but because they were squeezed between the left-wing societies and the Islamists, they failed to make an impact. During the 2011 unrest, several societies, like al-Wasat and the National Dialogue Society, joined the al-Fateh Coalition. Only a few small societies continue to occupy the center ground, with no national exposure whatsoever.

Shia Islamists

Shia Islamist activity goes back to the 1970s, the peak of the Shiite movements, such as the Religious Bloc in the 1973 Council. The 1979 Iranian Islamic Revolution radicalized these entities—and controlled them—leading to the Islamic Front for the Liberation of Bahrain's Iran-backed coup attempt in 1981. Those who were found guilty by the court were jailed or exiled, and their political activity went underground. In 2002, these trends formed al-Wefaq and Amal, although unregistered radical groups like Haq and al-Wafa broke away. Al-Wefaq boycotted elections in 2002 and participated in 2006, winning 17 seats. During the 2011 unrest, al-Wefaq resigned their 18 seats in the Council of Representatives and retained their municipal seats until 2014, and they have yet to return. As of 2016, two of the key Shia sectarian societies—Al-Wefaq and Amal—have been legally dissolved by court orders.

Sunna Islamists

Sunna Islamic societies first formally came to being in 2002, and the two leading societies, the Salafist al-Asalah Islamic Society and the pro Islamic Brotherhood, al-Minbar al-Islami Society , won twelve seats between them. Although both societies have remained socially and politically active, their political support has gradually depleted to the point where both today only have three formally serving members.

Orientation

Three main political orientations were shaped during and after the 2011 unrest; based on their goals and what they tried to achieve then and there, they took a corner of the arena that served them best:

Opposition

Public figures, societies, movements, and a big part of the Shiite community announced their boycott of the entire political life in 2011, which continues today for most of the groups mentioned above. An opposition, in political terms, usually referred to parliamentarian minorities that carry different values or have unorthodox means, such as the Greens in some parts of the world. However, in the Kingdom of Bahrain, that name is given to different groups that call for a coup and others who boycott without having a backup plan. In principle, it refers to those who have always been against the tide since the '50s.

Pro-Government

Pro-Government is a term used in Bahrain to identify the groups that favor the Government and supported it in the 1990s, in 2011, and afterwards. As a definition, such groups favor the system and resists radical change, especially the kind that has no manifesto or clear message. Despite the name-calling, these groups have a clear vision: they consider the ruling family the rightful rulers of Bahrain and seek real reform at the same time. These groups consist of almost all sects and political backgrounds in Bahrain but have a Sunna majority.

Silent Majority

By definition, the silent majority is the unspecified large group of people in a country that does not express its opinions publicly. In Bahrain, this group became the biggest in terms of numbers after 2014. Most felt they had been let down by those they followed, others concluded that politics was not for them, and the rest had just given up.

Pre-2002 Movements

Al-Nadi al-Islami
The Islamic Club

Considered the first Islamic society in Bahrain, being established in 1910 after calls by Mohamed Rasheed Redha in Cairo. He called for the establishment of Islamic clubs and societies in response to missionaries in the Middle East. Educated people, as well as merchants, responded to these calls, including Sheikh Mohamed Muqbil al-Thikeer, who, instead of preaching to the poor against the missionaries and their charities, which included the only hospital in town, enlightened them through counter-establishments such as the Islamic Club. The club was located in the *Souq* 'market' and opposite the missionary library.

Al-Muntada al-Islami
Islamic Forum

Established in 1982 by young men, including Ali Kanoo, Mohamed al-Wazzan, Ebrahim Khonji, Saleh al-Sehemmi. Its members were influenced guided by the Society of Muslim Youth in Egypt on the structure and legal paperwork. Shaikh Mubarak bin Hamad al-Khalifa was elected its first president. The group's primary focus was standing up to missionaries, as they were connected to the Islamic Brotherhood in Egypt, but they were not necessarily influenced by them.

Jameyat Etihad Arab al-Khaleej
Society of the Gulf Arabs Union

The first reform movement came in 1938 triggered by the Palestine-Israeli conflict and the emergence of the Patriotic Bloc in Kuwait, which called for basic demands such as a representative Council, a Constitution, and replacing the police force with locals instead of Iranians and Indians. Amongst their demands was banning Jews from entering the country and stripping the Bahraini Jews of their citizenship. In retaliation, Bapco fired 18 workers for participating in the society's activities, and their leaders were captured by the authorities, including Saad al-Shamlan, Ahmed al-Shirawi, and Ali al-Fadhel, only to re-establish it in Iraq in 1939. However, it did not last long due to the Second World War.

Jameyat al-Islah
Islah Society

The Jameyat al-Islah 'Islah Society' was founded in 1941 as the Students Club in Muharraq. The name changed to the Islah Club in 1948. Known as the Islamic brotherhood's front in Bahrain, the name again changed in 1980 to the Islah Society. Islah is the Arabic term for reform. The society focused -just like the other Sunni movements- on fighting missionaries and preparing youths to be active Muslims in their religious communities. Only after the establishment of their political society, Jameyat al-Menbar al-Islami did it became known that their agendas were politically focused and that they were using their charitable work as a means to gain public support.

Haya'at al-Itihad al-Watani
National Unity Commission

The '50s were wrought with issues on the island like no other era in its history. The Aramco strike of 1953 and the 1954 Sitra unrests that led to the death of four Sunnites forced the leaders of both sects to take vital measures to stop the civil unrest and establish what is known as the National Unity Commission (NUC). Other movements were founded after the NUC, but they failed to unite the sects of the community peacefully.

The NUC was considered the first coalition of its kind in Bahrain, as it unified the Shiites and the Sunnites, the liberals and Baathists, despite the growing tension between both sects in the 50s. It was the alarming events of 1953 that alerted the founders to the importance of such unity, especially after the Bahrain Petroleum Company (Bapco) and Muharram incidents.

With a national patriotic responsibility, the NUC lined up meetings in mosques to help unite all groups as Bahrainis, with the first meeting held in the Juma'a Mosque in the city of Muharraq. Unfortunately, the meeting was banned and did not take place as it went against the Government and colonial Britain's plans. Despite the ban, they met in smaller groups in scattered mosques all over the island.

Al-Haya'a al-Tanfeethya al-Ulya
High Executive Committee (HEC)

In October 1954, the bin-Khamis Mata'am held the largest meeting with leaders of both sects when they decided to form the coalition to stand their ground against Charles Belgrave. A week later, another meeting was held in Sanabis to elect the commission's leadership and prepare their followers through the al-Qafila newspaper. One hundred and twenty men were chosen to form the coalition, with a high executive committee of eight men (four Sunnites and four Shiites) with a second and third set of eights in case the first was caught. The chosen leaders were:

Sunnites:

1. Abdulrahman al-Bakir
2. Abdulaziz al-Shamlan
3. Ebrahim bin Mousa
4. Ebrahim Fakhro

Shiites:

1. Abdali al-Alaiwat
2. Sayyed Ali Kamaluddein
3. Abdulla Abu Deeb
4. Muhsen al-Tajir

At this time, the NUC eliminated the sectarian stress and transformed itself into an organized civil movement. They are credited for transforming the community into key supporters of the Arab nationalism causes, as well as increasing the awareness of workers' rights, which eventually led to the first Labor Law of Bahrain by establishing labor unions as a first step.

Jabhat al-Tahreer al-Watani-Bahrain
National Liberation Front-Bahrain

Founded in February 15, 1955, and was the first leftist party in the Arabian Gulf. They considered themselves to be clandestine Marxist-Leninists. In the 1960s and '70s, the NLF, headed by Ahmed al-Thawadi—known by his peers as Saif al-Bin Ali—who was assisted by Yousif Ajaji and Abdulla Rashid bin Ali, played a leading part in two main events. The March uprising of 1965, in which nationalist forces revolted against British colonialism, and the labor movement of the early 1970s.

By the first half of the 1970s, the NLF was a major political force in the country, and following the 1974 parliamentary election, it succeeded in having eight members in the first Bahrain National Assembly. In 1976, however, Parliament shut down. The NLF went underground, and many of its members went into voluntarily and non-voluntarily exile.

Despite the unprecedented political circumstances that faced the surviving activists of the NLF, a handful of fighters remained, though they participated in different activities—some chose to remain in exile, while others chose to still carry firearms, and the rest decided to participate in the legal, political space they were given.

In the early 2000s, after the National Charter took place, exiled leaders could return to Bahrain to exercise their political work of choice by the force of the law. It was this climate that made them establish the Progressive Democratic Tribune before the first parliamentary elections since 1973, winning two seats in 2002, including deputy speaker.

Harakat al-Qawmeen al-Arab
The Movement of Arab Nationalists

Was established in 1959 in Bahrain, where the movement started to frame itself within Bahraini society at the hands of local students who received their higher education in areas where strong nationalists movements existed, such as Cairo, Beirut, Baghdad, and Damascus. Among these students were Ahmed Humaidan and Abdulrahman Kamal, who returned after completing their higher studies and started the movement. The movement was fueled by their direct, undeniable ties to the headquarters of similar movements in the capitals mentioned earlier, and they were urged by those groups to channel their actions against the British existence in Bahrain and the region and stand firmly against Iranian migration to Bahrain. They considered migration a chief threat to the sovereignty of the state and its identity and believed it should be fought aggressively. They also demanded that such immigrants have no rights.

Hezb al-Dawa'a al-Islamiya
Islamic Call party

Bahrain's chapter of *al-Dawa'a* was established in 1968 exclusively by Bahraini college graduates from Iraq. Representatives from the party participated in the 1972 elections. In 1983, the leaders of the party were prosecuted by the authorities for being associated with the party in Iraq and, therefore, went underground until al-Wefaq was established.

Jamiyat al-Irshad al-Islami
Islamic Guidance Society

Jamiyat al-Irshad al-Islami was founded in 1969 at al-Urrayedh Shrine in Manama as the Youth for Islamic Irshad Society, which was later changed to the Islamic Irshad Society. It was denied licensing due to the contradiction it had with the shrine.

Jamiyat al-Taweya'a al-Islamiya
Islamic Awareness Society

Al-dawa'a Islamic party's religious arm was licensed in 1972 as an Islamic awareness society with religious classes and Quran recital lessons in Duraz. Sheikh Isa Qasim became its first leader while still a member of the National Council. The society played a vital role in politicizing the Shiite crowds and electing their National Assembly's candidates during the rallies.

The society also played a leading role against the leftists. Months before the Islamic Revolution in Iran, the society leaders had their first contact with Ayatollah Khomeini while he was in the holy city of Najaf, where the society (both Iraqi and Bahraini) assisted him financially and morally. After the revolution, Sheikh Isa Qasim, Sheikh Abdulamir al-Jamri, and Sheikh Abbas al-Rayes flew to Tehran to congratulate the Ayatollah in person. Support continued through the spreading of the revolutionary ideology in Bahrain and by linking it to the martyrdom of Imam Hussein ibn Ali and accusing everyone who did not support them of being enemies of the imam.

The authorities prosecuted the leaders of the society and shut it down in 1984. It resumed its activities in March 2001 and operated until May 2017, when it was shut down again for the same reasons as before.

Al-Sundouq al-Husseini al-Ijtemaie
Husseini Social Fund

The Husseini Social Fund was founded by Shiite clerks and college graduates in 1972. It was considered an arm of the Islamic Irshad Society and was led by Sayyed Jaffar al-Alawi. Because it failed to get a license to practice, it worked through the Islamic Culture Public Library. In 1976, the fund was forced to separate itself from the library due to noteworthy violations, including spreading its ideology by giving books of Sayyed Hadi al-Modaressi away. It got its name after the separation and started to call for revolutionary acts, joining hands with the Islamic Front for Bahrain's Liberation by recruiting and preparing jihadists to join the front when ready.

Al-Jabha al-Shabbiya fe al-Bahrain
Bahrain's People Liberation Front

The Bahrain's People Liberation Front was an underground political party established in 1974 by members of the Occupied Arabian Gulf Liberation Front, which had two branches later on: the Oman's People Liberation Front and Bahrain's People Liberation Front, whose members formed the BPLF after taking part in the armed struggle of Dhofar in the Sultanate of Oman. The BPLF established the National Democratic Action Society (Wa'ad) after the National Action Charter was passed, and it became the first licensed political society in the Arabian Gulf states.

Jamiyat al-Tarbiya al-Islamia
Tarbeia Islamic Society

The Society was instituted mainly as a response to the extreme conservatism of the Islah Society in 1979. It focused on charity and later used this as a means to attract support for its political arm, the al-Asalah Islamic Society. Among its founders are Sheikh Abdullatif al-Mahmoud and Sheikh Salah al-Jowdar, who were on the original crew of the Elite's Charter.

Harakat al-Wehda al-Islamiya
Islamic Unity Movement

Established on February 14, 1980, by Sheikh Abdulazeem al-Muhtadi al-Bahrani and was exposed by the authorities when captured. The movement was identical to the Liberation Front; hence, its members joined the Liberation Front afterwards..

Harakat al-Shuhada'a al-Islamiya
Islamic Martyrs Movement

Founded by Sheikh Jamal al-Asfoor in 1980 and was dismantled a few weeks after its inception due to a lack of members and funding. Its members joined the Liberation Front as well.

Al-Areedha al-Nakhbaweya
Elite's Charter

Three hundred and sixty-five signees were represented by Sheikh Abdullatif al-Mahmoud, Sheikh Abdulamir al-Jamri, Mohsin Marhoun, Mohamed J. Sabah, and Abdulwahab Hussein. On November 15, 1992, they handed a letter to the late Emir Shaikh Isa bin Salman al-Khalifa requesting his consensus to reactivate the 1973 National Assembly. The Emir made it clear they only represented themselves and did not represent a *Popular Mandate*.

To overcome the matter, they decided after three meetings that the Elite's Charter would become the *Popular Charter*. Twenty-three thousand citizens signed a petition to support this endeavor, of which most were Shiites, which resulted in the notable efforts their scholars made for it to be successful. Time proved their real intentions when they hijacked the command and the initiative after the Marathon incident and made the peaceful attempt a violent one, igniting the unrest of the 90s.

Political Societies

Licensed Movements

Jamiyat al-Wefaq al-Watani al-Islami
Al-Wefaq National Islamic Society

Founded: 2001

Closed: 2018 by court order after exhausting all legal options due to critical violations.

Ideology: Shia Revolutionary Islam

Orientation: Shia Theocratic Opposition

Ideological Affiliation: Islamic Republic of Iran

Location: Adhari Area

Members Count: 1500

Female Headcount: 342

Number of Secretary Generals: 2

Parliament Representation(s):

2002 – Boycott

2006 – 17 Seats

2010 – 18 Seats

2014 – Boycott

2018 – Ceased activity by court order

Al-Wefaq was founded in November 2001 when many Islamic opposition figures returned from exile in the context of King Hamad's amnesty. The decision-making apparatus of this society is dominated by Shia clerics. Its spiritual leader is Sheikh Isa Qasim. The organization's secretary-general is the cleric Sheikh Ali Salman, who was jailed in 2015. Al-Wefaq boycotted the 2002 elections but participated in 2006 and 2010. Al-Wefaq had 18 MPs in the 2010 CoR before its walkout in 2011. Al-Wefaq boycotted the parliamentary elections in 2002 but participated and won 17 seats in 2006. In June 2016, it was announced that al-Wefaq would be shut down, with the Justice Ministry accusing the society of fueling sectarianism and extremism. It was officially closed in 2018.

جمعية العمل الوطني الديمقراطي **وعد**
WAAD National Democratic Action Society

Jamiyat al-Amal al-Watani al-Democrati
National Democratic Action Society (WA'AD)

Founded: 2001

Closed: 31 May 2017 by court order after exhausting all legal options due to critical violations.

Ideology: Nationalist Progressive Left

Orientation: Liberal Opposition

Ideological Affiliation: Lebanon

Location: Umm al-Hassam

Members Count: 291

Female Headcount: 78

Number of Secretary Generals: 4

Parliament Representation(s):

2002 – Boycott

2006 – 0 Seats

2010 – 0 Seats

2014 – Boycott

2018 – Ceased activity by court order

This left-wing society has a long history of political action, considering themselves to be a continuum of *Harakat al-Qawmeen al-Arab*. Despite having enjoyed support among moderates and the middle classes, the society consistently fared severely in parliamentary elections. Under its previous secretary-general, Ibrahim Sharif, Wa'ad fatefully joined forces with al-Wefaq during the 2011 uprising, losing most of its mainstream support in the process. The last leader, before shutting down was Fouad Seyadi, succeeding Radhi al-Mosawi.

جمعية العمل الإسلامي
Islamic Action Society

Jamiyat al-Amal al-Islami
Islamic Action Society (AMAL)

Founded: 2002

Closed: 2012 by court order after exhausting all legal options due to critical violations.

Ideology: Shia Revolutionary Islam

Orientation: Shia Theocratic Opposition

Ideological Affiliation: Islamic Republic of Iran

Location: Qufool

Members Headcount: 106

Female Headcount: 11

Number of Secretary Generals: 1

Parliament Representation(s):

2002 – Boycott

2006 – Boycott

2010 – Boycott

2014 – Ceased activity by court order

2018 – Ceased activity by court order

The Islamic Action Society is associated with the Shirazi segment of the Shia community in Bahrain (who followed the leadership of Mohamed Al-Shirazi and were associated with Hadi al-Modarrissi—Amal's spiritual leader. The Shirazi's have a history of radical political activism in Bahrain dated back to the 1970s, notably in the form of the Iran-sponsored Islamic Front for the Liberation of Bahrain, which was dissolved after staging a coup attempt in 1981. Amal brought these trends together in the context of King Hamad's reconciliation program and the movement it formally registered. Amal boycotted all the parliamentary and municipal elections and aligned itself with the opposition movement in 2011, before being closed down by court orders in 2012.

Jamiyat al-Menbar al-Taqadomi al-Democrati
Progressive Democratic Tribune

Founded: 2002

Ideology: Progressive Left

Orientation: Liberal Opposition

Ideological Affiliation: CCCP

Location: Isa Town

Members Count: 342

Female Headcount: 61

Number of Secretary Generals: 3

Parliament Representation(s):

2002 – 2 Seats

2006 – 0 Seats

2010 – 0 Seats

2011 – Boycott

2014 – Boycott

2018 – 2 Seats

Jamiyat al-Menbar al-Taqadomi al-Democrati is a left-wing society which was formally established in 2002 as a continuation of the National Liberation Front (NLF), which was first established in 1955, making it the oldest active political society in Bahrain. The membership is said to be small and mostly elderly, made up of those with a history of left-wing and communist activism. It retains influence within the trade union movements.

In 2009, the PDT affiliated itself with Wa'ad and the NDA to form the Nationalist Democratic Movement, which is described as a secular, democratic opposition. In 2011, the PDT, Wa'ad, and the NDA united with the Shia Islamic society al-Wefaq in boycotting the political process. However, since 2014, the PDT broke away from the other opposition societies. In December 2017, the secretary-general announced to the press that they would cross the boycott and participate in the elections in 2018. They won 2 seats.

جمعية المنبر الوطني الإسلامي
Al-Menber Al-Watani Al-Islami Society

Jamiyat al-Menbar al-Watani al-Islami
Al-Menbar al-Watani al-Islami Society

Founded: 2002

Ideology: Islamic Brotherhood

Orientation: Theocratic Pro-Government

Ideological Affiliation: Egypt

Location: Muharraq

Members Count: 250

Female Headcount: 9

Number of Secretary Generals: 4

Parliament Representation(s):

2002 – 7 Seats

2006 – 7 Seats

2010 – 3 Seats

2014 – 1 Seat

2018 – 0 Seats

This is a Sunni society with close links to the Muslim Brotherhood. In the 2002 parliamentary elections, it gained six seats. However, it has struggled in more recent years, only gaining one or two seats in the last two rounds of elections, and it came up emptyhanded in 2018. Although the society enjoys widespread support, its link to the Muslim Brotherhood has arguably been a hindrance in the last couple of years. Its last MP, Mohamed al-Ammadi, generally tended to avoid Islamic issues altogether in Parliament and became its secretary-general after failing to get re-elected in 2018.

Jamiyat al-Asalah al-Islamiyah
Al-Asalah Islamic Society

Founded: 2002

Ideology: Islamic Salafism

Orientation: Sunni Theocratic Pro-Government

Ideological Affiliation: Kingdom of Saudi Arabia

Location: Isa Town

Members Count: 2000

Female Headcount: 100

Number of Secretary Generals: 3

Parliament Representation(s):

2002 – 7 Seats

2006 – 7 Seats

2010 – 5 Seats

2014 – 5 Seats

2018 – 3 Seats

This Salafist society has been an influential political force, having won six seats in the 2002 elections. However, in the last two rounds of elections, it only succeeded in winning a couple of seats (although, customarily, several independent Islamist MPs have associated themselves with this society). Despite only representing a narrow fringe of Bahraini society, al-Asalah has tended to be highly influential when campaigning on social issues. Al-Asalah separated from the al-Fateh Coalition in 2013, following differences over how to pursue participation in the National Dialogue.

Jamiyat al-Rabitah al-Islamiyah
Islamic League Society

Founded: 2002

Ideology: Najaf Institutional Shiism

Orientation: Shia Theocratic Pro-Government

Ideological Affiliation: Republic of Iraq

Location: Jiddhafs

Members Count: 100

Female Headcount: Unknown

Number of Secretary Generals: 2

Parliament Representation(s):

2002 – 3 Seats

2006 – 0 Seats

2010 – 0 Seat

2014 – 1 Seats

2018 – 0 Seats

    This moderate Shia society was last represented by MP Ali al-Atish in the 2014 CoR. The society was active following the 2001 new Constitution and gained three seats in 2002. However, it has been less visible as a coherent society in recent years.

تجمــع الوحــدة الــوطنية
National Unity Assembly

Tajamo'a al-Wehda al-Wataniya
National Unity Assembly

Founded: 2012

Ideology: None

Orientation: Pro-Government

Ideological Affiliation: None

Location: Busaiteen

Members Count: 121

Female Headcount: 28

Number of Secretary Generals: 1

Parliament Representation(s):

2002 – 0 Seats

2006 – 0 Seats

2010 – 0 Seats

2014 – 0 Seats

2018 – 1 Seat

This society, appearing in response to the 2011 unrest, primarily featured Sunni loyalists and was led by Abdullatif al-Mahmoud, who transformed it from a coalition into a political society. It quickly gained vast amounts of funding, support, and attention. However, by 2014, despite a high-profile campaign and reliable candidates, it failed to gain any seats at all in the parliamentary and municipal elections. In 2015, it recorded a 90% fall in donations, and relatively little has been heard from the movement in the media. In 2018, it put forward a smaller number of candidates: three for CoR and three for municipal. One of each category won, both in Hamad Town.

Jamiyat al-Tajamo'a al-Watani al-Destori
National Constitutional Assembly

Founded: 2002

Ideology: Arab Nationalism

Orientation: Liberal Pro-Government

Ideological Affiliation: Egypt

Location: Sanad

Members Count: 102

Female Headcount: 48

Number of Secretary Generals: 3

Parliament Representation(s):

2002 – 0 Seats

2006 – 0 Seats

2010 – 0 Seats

2014 – 0 Seats

2018 – 0 Seats

The National Constitutional Assembly '*al-Tajamo'a al-Watani al-Destori*' has never been a high-profile society, but it has continued to maintain a presence since being established in 2002. Its long-time serving secretary-general was Abdulrahman al-Bakir, who was recently replaced by Khalid al-Kalban.

النACTIONAL ACTION CHARTER SOCIETY

Jamiyat Meethaq al-Amal al-Watani
National Action Charter Society

Founded: 2002

Ideology: Arab Nationalism

Orientation: Liberal Pro-Government

Ideological Affiliation: Egypt

Location: Hidd

Members Count: 80

Female Headcount: 20

Number of Secretary Generals: 3

Parliament Representation(s):

2002 – 0 Seats

2006 – 0 Seats

2010 – 0 Seats

2014 – 0 Seats

2018 – 0 Seats

The society was set up in 2002 in support of the King's new Constitution and campaigned hard but unsuccessfully in the 2002 parliamentary elections. However, 16 members, including technocrat and business figures, gained seats in the Shura Council. This liberal society has supported progressive causes and was closely associated with the al-Muntada Society in the years prior to 2011. The society spoke out against the opposition in the 2011 unrest and, consequently, affiliated itself with al-Fateh Coalition.

Al-Tajamo'a al-Watani al-Democrati al-Wehdawi
Unitary National Democratic
Assembly (al-Wehdawi)

Founded: 2002

Ideology: Arab Nationalism

Orientation: Liberal Opposition

Ideological Affiliation: Syria

Location: Adliya

Members Count: 376

Female Headcount: 63

Number of Secretary Generals: 3

Parliament Representation(s):

2002 – Boycott

2006 – Boycott

2010 – Boycott

2014 – Boycott

2018 – Boycott

The Unitary National Democratic Assembly is associated with the opposition and has boycotted the political process since 2011. In 2015, the Justice Ministry issued a statement announcing that the organization would be shut down for violations of the Constitution and undermining security, but since they rectified their situation, all charges have been dropped.

Jamiyat al-Ekha al-Watani
Al-Ekha National Society

Founded: 2002

Ideology: Persian Nationalism

Orientation: Liberal Opposition

Ideological Affiliation: Islamic Republic of Iran

Location: Adliya

Members Count: 120

Female Headcount: 7

Number of Secretary Generals: 2

Parliament Representation(s):

2002 – 0 Seats

2006 – 0 Seats

2010 – 0 Seats

2014 – Boycott

2018 – Voluntarily Dissolved

The al-Ekha National Society (Al-Ikha) emerged in 2002, primarily among Bahrainis with Iranian roots 'Ajam' living in Muharraq. Its secretary-general is Musa Ghulum al-Ansari. It participated in the 2002 and 2006 legislative elections but won no seats. The society affiliated itself with the opposition in boycotting the political process after 2011. However, many Bahrainis from the Ajam community, particularly well-established figures, were reluctant to associate themselves with the opposition and distanced themselves from al-Ikha. As a result, in June 2016, this society eventually decided to shut down after failing to find sufficient active members to fill executive positions.

التجمع القومي الديمقراطي
National Democratic Assembly

Al-Tajamo'a al-Qawmi al-Democrati
National Democratic Assembly

Founded: 2002

Ideology: Baathist Progressive Left

Orientation: Liberal Opposition

Ideological Affiliation: Republic of Iraq

Location: Zenj

Members Count: 280

Female Headcount: 60

Number of Secretary Generals: 3

Parliament Representation(s):

2002 – 0 Seats

2006 – 0 Seats

2010 – 0 Seats

2014 – 0 Seats

2018 – 0 Seats

Hasan al-A'ali leads the National Democratic Assembly, and Mahmoud al-Qassab is deputy secretary-general. This Baathist society was established by Bahrainis who had studied in Iraq during the 1960s and 1970s. The society gained two seats in the 2002 parliamentary elections but failed to win seats in subsequent elections. Since 2011, it has boycotted the parliamentary process.

جمعية الوطن
Alwatan Society

Jamiyat al-Watan
Al-Watan Society

Founded: 2014

Closed: Voluntarily Dissolved in 2015

Ideology: None

Orientation: Pro-Government

Ideological Affiliation: None

Location: A'ali

Members Count: 50

Female Headcount: 13

Number of Secretary Generals: 1

Parliament Representation(s):

2002 – 0 Seats

2006 – 0 Seats

2010 – 0 Seats

2014 – 0 Seats

2018 – Voluntarily Dissolved

The al-Watan Society was formed in 2014 for the sole purpose of participating in the parliamentary elections by ex-one-term MP Ahmed al-Sa'ati. The society was shut down later that same year when its secretary-general and founder was appointed as an ambassador to Russia. The society was formed with no ideology, and none of its members had any political experience or exposure (aside from its founder's one term in the Council of Representatives). Its members were businessmen and women and academics. The society applied to be dissolved in 2015 and was granted permission by the justice Minister.

Jamiyat al-Saff al-Islami
Islamic Saff Society

Founded: 2007

Ideology: Islamic Salafism

Orientation: Sunni Theocratic Pro-Government

Ideological Affiliation: Kingdom of Saudi Arabia

Location: Riffa

Members Count: 102

Female Headcount: 19

Number of Secretary Generals: 1

Parliament Representation(s):

2002 – 0 Seats

2006 – 0 Seats

2010 – 0 Seats

2014 – 0 Seats

2018 – 0 Seats

The Islamic Saff Society is a smaller conservative Sunni Islamist society established in 2007. Its secretary-general, Abdullah Bughammar, has recently complained about the difficulty of attracting funds and remaining politically active.

Harakat al-Adala al-Wataniya
National Adala Movement

Founded: 2006

Closed: Voluntarily Dissolved in 2019

Ideology: Nationalism

Orientation: Sunni Opposition

Ideological Affiliation: None

Location: Arad

Members Count: 600

Female Headcount: 0

Number of Secretary Generals: 1

Parliament Representation(s):

2002 – 0 Seats

2006 – 0 Seats

2010 – 0 Seats

2014 – 0 Seats

2018 – 0 Seats

This society describes itself as a secular movement with liberal and left-wing tendencies. It was established in 2006 with Abdullah Hashim (a founding member of al-Wehdawi) as its secretary-general. The organization has been outspoken against Islamic societies like al-Wefaq and al-Asalah. It has been less visible in recent years and filed for shutting down in July 2019.

جمعية الوسط العربي الاسلامي

Jamiyat al-Wasat al-Arabi
Al-Wasat Al-Arabi Society

Founded: 2002

Ideology: Conservative Nasserite

Orientation: Sunni Pro-Government

Ideological Affiliation: Egypt

Location: Hidd

Members Count: 87

Female Headcount: Unknown

Number of Secretary Generals: 1

Parliament Representation(s):

2002 – 0 Seats

2006 – 0 Seats

2010 – 0 Seats

2014 – 0 Seats

Al-Wasat Al-Arabi is a centrist Arab nationalist society that joined the al-Fateh Coalition in 2011, adapting Nasserite ideology. Al-Wasat's al-Fateh membership has been suspended since October 2014, and the leadership has, on occasion, hinted at discomfort in being associated with a coalition that was sometimes accused of having sectarian leanings. Al-Wasat's secretary-general, Ahmed al-Binali, resigned in 2014 in the context of the parliamentary elections. Since then, the society has been relatively dormant, with only an interim secretary-general, Jassim al-Muhazza.

جمعية الشورى الإسلامية

Jamiyat al-Shura al-Islamiya
Islamic Shura Society

Founded: 2002

Ideaology: Azharian Islam

Orientation: Sunni Theocratic Pro-Government

Ideological Affiliation: Egypt

Location: Arad

Members Count: 102

Female Headcount: 0

Number of Secretary Generals: 1

Parliament Representation(s):

2002 – 2 Seats

2006 – 0 Seats

2010 – 0 Seats

2014 – 0 Seats

The Islamic Shura Society is a political society of Sunni Islamic orientation. It won two seats in the 2002 parliamentary elections but has been a less visible presence in recent years. The Secretary-General Sheikh Abdulrahman Abdulsalam recently expressed his frustration at the problematic climate political societies are facing. On 18th July 2019 the Ministry of Justice announced through the official gazette the voluntarily dissolvement of the society.

جمعية الحوار الوطني

Jamiyat al-Hiwar al-Watani
National Dialogue Society

Founded: 2012

Ideology: None

Orientation: Pro-Government

Ideological Affiliation: None

Location: Riffa

Members Count: 55

Female Headcount: Unknown

Number of Secretary Generals: 1

Parliament Representation(s):

2002 – 0 Seats

2006 – 0 Seats

2010 – 0 Seats

2014 – 0 Seats

This society was set up in support of the post-2011 National Dialogue process. Following its affiliation with al-Fateh, it has been less visible as a separate entity.

Jamiyat Al-Iradah wa al-Taghiyr al-Wataniyah
National Will for Change Society

Founded: 20 February 2012

Ideology: None

Orientation: Pro-Government

Location: Manama

Members Count: 50

Female Headcount: 20

Number of Secretary Generals: 1

Parliament Representation(s):

2002 – 0 Seats

2006 – 0 Seats

2010 – 0 Seats

2014 – 0 Seats

The National Will for Change Society is a society which was active between 2012 and 2014. Has no visible accomplishments and said will dissolve itself voluntarily during the 2018 legislative elections if it won no seats.

جمعية الفكر الحر

Al-Fikr al-Watani al-Hurr
Free National Thought Society

Founded: 2002

Ideology: Egypt

Orientation: Liberal Pro-Government

Location: Riffa

Members Count: 98

Female Headcount: 46

Number of Secretary Generals: 1

Parliament Representation(s):

2002 – 0 Seats

2006 – 0 Seats

2010 – 0 Seats

2014 – 0 Seats

Al-Fikr al-Watani al-Hurr is considered to be a moderate and liberal opposition society, which has spoken out against violence. It has never been successful in elections but has gained Shura Council seats. The Secretary-General is Layla Rajab, making her the only woman chairing a political society.

Jamiyat Al-Adalah Wal Tanmeyah
Justice & Development Society

Founded: 2011

Closed: Voluntarily Dissolved in 2015

Ideology: None

Orientation: Liberal Pro-Government

Location: Muharraq

Members Count: 50

Female Headcount: 7

Number of Secretary Generals: 1

Parliament Representation(s):

2002 – 0 Seats

2006 – 0 Seats

2010 – 0 Seats

2014 – 0 Seats

2018 - Voluntarily Dissolved

A moderate political society conceived by elitists, by forming a national political society representing outstanding and reputable technocratic leadership from professional, business, economic and social backgrounds; the members were sons and daughters of prominent Bahraini families. Established by Businessman Khadhim al-Saeed during the 2011 unrest to run for the byelections and filed for dissolvement in 2015 with an excuse that the members have no time to run the society since they are committed businesspeople.

Unlicensed Movements

Harakat Ahrar al-Bahrain al-Islamiya
Bahrain Freedom Movement

Longtime opposition leader Saeed al-Shehabi leads the Bahrain Freedom Movement out of London. It is considered the oldest movement abroad. It calls for a total change toward both the ruling family and the Government and is against any negotiations or amicable settlement. It is widely known that al-Shehabi has strong ties with Iran and managed an Iranian Government-owned magazine that later became a TV channel well known for its daily coverage of Bahrain since 2011. Saeed al-Shehabi is known for his radical views, having attacked his opposition peers in Bahrain in the past.

Harakat Haq
Haq Movement

After quitting al-Wefaq, Hasan Mushaima formed the *Haq Movement* Rights Movement in protest of al-Wefaq deciding to participate in the 2006 parliamentary elections. During that time, he claimed it was useless, and then the authorities banned it after it adopted fundamental objectives and techniques. Mushaima was jailed after being convicted for inciting disorder and attempting a coup. The Haq Movement is now led by his son Ali Mushaima while he serves time for another attempted coup. It is operated out of London.

Taya'ar al-Wafa al-Islami
Al-Wafa Movement

The al-Wafa Movement was established in 2009 by Abdulwahab Hussein, who was well known throughout the 90s for leading violent protests. He is serving a jail sentence for his role in radicalizing the protests in 2011, and Sayyed Murtadha al-Sindi has led the movement from Iran. He is known for his radical views and revolutionary ideology and for broadcasting videos in 2017 after the execution of three Bahrainis charged with killing an Emirati police officer, inviting Bahrainis to join his armed movement to overthrow the Government.

Hezbollah al-Bahrain
Hezbollah Bahrain

Hezbollah Bahrain was considered a proxy movement to Lebanon's protuberant organization. It is believed to have been formed after its counterparts in Saudi Arabia and Kuwait. In June 1996, a sleeper cell was exposed by the authorities, uncovering a well-connected movement that had plans to not only destabilize Bahrain but the whole Gulf region as well.

Saraya al-Ashtar
Al-Ashtar Brigades

Saraya al-Ashtar was founded in 2012 as an armed radical movement by Ahmed Sarhan and Jassim Ahmed Abdulla, both residing in Iran. The movement is on the list of terrorist groups, and its members are fugitives wanted by Bahrain, KSA, Egypt, UAE, and the United States of America.

Saraya al-Mukhtar
Al-Mukhtar Brigades

This Shiite militia is said to have been formed at the end of 2011. It adopted guerilla warfare methods and conducted and claimed responsibility for a handful of terrorist attacks. It aims to overthrow the Government and establish an Islamic Republic, just like in Iran. The founder, Sheikh Maitham al-Jamri, is an active member of the Iraqi Shiite militia Popular Mobilization Units (PMU).

Saraya Wa'adullah
Wa'adullah Brigades

Saraya Wa'adullah was formed in 2015 and claimed responsibility for a car explosion on July 28 of the same year, killing one policeman and severely injuring seven others. They are considered radical revolutionary Shiites who are attempting a coup to overthrow the Government by destabilizing society like a few other illegal movements and organizations.

Monathamat al-Kefah al-Thawry
Revolutionary Struggle Organization

The Revolutionary Struggle Organization was established in December 2016 as a radical armed group to free prisoners and overthrow the Government. It has strong ties with the al-Wafa Movement and is believed to have been established by them.

etila'af Thawrat 14 Febrayer
Coalition Youth of 14 Feb Revolution

Coalition Youth was named after the date of the beginning of the attempted uprising on February 14, 2011, and is allegedly led by anonymous individuals who plan and organize protests mainly via Social Media sites. The coalition first appeared on the popular online forum *Bahrain Online* in 2010, where they distributed their call for a revolution plan with a precise calendar that escalates their moves every time the authorities do not respond. They were raided by the authorities days after they organized a sit-in outside his the King's palace. It is notable that the King did not order these raids but received the group with traditional hospitality, serving them milk and dates.

Al-Muqawama al-Islamiya fil Bahrain
Islamic Resistance of Bahrain

The Islamic Resistance of Bahrain is another armed group that claims roots in Saudi's Eastern Province and has close ties with Hezbollah in Lebanon and, hence, the Islamic Republic of Iran. They claimed responsibility for a few armed operations in some of the villages—mainly Budaiya and Sitra.

Al-Jabha al-Islamiya Litahreer al-Bahrain
Islamic Front for the Liberation of Bahrain

The Islamic Front for the Liberation of Bahrain calls for a theocratic rule over Bahrain. It was established in 1981 by Sayyed Hadi al-Modarissi, who attempted a coup the same year. It was funded by the Iranian Intelligence Unit and was based in Tehran. It voluntarily ceased it's operations in 2002 when the King pardoned its jailed and exiled members.

Tayaar al-Amal al-Islami
Islamic Labor Group

The Islamic Labor Group claims to be the first revolutionary Islamic movement in the Kingdom. It was formed in 1976 and was the first to call for a Shiites Islamic Republic in what they call Greater Bahrain, i.e. Saudi's eastern Province and the Kingdom of Bahrain. There is little information available on them, but they are believed to be part of the Shirazites movement, with close ties to Sayyed Hadi al-Modarressi.

Al-Kateeba al-Haydariya
Al-Haydariya Platoon

It has unknown origins and claims to have been established in 2015. It was behind damaging security force cars in Muharraq.

Saraya al-Karrar
Al-Karrar Brigades

This group is linked to Saraya al-Ashtar and has no exact date when it was instituted. Its founder was sentenced to death twice in one day by the Supreme Criminal Court on April 28, 2016.

Coalitions

Al-Kutla al-Deeniya
Religious Bloc

The Religious Bloc was founded upon the announcement by the authorities of establishing a representative Council in 1972. It was led by a prominent Sharia court judge, Sheikh Abdulamir al-Jamri. He managed to gather the scattered religious Shiites groups into one bloc, including Sheikh Isa Qasim, Abdulla al-Madani, and Abbas al-Rayes. They called for the support of Labor Unions, banning alcohol, gender-separated educational systems, banning women from civil societies, workplaces, and voting. They won nine seats.

Tajamo'a al-Fateh
Al-Fateh Coalition

The six political societies below formed the Al-Fateh Coalition in response to the February 14 movement of 2011, right after it became radical and started calling for a refined change. It was formed by five Sunni societies. Salafist al-Asalah left the coalition in 2013, and in 2014, al-Wasat suspended its membership due to Sheikh Abdullatif al-Mahmoud's bold move to form a society initially under the name of al-Fatih, which was later changed to the National Unity Assembly.

The Coalition founders were:

- National Constitutional Assembly
- National Dialogue Society
- Islamic Shura Society
- National Action Charter Society
- National Unity Assembly
- Al-Menbar al-Watani al-Islami

Tahalouf min ajl al-Jumhouria
Coalition for a Republic

The Coalition for a Republic was formed in 2011 right after Hasan Mushaima returned from his exile in London (through Lebanon, where he met Sayyed Hasan Nasrullah of Hezbollah). It calls for the Islamic Republic of Bahrain instead of finding ways to build and fix the problems. They did not present a plan nor ways to reach their goal but instead participated in a civil uprising that later led to armed conflicts through militias that were led by at least one of the coalition societies.

The members of the coalition are:

- Haq
- Al-Wafa
- Bahrain Freedom Movement

Al-Haraka al-Wataniya al-Democratiya
Nationalist Democratic Movement

The founders of this coalition are participants of the six societies' coalition. They formed this group to distinguish themselves from the Islamists in the broader coalition, distinguishing themselves by rejecting the theocratic approach of their peers, defending women's rights, and calling for a civil state.

The Nationalist Democratic Movement was formed by:

- National Democratic Action.
- Society.
- Progressive Tribune.
- National Democratic Assembly.

Al-Jamiya'at al-Set
The Six Societies

This coalition was formed amid the 2011 unrest right after it was known to all that the February 14 movement was leaderless. The societies listed below formed this coalition to take charge of the uprising and form a committee that leads and negotiates with the Government on behalf of the protesters.

These societies are:

- Al-Wefaq National Islamic Society.
- Islamic Action Society.
- National Democratic Action Society.
- Progressive Tribune.
- National Democratic Assembly.
- Al-Ekha National Society.

Political Unrest

Pearling in Political History
Protesting taxation, interests and customs tariffs
Lands, Labor and Law
The Roaring 20s: Revolts, a Forced Succession,
and Reforms Forced Succession
Oil Prosperity & Political Protests: The 1930s
The Period of 1953-1956: High Executive Committee (H.E.C)
Effects of Arab Nationalism in Bahrain: 1956–1971
Independence and the First Parliamentary Experiment: 1971-1975
The Effects of the Iranian Revolution 1976-1979
Attempted Coup of 1981
The 1994-1999 Unrest
Political Reforms
Municipal and Parliamentary Elections of 2002
Lebanese Style Protest & Socio-Economic
Challenges to the Political Process
Parliamentary Elections 2006
Parliamentary Elections 2010

Bahrain's early modern history is one of independence until the Portuguese occupied the country from 1521–1602, followed by the Persians, who occupied the country intermittently and indirectly until 1782. In 1783, the Persians were expelled by the Bani Utub, a Sunnite clan that originated from central Arabia. The Sunnite clan's leading family, the al-Khalifas, became the independent Shaikhs of Bahrain and have ruled Bahrain ever since, except for a brief period before 1810.

To allow some form of political participation, Emir Isa bin Ali al-Khalifa, the tenth ruler of Bahrain, vowed to rule in accordance with the Islamic principle of consultation, or *Shura*. He kept his promise and discussed all political, social, and economic issues with his people via the following:

- *Al Majlis* 'open door': This tradition was and continues to be held. Rulers open their *Majlis* to the public to discuss matters of mutual interest, as well as the specifics of their policies. The people of Bahrain meet on a regular basis in their own *Majlis* for the same purpose.
- *Al Moktar* 'mayor': A tribal system where an elected person acts as a liaison between the tribe and the ruler. The *Moktar* collects his people's requirements and suggestions to discusses them with the ruler. It was developed by Decree No. 16 of 1996 to establish the Governorates system, which assists Ministries and other Government institutions.

In 1820, Britain guaranteed the protection of Bahrain as part of the *General Treaty of Peace*, ratified in 1861, to establish British hegemony in the Gulf and put an end to the piracy that threatened British trading routes to India. Between 1870 and 1874, the Ottomans presented their claims to Bahrain, and to counter these moves, further treaties were signed with the British in 1880 and 1892. A British political agent was assigned to Bahrain in 1902 replacing the earlier local commercial agents who had represented the East India Company in the past, and the British signed a convention with the Ottomans in 1913 to ensure Bahrain's independence from the Ottoman Empire. In 1916, they signed another agreement with Shaikh Abdulaziz al-Saud to guarantee the protection of Bahrain's independence once again.

Pearling in Political History

During the period between 1830 to 1930, pearling was an essential factor in the political history of the islands. Since Bahrain was the center of the pearl industry in the Gulf and pearl fishing was the most significant element of commerce in the eastern world at the beginning of the 16th century, Bahrain was labeled the *Pearl of the Gulf*. Pearl divers were Arabs who lived on both the eastern and western coasts, and during the pearling season, about 4,500 boats and ships were active, with more than 30,000 people working in the industry. Many of them farmed the land in winter and dived for pearls during the summer. The pearling seasons went from mid-May until the end of September every year. The pearls were then sold on board the ships in Bahrain, Qatif, and other neighboring towns on the Arabian coast.

Protesting taxation, interests and customs tariffs

Pearl-diving was a capital-intensive industry. The *Naukhadas* 'fleet owners,' had to fit and provision their boats for the five-month-long pearling season and pay the crew in advance, meaning they had to take out a *Salaf* 'loan' so the crewmembers could support their families while they were away. At the end of the season, the divers got another payment called *Tisgam* 'maintenance,' and during the winter, when diving did not take place, they received *Karjiyah* 'pocket money,' as an incentive to dive for the same captain the following year. These cash advances were recorded and compelled the divers to come back the following year. Rarely did a diver earn enough to pay off these debts, and the outstanding amounts would, therefore, be carried forward to the following year, with interest. The running of expeditions and financing of the pearl industry throughout Bahrain's history proved to be socially disastrous to various sectors of the community, especially the direct workers in the industry, including the divers, pullers, amongst others.

The divers were illiterate, the captains, as well as the Arbitration Court—which dealt with disputes in the pearl industry—took advantage and abused the system. The captains would falsify the accounts, leaving divers in permanent debt with no choice but to return and work each season.

Taxation and interests in the pearling industry played a crucial role in the protests of the 1920s. Until 1923, when general reforms in the administration began in Bahrain, even death was not an exit from one's debts, as they were then inherited by one's sons or brothers, forcing them to enter the pearl industry themselves unless they had money or property with which to clear the debt. Captains were also in debt as they were often forced to obtain financing from merchants to equip and provision their boats and pay the divers in advance. The merchants commissioned interest on their money, and the captains passed this down to the divers.

Nevertheless, cash advances were restricted to Rs100 to the diver and Rs 80 to the puller. Divers considered this amount insufficient, and they regularly held demonstrations at the start of every season to protest low advances, ill-treatment, and high tax payments. Demonstrations and disturbances continued at the start of every season until they reached a climax with the riots of 1932.

Lands, Labor and Law

In the winter, these indigenous inhabitants supplied the agricultural workforce for the Shaikh and held the land they usually worked only in return for *Sukhra* 'unpaid labor,' and were also assessed for service based on their possessions e.g., boats and animals. Strong feelings of unjust treatment emanated from this population, who felt they were turned into virtual serfs. There was little incentive for them to improve their lands, as one of the most significant abuses was the system of land rents. Those who managed to purchase their gardens continuously lived in fear of local agents possibly taking it upon themselves to appropriate the holding. For example, if the Bedouin tribesmen stole the property of a Shiite, the latter could not rely on the political chiefs to obtain reparations on his behalf. They were also subject to paying extra taxes, especially for palm trees and fish. A noteworthy contribution to ruling revue, other than the customs tariffs, was claimed to be the inequitable taxation of the Shiites . These included date garden taxes, which were collected quite arbitrarily and practically from the Shiites only, as well as a poll tax and fixed tax levied mostly on the Shiites at varying rates in different villages. The majority of the population being Shiites at the time could also explain the reason for this inequitable taxation.

However, there were no other means of earning a livelihood, especially for a Shiite, before the oil era, except as either a peasant or diver. Because, in the latter occupation, there was greater competition for employment with the Sunni section of the community, most of the Shiite population worked on the land and accepted the conditions imposed. The peasant families were living under extremely insecure circumstances, either out of fear of being deprived of their tenancy or of going into debt. Besides, their insecurity was often increased by the vague terms of their contracts, which were often subject to alteration by the owner. This latter condition was one of the grievances presented to Shaikh Isa bin Ali in 1922, along with other demands for reform.

The Roaring 20s: Revolts, a Forced Succession, and Reforms

By 1921, public agitation had been building for some time, owing to multiple factors, such as judicial corruption, political murder, and money extortion. Therefore, on December 21, 1921, several thousand Bahrainis, Sunnites and Shiites, made their way to the British Agency in Manama to raise complaints to the political resident. However, reluctance from the British to become involved led the Shiite community to take matters into their own hands by exerting political pressure. The discontent continued until an uprising took place on February 16, 1922, in which Shiite and Sunni sects protested the ill-treatment and discrimination they were suffering, and eight demands were presented to Shaikh Isa by a Shiite deputation and several leading Sunni personalities. These demands called for an end to ill-treatment, paying extra taxes imposed explicitly on the Shiites, ending the era of *Sukhra*.

Tensions continued in March 1923 when the Shiite village of Barbar was attacked by the Dawasir of Budaiya. Later, on April 20, 1923, a clash took place in the Manama bazaar between a Najdi and a Persian, which developed into a riot between the two groups. The British Agency reported that the clashes were instigated by bin Saud's commercial agent, al-Qusaibi, who had incited the Najdis to commit violence against the Persians. Between May 10 and 15, 1923, the riots continued intermittently and resulted in four Persian and two Najdi casualties. To alleviate this threat to British interests, the British resident suggested the rearrangement of the political system to better the situation, including the abdication of Shaikh Isa as Governor.

Forced Succession

On May 26, 1923, the ceremony to transfer the power from Shaikh Isa to his son Shaikh Hamad was held at the British Agency. Resident S.G. Knox assembled two to three hundred commercial and community leaders from both Sunni and Shiite backgrounds to attend. At the ceremony, Knox announced the forced abdication of Shaikh Isa and the appointment of Shaikh Hamad as deputy ruler.

Upon the enforced abdication of Shaikh Isa came a series of incidents of political unrest. These came from two quarters: first, from the more conservative elements, such as the Dawasir tribe and some al-Khalifas, and secondly, from some of the embryonic politicians of the islands, who, although moderate in their views, regarded the recent changes as detrimental to the future development of the island. It was the second opposition party that preferred to make political moves, instead of fighting, to ensure their grievances were heard. Once the diving season finished, they gathered support for their proposed actions and demands at a meeting held under the name of the Bahrain National Congress on October 26, 1923.

The National Congress' demands, although moderate, were at that time considered radical. The representatives submitted their demands to Resident Trevor in the hope he would be more reasonable than Knox. Instead, on November 7, 1923, under the guise of a discussion of their demands, British Political Agent Trevor invited the representatives to an assembly at the British Agency and detained Abdul Wahab al-Zayani and Ahmed bin Lahij, who were deported that same night to India. The Dawasir tribe was given ten days to evacuate Budayyia completely. If they did not, Trevor threatened to bombard the town. In the face of this threat, the Dawasir evacuated from Bahrain altogether, after which the state confiscated their properties.

After these events, the situation in Bahrain became more stable as reforms were implemented, and Bahrain started to have a modern and more efficient administration. These would be solidified between 1926–1957, a period dominated by Charles Belgrave, the British advisor to the ruler. Much despised by locals, he was initially brought in by the Emir on a private contract to oversee budgetary matters of the Government. He would quickly take over most administrative duties on the island. The reforms enacted would become the first serious attempt to introduce organized systems of bureaucracy into the country. Efforts were made to centralize the administration, moving it away from the existing devolved feudal system. Conditions in the labor force were reformed, with particularly harsh practices banned. Formal education, first introduced in 1919, was expanded, and directorates were set up for the provision of electricity, hospitals, and telephones. Municipalities, as well as courts, were established.

Political resentment, however, did not die but continued to simmer below the surface, breaking out into occasional acts of violence, and these reforms encountered resistance from the local population. On May 26, 1932, a divers uprising took place after several divers were arrested following disturbances over the payment of *Salafiyh* and were imprisoned in Manama. One thousand five hundred of their colleagues crossed from Muharraq to Manama to obtain their release by force, looting several shops on their way. The police, the British adviser to the Emir, Belgrave, and the political agent, Captain Bray, unsuccessfully tried to prevent them, and the police were forced to open fire, resulting in several causalities. It was the last incident of this type, partly due to the setting up of a centralized *Sulfah court* 'loan court,' where the amount of advances could be fixed and grievances aired, and partly because of the new opportunities for work outside the pearl industry created by the booming oil industry. Other protests took place were students stood for educational reforms and these of agricultural workers; however, these were not as large.

Oil Prosperity & Political Protests: The 1930s

After discovering the first profitable oil supply in the Gulf region in 1932, a group of eight notable Baharna began to engage with other sections of Bahraini society, seeking genuine reforms to lay the foundations for a modern state. In December 1934, these eight dignitaries submitted a petition to the ruler, Shaikh Hamad bin Isa al-Khalifa, calling for the following reforms:

- Reforming the courts of law and the codification of the provisions adopted by the judges.

- Introducing proportional representation so the number of Shiite representatives in municipal and *Tijarah Councils* 'chambers of commerce,' would be increased.

- Provide schools in Shiite areas.

In response, oil revenues were used by the Government to create new departments and lay the foundations for a modern state. Bahrain became a rentier state, an interest-rate state that receives its income from the sale of natural resources. These returns were then primarily used to share the profits with the citizens in the form of cost-free health and education, as well as the subsidizing of food, housing, and electricity and the creation of sufficient Government jobs. The education system, initially a grassroots venture, expanded quickly. In 1930, there were 600 students enrolled in schools, and by 1938, this number had tripled.

Several cultural and sporting clubs also flourished at the time and played essential roles in the absence of political parties, although this was not their original function. They provided the environment for the public to develop and articulate political opinions. The increase in the number of clubs and the intensification of their political role was directly related to the emerging political consciousness following the end of World War II. They became where the educated met, the clubs, though strictly non-political, became political centers.

Employment opportunities, which were desperately needed since the decline of the pearl industry, also became available when the Bahrain Petroleum Company (BAPCO) started recruiting. The labor movement brought about significant changes. As the former pearl divers became oilfield workers, and the date cultivators left their rural areas to join them in the towns, the old barriers compartmentalizing the population began to break down. However, the transition to an oil-based economy was accompanied by new problems.

With no experience in industrial employment and high levels of illiteracy, most Bahrainis were unfit to occupy technical and clerical positions in the new industry. In the first decades of its existence, BAPCO relied primarily on Iranian laborers. A significant population of them already resided in Bahrain, and many had experience in the oil industry in their home country. They also had lower salary expectations and had no formal contracts with the company, thus providing a flexible labor force that was easy to recruit and dismiss. Indian laborers were contracted through lengthy bureaucratic procedures; they were costlier to recruit and required a one to a three-year contract. However, due to the political concern of an increased Iranian presence on the island that might foster the existing Shah's claim over Bahrain, they hired more Indian laborers. Nevertheless, labor in the company remained segregated and stratified along strict ethnonational lines, and Bahrainis were a minority among BAPCO employees and worked on a daily, non-contract basis—a grievance that would later surface in the 1930s.

In 1936, there was a brief economic boom when American engineers arrived to work on the establishment of an oil refinery, leading to increased local employment opportunities and shops enjoying a brisk trade. However, once the oil refinery was completed in 1937, a sudden depression set in. Young, educated men unable to find employment at BAPCO and merchants on the verge of bankruptcy after the dramatic fall of shop prices were particularly affected. This contrasted sharply with the ruling family's newly acquired wealth from oil revenues, and the people were resentful. In addition to these problems, the new complexity of Government administration began to contribute to a growing gap between the different classes of the community. Whereas previously, most Bahrainis could approach their ruler personally with any issues, they now had to go through the labyrinth of Government bureaucracies.

Other significant complaints revolved around the following:

- Ineffectiveness of the educational system, which was not producing graduates for either the Government or the oil industry.

- Inefficiency and injustice of the law courts.

- Unsatisfactory employment conditions at BAPCO. Which discriminated against nationals. While the term did not appear as such, Bahrainization, or the idea that Bahrainis should be given priority over foreigners for employment, became a core demand for political mobilization.

In the political sphere, despite official suppression and the disapproval of the British, the aspirations of the National Congress had not faded away. A widely supported movement started in 1938, calling for reforms at the same time as their neighboring Gulf States, Kuwait and Dubai. Although the initial demand was for the establishment of a Parliament like the one recently set up in Kuwait, this was not pursued long. Instead, they focused on more specific issues such as Belgrave's omnipotence and the chaos and inefficiency of most reformed bodies under his direction, like the police, prisons, and passport office. The movement, launched as an initiative to demand the establishment of a legislative body, gathered momentum when students and oil workers from BAPCO joined forces. The merchants, in their nascent struggle for power, were amenable to the incorporation of some of the specific demands of Bahraini BAPCO workers into their agenda.

In November 1938, there were strong rumors that BAPCO workers were planning a strike in support of the reform movement. Aware of the trends in Dubai and Kuwait, the Government acted firmly to curb the opposition. Two men were accused of being the instigators of the proposed strike and were deported. That provoked widespread disapproval, agitation grew, and several opposition bodies were formed:

Sir Charles Belgrave talking with Yousuf Ahmed al-Shirawi

- The Representatives of the People.
- The Society of Free Youth.
- The Secret Labor Union.

However, these were unable to hold on for long against Belgrave, the political agent, and BAPCO, who dismissed any employee that went on strike.

The movement eventually dissolved after their demands were met. The Government sanctioned the formation of a national labor committee and appointed a labor relations representative to BAPCO. It also sought the advice of education experts on improving the system, making it more relevant to the needs of the population. Although political activity subsided during the Second World War, yet there were still some prevailing tensions. The main arenas for their expression were the *ma'atam* 'Shiite mourning shrines,' and the clubs. Other sources included the first newspaper to be published in the Gulf in 1939, *Bahrain*, and the Bahrain Broadcasting Station, established by the Ministry of Information to counter Axis propaganda in 1940. Both sources had a profound local impact, especially the radio, as it appealed to a population that was still mostly illiterate. British slogans concerning freedom and democracy were readily accepted by the people of Bahrain, who sought to apply these principles for themselves.

The Period of 1953-1956: High Executive Committee (HEC)

After World War II, political activism became increasingly visible with the establishment of more civil society organizations. Regionally, this was the period of revolution and rising Arab nationalism. Political developments in other parts of the Arab world echoed strongly in Bahrain, where people took to the streets to demonstrate their support for the Arab cause in late 1947.

Internally, the improved education system had created some individuals who attempted to bundle forces with the intention of convincing the ruling family of the need to implement political reforms. According to them, Bahrain needed an elected Parliament, autonomous courts, and unions to serve the interests of the people. Consequently, the early 1950s witnessed the most substantial public mass movement in Bahrain's modern history. The combination of three elements incited the discontent that would lead to the movement:

- Westerners were in management positions and Bahrainis at the bottom in lower clerical and labor jobs.
- Anti-colonial sentiments were spreading.
- Prosperity brought about by oil had a much minor impact in Bahrain than it had in neighboring countries, and Bahrainis, especially those who had experienced the higher wages and standards of living of the oil workers of the mainland, considered their situation to be humiliating in comparison.
- General frustration with the sociopolitical status of Bahrain, fused with nationalism and anti-British sentiment, resulted in open defiance of the Government. The latter, with the aid of British forces, imposed a state of emergency and forbade all political activity.

HEC members - 1954
L-R (back): a-Aaiwat, bin Mousa, al-Bakir, Fakhro, al-Shamlan; (front): al-Tajir, Abudeeb, Kamaluddin

Soon, the cultural gap between Shiites and Sunnis reared its head. In September 1953, several clashes broke out between Shiite participants and *Fdawiya* 'strongmen under the command of the Shaikhs' during the religious march of *Ashura* 'the Shiite commemoration of the martyrdom of Imam Hussein'. That sparked a period of political unrest with intermittent clashes. The main incident happened in June 1953 at a Sitra camp between the two groups, during which there was a Sunni casualty. This led to the arrest of the alleged Shiite ringleaders, and after a trial, they were sentenced to various periods of imprisonment. The Shiite community thought this response to be excessively harsh, leading to a series of heated meetings and demonstrations on July 2, 1954, and a march to Manama Fort in an attempt to free the prisoners. The police, apparently apprehensive at the fervor of the demonstration, opened fire, which resulted in four Shia casualties. Consequently, for a week, a general business shutdown occurred due to fear and the industrial action of sympathizers. Shaikh Salman ordered an investigation of the incident, but this came to nothing other than a reprimand of the police for their actions.

The significance of these clashes and their effects on the country highlighted the need for a greater understanding between the two communities and for the establishment of a rapport to lay the foundations of future joint action and co-operation. Therefore, by the end of the year, the two sides established tentative contacts with each other, and from October 1954, a series of public meetings in the bin-Khamis Mata'am in Sanabis occurred. These meetings actively involved Abdulrahman al-Bakir, head of the board of directors of the Cooperative Compensation Society, as well as members of all the various clubs and societies and local notables both from the Shiite and Sunnite communities. The significance of this step was not just a commercial one; for the first time, it brought together the Sunnite and Shiite working classes on a co-operative, working basis.

Abdulrahman al-Bakir became a national hero, and to counteract the rising tensions, on October 13, 1954, al-Bakir and his friends from the two sects succeeded in holding a rally in the Mata'am of Sanabis village, where they announced the formation of a General Assembly composed of 120 members to represent the two sects. This assembly would appoint eight prominent Bahraini citizens—four Sunnites and four Shiites—to create the Higher Executive Committee (HEC).

This committee was elected to put forward demands seeking more political participation. They centered on a legislative Council, a general legal and civil code, labor unions, and the establishment of a Supreme Court, a higher appeals court. A petition was also drafted in which the foundation of an elected Parliament was advocated, as well as independence from Britain. On November 17, 1954, during the celebration of the anniversary of the Prophet's birth, the HEC seized the opportunity to mobilize the public actively. Thousands of Sunnites and Shiites gathered at this meeting in a mosque in Manama, signing a petition authorizing the HEC leaders to speak on their behalf. At the time, the political movements were centered in the urban cities of the capital Manama and the rural city of Muharraq, while the villages were seen as more conservative and less prone to the political momentum sweeping the region. Still, the HEC was able to collect 25,000 supporting signatures—an extraordinary achievement in a country whose citizens barely numbered 100,000.

Even though the authority of the ruling family was in no way questioned, the rulers refused to recognize the HEC. However, popular support for the HEC forced the Government to reconsider its position, and clandestine talks took place with some concessions granted by the latter, such as the promise of setting up elected committees to supervise—but not administer—health and education services. Although certain other concessions were won, it appeared that the talks with the Government did not make any progress with the primary demand for a legislative Council. As a result, the HEC called for another one-week general strike starting December 4, 1954, and the majority of the public responded to the call with 90% adhering the call . The strike was extraordinarily competent and brought Bahrain to a complete standstill.

Within a day of the lifting of the strike, Shaikh Salman announced in a proclamation the formation of an ad hoc committee to supervise education, health, and police services. The proclamation went on to cite the latest improvements in the administration, such as the appointment of a British judicial adviser, two British officers to the police, an additional doctor in the hospital, and the forthcoming elections for a new Municipality Council. The HEC acknowledged these reforms but defended their position by reprimanding the Government's suppression of the *al-Qafilah* newspaper and their encouragement of employers not to pay the wages of the strikers. They repeated their original demands, threated to boycott the municipal elections planned for February 19, 1955, and presented the Government with an ultimatum. On February 21, 1955, the HEC handed a memorandum containing their demanded reforms to the British political resident to forward to the foreign secretary. They received a response on March 17, 1955, in which the foreign secretary advised that close cooperation with the Government would be in their best interest.

As they were at a standstill on the political front, the HEC took on social affairs to maintain support. Their greatest successes included establishing several scholarships to Bahrainis from the University of Cairo, helping merchants, BAPCO workers, and the administration employees form the National Union Committee, helping to mobilize and set up Bahrain's first Trade Union, the Bahrain Labor Federation in October 1955, and drawing up their labor legislation.

At this point, the Government was also working on reforms as promised. The Labor Law Advisory Committee was set up, as were proposals for permanent councils to supervise health, education, and a criminal code of law. The latter was suspended by pressure from the HEC, though they agreed to participate in the proposed committee. On polling day for the Education Council, February 9, 1956, 80% of the electorate attended, and the HEC won 92% of the votes. Committees were agreed to involve half elected members and half Government nominees. However, HEC candidates were unhappy with the choice of Government appointments and refused to take their seats on the Council until these nominees were changed. The Government conceded, yet the appointment of Shaikh Abdulla bin Isa, the ruler's uncle, as chairman of the Council, caused the HEC to continue their refusal.

During this time, incidents were ongoing, and the atmosphere on the island was agitated. On March 2, 1956, the car of a British citizen, was mobbed in an anti-Belgrave demonstration, and the British condemned the HEC for it. On March 11, there was a severe riot in the vegetable market near the Municipality in which officials and stallholders clashed, killing three and wounding many others. These killings and the lack of formal recognition of the HEC led to another general strike, putting Bahraini businesses at yet another standstill. After the success of this strike, the authorities—with British mediators—started to negotiate with the HEC from March 13–16, 1956. The negotiations led to the following concessions from the two sides:

- HEC would drop their demand for a legislative Council for the time being and not press for Sir Charles Belgrave's dismissal.

- The Bahraini Government would recognize the HEC provided it changed its name (as it was linked to previous troubles) and its secretary-general, Abdulrahman al-Bakir, would go into self-imposed exile for six months.

The committee changed its name to *Hai'at al-Itihad al-Watani* 'the National Union Committee' or NUC, and under the new Secretary-General, al-Shamlan received official recognition on March 18, 1956. The NUC is considered to be the first political group based on a non-sectarian foundation in the history of modern Bahrain. However, the NUC was continuously outspoken about their lack of role in consultation on specific reforms and attacked the Council for its composition and aims. In July 1956, they issued a bulletin outlining their differences with the Government, expressing the refusal to accept the Administrative Council, resentment to Belgrave's continued presence in meetings between the NUC and Bahraini Government, and strong objection to the new Press Law, which implemented specific censorship. In conclusion, the NUC's most eminent activities were to issue statements against the Government and hold rallies by the two main sects.

On July 26, 1956, Egypt's Jamal Abdulnasser's announcement of the nationalization of the Suez Canal led to a confrontation between Egypt and Britain, an action that echoed loudly in Bahrain. Al-Bakir made several violent anti-British speeches in Cairo and Beirut. In November 1956, protests broke out in Bahrain denouncing the tripartite aggression on Egypt. These events led to the implementation of a state of emergency in the country and the arrest and deportation the NUC leaders to the St. Helena Island, sending the organization to its deathbed.

Nevertheless, the NUC created a long-lasting legacy that has survived to this day. Foremost, it was the first popular political movement to be recognized by any Government among the Gulf Arab states, and arguably constituted the birth of modern Bahraini nationalism. It led to wide-ranging reforms in the legal and civil codes of the country, as well as successfully forming Bahrain's first labor union, the Bahrain Labor Federation with 6,000 members. Although it was later suppressed, apparent efforts to address labor demands were introduced. BAPCO modified its recruitment policy, shifting to a paternalistic management model that resulted in the stabilization of a Bahraini workforce through intensive professional training, as well as generous social benefits. Rulers also acceded to specific demands made by BAPCO workers, the most significant being the drafting the Labor Ordinance Law, passed in 1957, establishing workers' rights.

Effects of Arab Nationalism in Bahrain: 1956-1971

The fall of the NUC heralded a new era in Bahraini political movements. In essence, the NUC's demands and activities reflected grievances directed at both the British presence and the rulers, and it never went beyond asking for political reform within the system. Many saw the NUC's aims as not reaching far enough. In subsequent political movements, the NUC went underground and took a much more radical stance, with their outlook becoming distinctly anti-colonialist and anti-Government. Their goal was no longer partial system reform but the

Civil protest in Muharraq supporting Arab Nationalism in 1953

overthrow of the ruling Government using armed conflict.

Foreign political movements heavily influenced the development of political unrest between 1956 and Bahrain's independence in 1971. Two major clandestine movements, largely secular in composition and outlook, which developed in Egypt, Iran, and Iraq, saw their influence propagated in the Bahraini political scene:

– *Harakat al-Qawmeen al-Arab* - **Movement of Arab Nationalists (MAN)**

Originated in the American University of Beirut (AUB) to establish a vanguard movement directed at the liberation of Palestine and rest of the Arab world using revolutionary means. Between 1958 and 1959, a group of Bahraini students at the American University of Beirut (AUB) and the University of Cairo (UOC) approached youth groups in Bahrain with Arab nationalist leanings to bring them under the wing of the MAN. Within a few months, the movement expanded hugely, encompassing several hundred members. In 1974, their offspring formed the People's Liberation Front (PLF).

– *Jabhat al-Tahreer al-Watani* - **Bahrain National Liberation Front-Bahrain (NLF)**

NLF was the communist movement in Bahrain that formally established itself on the island in 1955. Its creation was heavily influenced by its contacts with the Iranian Tudeh Party and the Communist Party of Iraq, resulting in influence, logistics, and funding.

Both movements played an active role in opposing the Bahraini Government, relying mainly on support in the urban cities of Manama and Muharraq, which were still the main hotbeds of opposition. However, the relationship between them was ambivalent from the start due to ideological differences. The MAN saw the Arab world as its natural home and the main aim of its struggle and viewed the NLF and as an international agent that did not have the Arab world's interest at heart. Inversely, the NLF saw the MAN as a regional upstart clouded with nationalist xenophobia. The idea of Arab Nationalism did not sit well with it.

The activities of the two groups reached a climax with the uprising in March 1965. Events ignited when the local oil company, BAPCO, announced plans to lay off several hundred local workers. That quickly spiraled into nationwide protests and civil disobedience, focused mainly in the cities of Manama and Muharraq. The uprising lasted some three months. The Government's report states that:

Toward the end of March, certain subversive elements took advantage of a strike by the oil company workers over redundancy to carry out acts such as the attempted blowing up of the oil pipeline to the refinery, the burning of oil company buses, stoning of European's cars, and the destruction by fire of a European national's car. The strike was settled, and with the capture and arrest of the ringleaders of the subversive elements, everything was back to normal by mid-April.

The quickly escalating protests caught the MAN and the NLF by surprise and with little preparation; therefore, cadres from each organization tried to work together to coordinate on tactics. Nevertheless, the hastily assembled coalition quickly fell apart.

In June 1967, the defeat of the Arab forces in the War against the State of Israel damaged the image of the Egyptian president, Jamal Abdulnasser, and was the final death knell in the

MAN movement. This heralded the rise of the leftist forces within the MAN. A new movement was born in the late 1960s, which would eventually solidify under the banner of the Popular Front for the Liberation of Oman and the Arabian Gulf (PFLOAG). The main differences were:

- The refocus of the movement on the Arabian Gulf instead of the broader Arab world
- The adoption of Marxism-Leninism as an official ideology
- The endorsement of armed struggle

The explicit aim became the overthrow of the sheikhdoms through violent means. The PFLOAG became increasingly active in the Dhofar movement, which was active in Oman from 1965 to 1976, with several Bahraini cadres actively joining their Dhofari comrades. During this period, the PFLOAG also had a Bahraini branch, which witnessed a decline and was supplanted by Shiite Islamic movements as the main opposition force. These movements emerged in the late 1960s and early 1970s as the offspring of Iraqi-based movements, *Hezb al-Da'wa al-Islamiyah* 'the al-Da'wa Islamic Party,' who later became pro Ayatollah Khomeini, and *al-Haraka al-Risaliyya*, 'the Message Movement,' that became widely known as Shirazites and whose local branch came to be known as the armed group Islamic Front for the Liberation of Bahrain (IFLB).

They contributed to politicizing the Sunnite/Shiite divide. This defining divide within Bahraini society has been transcended by the leftist and Arab nationalist movements, which recruited in both sects. As for the Shiite Islamic movements, their recruitment was, of course, exclusively sectarian since they developed a viewpoint that emphasized the sectarian structure of power whereby a Sunnite dynasty ruled a society where the Shiites claimed to outnumber Sunnites. These Shiite Islamic movements, focusing on identity issues, came at a period of prosperity in the country, when the grievances, which had generated previous labor conflicts through 1968 affecting practically every key and medium-sized employer, had virtually disappeared due to the rise of petroleum prices in the early 1970s and the first parliamentary experiment 1973–1975. Therefore, these movements would only gain influence and relevance after the effects of the Iranian Revolution in 1979 and, later, in the 1990s due to the conflict between them and the leftists.

After political independence in 1971, issues like social justice, democracy, human rights, women's equality, Arab (and Gulf) unification, elimination of any foreign military presence, and economic development became gradually more prominent in the political literature of the underground networks. The opposition suffered from a split over the course and means of struggle. While the Bahraini section of the PFLOAG advocated armed action, the NLF advocated the buildup of opposition forces through civil actions. These differences determined their attitudes toward the parliamentary elections of 1973. The PFLOAG viewed the elections as diversionary and called for a boycott (a path they kept on pursuing until the present day), while the NLF formed the People's Bloc, an alliance with independent leftists, and campaigned on a rather moderate platform. Eight of its 12-man list were successful. Although the Popular Front later privately admitted that their course was an error, the disunity between these two underground forces persists today.

Independence and the First Parliamentary Experiment: 1971-1975

In 1967, the British had drawn up plans to withdraw from the Arabian Peninsula due to an economic crisis at home. A UN plebiscite was held in Bahrain to counteract the potential Iranian claims to the islands. On August 15, 1971, Bahrain became an independent state under the rule of Shaikh Isa bin Salman al-Khalifa, who ruled the nation since 1961 and became the head of state and the supreme commander of the armed forces.

His brother, Shaikh Khalifa bin Salman al-Khalifa, became the Prime Minister, and key ministerial portfolios were assigned to members of the al-Khalifa family. After independence from the British in 1971, the rulers of Bahrain continued meeting with people regularly through the *majlis*. The rapid growth of the population resulted in the call for a larger institution to represent its citizens. In his 1971 National Day Speech, the first since independence, Shaikh Isa bin Salman announced that the country would have a constitutional form of Government. Such a Constitution would protect society's unity and cohesion and would guarantee citizens their fundamental individual freedoms of education, work, social welfare, health, and expression of opinion. It also provided the people with the right to participate in the Government of the state.

March 1972 Uprising

Popular expectations were heightened further by proposals for political and social reforms offered by Bahraini representatives. However, prolonged Government action caused frustration and the turn of political activity toward civic coalition-based popular movements. That was spurred by the establishment of the Constitutive Committee (CC) for the General Federation of Workers in Bahrain, the first organized public mass movement after independence. The CC signaled a significant shift within the tactics of Bahrain's political movements. Although the Constitutive Committee for Bahrain Workers and Professionals Union (CCBWPU) was spearheaded by a coalition of individuals from PFLOAG, NLF, and MAN, it was not organized along party lines and included many independents among its ranks. The CCBWPU also took its work to the public rather than focusing on clandestine activity, organizing petitions for the establishment of a general labor union that garnered nearly 5,000 signatures. In this regard, it was the first genuinely secular public-coalition in Bahrain, where sect and religious issues did not play a notable role in its composition or goals.

When negotiations over legalizing labor unionization failed, and the authorities refused to recognize the CCBWPU, labor workers challenged the Government in the streets. The situation culminated in the March uprising of 1972, when workers at the local airline company, Gulf Air, went on strike after a group of expatriate workers were brought in from Pakistan. The strikes quickly escalated and spread nationwide. On March 11, the CCBWPU held a mass rally at the steps of the Government House in Manama. The significant demands revolved around improvement of labor laws, freedom of association (including the right to unionize), and the release of political prisoners and detainees. Eventually, the Bahraini military was deployed, and the protests were put down, with the members of the CC either taken to prison or exiled.

The March 1972 uprising accelerated the moves by the authorities to establish the promised

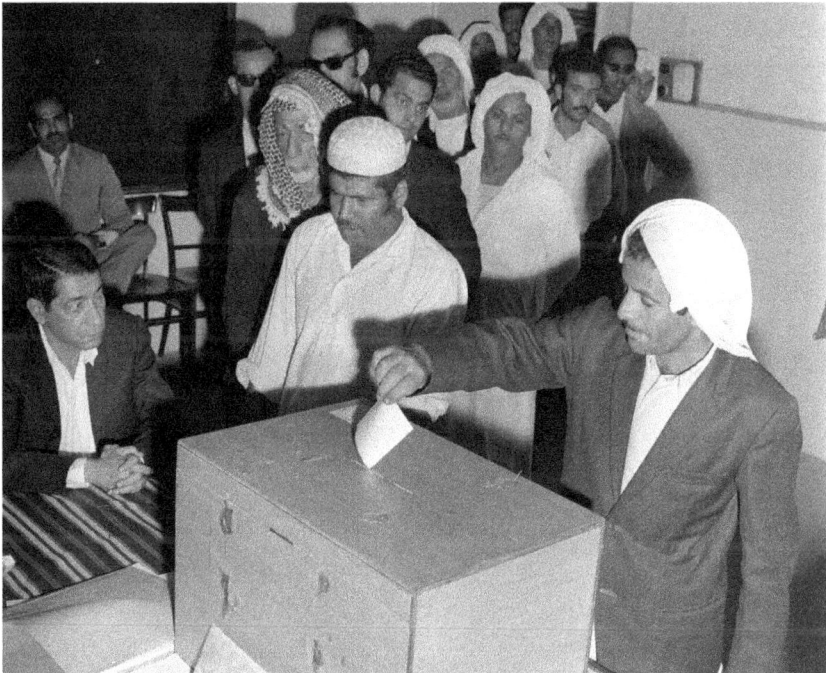

Citizens lining up to cast thier votes in the state's first Elections

Constituency	Elected Member	Bloc	Votes	Position
1	Rasool al-Jishi	al-Wasat	759	
1	Khalid Ibrahim al-Thawadi	People's	691	
2	Abdulhadi Khalaf	People's	711	
2	Hasan al-Jishi	al-Wasat	582	Speaker
3	Mohamed Salman Ahmed Hammad	People's	288	
4	Mohamed Abdullah Harmas	Independents	304	
4	Mohsin Hameed al-Marhoon	People's	221	
5	Ali Saleh al-Saleh	al-Wasat	468	
6	Hamad Abdullah Abul	al-Wasat	311	
7	Ali Ebrahim Abdula'al	Independents	207	
8	Abdullah Ali al-Moawada	People's	580	
8	Jasim Mohamed Murad	al-Wasat	596	
9	Ali Qasim Rabea'a	People's	573	
9	Mohamed Jaber al-Sabah	People's	341	
10	Isa Hasan al-Thawadi	People's	557	
10	Ibrahim Mohamed Hasan Fakhro	al-Wasat	488	
11	Khalifa Ahmed al-bin-Ali	al-Wasat	388	Deputy Speaker
12	Abdullah Mandoor Isa	Independents	650	

Table title: **Elected National Council Members 1973**

Constituency	Elected Member	Bloc	Votes	Position
	Elected National Council Members 1973			
13	Mustafa Mohamed al-Qassab	Religious	665	
13	Alawi Makki al-Sharakhat	Religious	633	
14	Abdullah al-Sheikh M al-Madani	Religious	771	Secretary
15	Isa Ahmed Qasim	Religious	1079	
15	Abdulamir al-Jamri	Religious	817	
16	Abbas Mohamed Ali	Independents	324	
17	Yousif Salman Kamal	al-Wasat	359	
18	Abdulaziz Mansoor al-A'ali	Independents	631	
19	Hasan Ali al-Mutawaj	Religious	585	
19	Salman al-Sheikh Mohamed	Independents	495	
20	Ibrahim bin Salman al-Khalifa	Independents	572	
20	Khalifa al-Dhahrani	Independents	250	

political and economic reforms. Shaikh Isa bin Salman issued a decree for the election of representatives to a Constituent Assembly in 1972, tasked with drafting and ratifying a Constitution. This constitutional Council was composed of fourty two members: twenty two elected by the people, eight appointed by the Emir, and the remaining twelve seats were provided for Government members from the Council of Ministers.

It was the first national election in the history of Bahrain, held on December 1972. In the electorate, 27,000 native-born male-only citizens aged twenty years and older were able to vote for thirty parliamentarians. This significant milestone in the country's political history was unfortunately boycotted by the Shehabi Bloc, a coalition formed of the NLF, the PFLAOG, and other Arab Nationalist elements, due to their internal differences.

Right after it was quickly followed by the elected legislative assembly, which was in session during most of 1973, it approved a Constitution of 108 articles. The Constitution, enacted by decree on December 1973, provided for the National Assembly, a legislative advisory body consisting of thirty members elected for a four-year term in addition to all the members of the Council of Ministers whose terms were not fixed.

The National Assembly had two sessions: the first lasted from December 1973 to June 1974, and the second started in October 1974 and lasted until June 1975.

Two main political groupings emerged during the short life of the National Assembly:

— **The People's Bloc**: the successor of the Shehabi bloc, sometimes referred to as leftist since it encompassed Arab nationalists, communists, and socialists. It was the largest single bloc in the assembly and strongly advocated for legislation for labor unions, the abolition of the Security Law, and pan-Arab policies. Support came from workers, students, and intellectuals, both Sunnites and Shiites. It was, in effect, the political successor of the Committee of National Unity. It won eight seats in the newly elected Parliament.

— **The Religious Bloc**: represented the rural Shiites. It supported labor reforms and various social restrictions, adopting a religious approach to matters such as co-education, the practice of Islamic rituals, and the ban on the sale of alcoholic beverages. It won six seats.

At this time, the population was prompted to claim its political and civil rights were guaranteed by the Constitution. Trade unions, the unemployed, and women's associations organized themselves through petitions to enforce their rights. The early 1970s was also a time of rising petroleum prices especially between 1973–74, which accelerated development in the Gulf region. In Bahrain, the oil and aluminum industries expanded, new industries were established, and the communication and transportation infrastructure developed.

When the Lebanese Civil War destroyed their banking system in the late 1970s, Bahrain developed a new financial sector and became the most important financial hub in the Middle East. The incredible growth of the 1970s gave the rulers a unique opportunity to accommodate the labor movement by responding positively to their demands for the Bahrainization of the workforce. Bahrain chose to use its oil money to expand the state apparatus and set up a generous welfare state for the redistribution of wealth among its citizens. In addition to

First session of the National Assembly on December 16, 1973

subsidized services like health care and housing, the public sector primarily employed Bahraini nationals, guaranteeing the provision of a public sector job for each male citizen. The rulers were able to solve endemic national unemployment momentarily.

Initially, electoral successes of the opposition forced a number of concessions, elevating opposition morale and extending networks of political agitation, which was reflected in the surge of labor-related actions.

Thirty-six strikes took place during the first six months of 1974, affecting all major employers on the island. Twenty-four of these lasted for ten days or more. The longest strike occurred at the drydock: it involved more than 400 workers and lasted for twenty six days. These strikes were instrumental in improving wage levels and working conditions. The minimum wage level was raised by one third. Most strikers obtained wage increases of ten to fifteen percent and paid for half of their strike days

Trade Unions were formed in four main areas: Aluminum Smelting, the Electricity department, the Ministry of Health, and the construction industry, which led to a head-on clash with the Government. The four unions significantly expanded their recruitment beyond initial expectations by taking advantage of loopholes in the 1955 labor code. On May 27, 1974, failed negotiations with management led to the welders in Aluminum Bahrain (ALBA), an aluminum venture with the Bahraini Government as a shareholder, to go on strike. The union made three demands: to end harassment by management, improve wages, and provide cold drinking water on worksites. Negotiations continued until the entire ALBA workforce went on strike, yet they reached a deadlock and caused losses worth twenty million Bahrain dinars.

The Parliament became a public forum for the leftists and their allies to express their ideas, grievances, and demands. Labor unrest gained an added impetus through the publicity offered by the press coverage and parliamentary debate. This ended in June 1974, when the security forces were again given a free hand in dealing with labor unrest. The authorities obtained considerable assistance in this effort from Kuwait, Saudi Arabia, and Jordan that marked the end of the first parliamentary session.

Several areas of friction between the National Assembly and the Government arose during the second parliamentary session, specifically between the People's Bloc and the Government, which was represented in the assembly by the members of the cabinet. Heated discussions revolved around the problems of inflation and housing, but two issues polarized both sides: the proposed security bill and the Juffair agreement.

The State Security Law issued in 1974 by Shaikh Isa was very controversial. The law allowed the Government to arrest and imprison any person suspected of being a threat to national security. As the only legislative body, the National Assembly regarded this law as an infringement of its authority and refused to pass it. The members of the Religious Bloc were the most prominent supporters and were keen on passing it, for it was a way to eliminate their leftist rivals, whom they had been attempting to take out since they considered them infidels. More so, it disapproved of the content of the law, with the memory of the unrest of 1956 and 1965 still present. The second primary source of conflict between the Government and the assembly was the Juffair agreement of 1971, whereby the United States Navy had been granted military and naval facilities in exchange for an annual payment of four million dollars.

Islamic bloc members - 1973
L-R: Qasim, al-Rayes, al-Jamri

Although the agreement was no secret and had been deposited with the United Nations, the fact that it had not been publicized locally aroused suspicion in the deputies. Members of the People's Bloc moved to discuss the agreement with the Government in a session held on camera, to which the assembly recommended reconsideration for the agreement, as it was not in the national interest. No action was taken at the time, as the assembly had three more sessions before dissolution. In 1977, though, the agreement was canceled in favor of other US-Bahrain contracts. There were also demands to rescind the 1965 Law of Public Security, as political parties were not permitted, which would also be a factor in Parliament's dissolution.

Following a boycott by the cabinet of the last session of the assembly, on August 26, 1975, the Prime Minister resigned, complaining of the continual obstruction of his work by the assembly. The ruler formed a new Government and dissolved the National Assembly by decree in August 1975. The decree also suspended particular articles of the Constitution, including those pertaining to the reelection of a new Parliament. All political activities were forced underground, and the country was put under a virtual state of emergency.

Many internal and external factors postponed elections to the new assembly until 1992:

- The Iranian Revolution of 1979 and the disorder that came prior to it, in addition to the claim on Bahrain by Iran.
- The Iraq-Iran War (1980–1988), which threatened the security and stability of the Arabian Gulf.
- The Israeli invasion of Lebanon in 1982 and the peace accord between Egypt and Israel, which saw Egypt withdraw from the Arab League.
- The attempted coup by the Islamic Front for the Liberation of Bahrain (IFLB).
- The Qatar-Bahrain border dispute that pushed the country to military readiness.
- The invasion of Kuwait by Iraq in 1990, which changed all GCC states' security and policies towards their neighboring states.
- Union strikes that caused colossal damage to entities like Alba and Gulf Air.
- The financial Institutions that fled Lebanon looking for a more secure environment and found that Bahrain was the best option except for the continued labor union strikes.
- State-owned land registration dispute.

The Effects of the Iranian Revolution 1976-1979

The sectarian divide has been a politically polarizing factor since the election of Bahrain's first Parliament in 1973. The shock of the assembly's suspension was absorbed by distractions that accompanied the new oil wealth in all Gulf countries after the 1973 Arab-Israeli War. However, socially, the new easy wealth created a cluster of men in most states whose main ambitions became the high commissions that led to corruption, the backlash of which was felt all over the Gulf States.

In 1975, the Shah of Iran, Mohamed Reza Pahlavi emerged as 'policeman' of the Gulf as part of U.S. policy in the region at the time -having already recognized Bahrain's independence-, while sustaining two seats in the Iranian Parliament with representatives from the island. However, like other oil-producing states, Iran was plagued with excesses and corruption. Much of the discontent in the vast country was channeled into the religious institutions, which thrived undeterred by the secret police, Savak. When the Shah was finally overthrown in early 1979, the Islamic Republic of Iran was established and with it, the revival of Islamic fundamentalism in Iran that was mainly exported to the neighboring Gulf states, Yemen, Iraq and Lebanon.

The Shiite militant Government of Iran now began to focus its attention on the Gulf states. Bahrain was particularly important to them because of old Iranian claims to its large Shiite population. Radio broadcasts targeting Bahrain urged the Shiites of Bahrain to overthrow their ruler. During 1979, Ayatollah Rouhmani revived Iran's claim over Bahrain and mentioned the possibility of annexing it. Tensions between the Bahraini and the Iranian Government emerged, and two main affiliations in Bahrain surely did not make it easier:

— **People's Bloc**

— **The Islamic Front for the Liberation of Bahrain (IFLB)**

Attempted Coup of 1981

In 1971, the first signs of a dispute between Shiites from Iranian descent, *Ajam*, and those from Arab descent, *Baharna*, appeared during the referendum, supervised by the UN, regarding the independence of the country. The former accused the latter of denying the existence of their sect and of being a victim of their nationalist fanaticism, while the latter accused the former of being Persians, foreigners to Bahrain, reinforcing the historical fact that Bahrain was a country first inhabited by Arabs and, therefore, independence is a natural right to them.

As Iran became a source of inspiration for Shiite Islamic movements in Bahrain, more confrontation between Shiite movements and the Government manifested. The London-based Bahrain Freedom Movement (BFM), gained prominence during the decade. The most motivating aspect of the movement campaign was the participation of both Shiites and Sunnites (those who had not benefited from the oil boom), having shared grievances and demanded political and economic reforms.

This unrest culminated in late 1981 when a plot to overthrow the Government and establish a Republic was discovered and blocked. They were all Gulf Arabs, some of whom had been supplied with military equipment by Iran, while others had been trained in Iran. The failed coup revealed the Islamic Front for the Liberation of Bahrain (IFLB), with headquarters in Tehran, of which 73 men—including Bahrainis, Omanis, Kuwaitis, and Saudis—were arrested, tried on camera, and imprisoned. It profoundly affected the employment of Shiites in the military due to the rising religious-political duality, which was not easily separated.

It is in this general context that the threat perception of the Government underwent a subterranean transformation. With the all-out use of the Shia religious identity for protesting against the Government, and then constituting a significantly large part of the population, the Bahraini rulers began to embrace a dogmatic definition of concepts of loyalty and disloyalty, being provoked to see any Shiite as potential threat. 1981, the coup attempt was critical in this respect.

The 1994-1999 Unrest

The unrest in the 1990s began due to a conflict of interest between those who established the committee that wrote a letter asking the late Emir Shaikh Isa bin Salman al-Khalifa to reinstate Parliament and the Shiite Islamists who hijacked the initiative, called it their own, and ousted the founders; taking the island to a whole new level of unnecessary violence and division.

It was June 1990 when Muharraq City witnessed discussions by nationalists and leftists regarding the deterioration of political, economic, and living conditions and the worsening of the unemployment problem. Furthermore, with the invasion of Kuwait in August 1990, the demand for democracy and participation in decision-making increased as constitutional legitimacy strengthened national cohesion and brought the morale of Bahrain's political elite forward.

The Emir established a Consultative Council in 1992, mainly composed of notables equally distributed between Sunnites and Shiites, whom he directly appointed and whose functions were to advise him on various policy-making issues.

In 1992, 365 social and intellectual elites signed a petition demanding the reinstatement of Parliament, a reintroduction of the Constitution, and amnesty for all political prisoners. A committee of five members was elected to present the petition to the Emir: Sheikh Abdullatif al-Mahmoud, Sheikh Abdulamir al-Jamri, Isa al-Jowder, Mohamed J Subah -who could not make it due to illness-, and Abdul-Wahab Hussein. The Emir received them in a friendly atmosphere, listened, discussed the subject with them, and then responded that he would not consider the opinion of 365 petitioners as the people's demand since they only represented themselves. A meeting was held the very next day between most of the participants and those who had were leading it, including Ali Rabea'a, Fadhel al-Hulaibi, and Ahmed al-Kuwari, among many more, provided them the time to think about the ways to tackle the issue. What they came up with was to change it from an elite's initiative to one that was more popular; hence, it became the *Popular Petition*, bearing the signatures of approximately 23,000. That was not possible without the assistance of their Shiite friends. Led by the Shiite leader Sheikh Abdulamir al-Jamri, the petition underwent some changes, including addressing authoritarianism, the stagnant economy, corruption and favoritism by the ruling family, and the repressive and largely foreign-staffed security apparatus. Spurred by Shia Islamic activists, in June 1994, unemployed Shia youth began to gather regularly in front of the Ministry of Labor to complain about their lot, accusing the Government of implementing a deliberate policy of favoring Sunnites over Shiites for jobs in the public sector. Sheikh Ali Salman, a young politicized Shia cleric who, in 2001, became the general secretary of al-Wefaq, began his political career leading such demonstrations. The leftists and the initiators of the petition were left out and were not even called to meetings or consulted. Sheikh Abdullatif al-Mahmoud brought up the matter of an annual marathon that takes place in Bahrain and is run through villages, with female participants who dress in offensive attire. He was asked to drop it under the excuse that it would deter from the cause and that it could easily lead to unnecessary riots.

That led to the country's lengthiest period of unrest, and aside from the socioeconomics involved in the turmoil, the focus of protestors changed from fundamental civil rights that needed to happen to a messy list of demands to release rioters and pardon leaders. It was initiated in an amicable manner that proved to be slightly effective but required patience, it ended up causing catastrophic violence with no results at all. When the idea was picked up by Sheikh Ali Salman, who started and participated in an unlicensed gathering in the Shia villages on December 5, 1994, the unrest started when stones were thrown at British runners participating in the annual charity marathon as they passed by the village, leaving four British citizens injured. A number of arrests were made, including that of Sheikh Ali Salman, as he was the instigator of the violence. As he had gained popularity among the Shiite communities, the arrest of Sheikh Ali Salman ignited protests over two weeks for his release, which spread throughout the Shia villages and Manama.

Protests demanding the release of Sheikh Salman started in Bilad al-Qadim and spread throughout the nearby villages and Manama, resulting in a few casualties in Duraz and Manama when protesters broke into the Bab al-Bahrain police station and nearby hotels, their justification being that the hotels served alcohol.

Unrest continued into 1995, with multiple new demonstrations taking place starting in mid-January. The Government sought to defuse the situation by expelling seven clerics to Dubai and then to London, amongst them Sheikh Ali Salman, Hamza al-Dayri, and Haydar al-Sitri. February was quiet, but the situation deteriorated in March and April of 1995. The protests continued to grow, riot police had to intervene, and the first prison sentences were handed down for those accused of sabotage. The situation continued to spiral downwards, with a death toll reaching thirteen civilians and three law enforcement officers. The first glimmer of dialogue occurred in August and September. Interior Minister Shaikh Mohamed bin Khalifa met with jailed leaders, including Sheikh Abdulamir al-Jamri, Sheikh Hasan Sultan, Abdalwahab Hussein, Hasan Mushaima, and Sayyed Ibrahim.

In return for a pledge by Shia leaders to end all violence, the Government promised it would free all detainees by the end of September.

Resentment was particularly high against the security forces' recruitment policy; the security apparatus was seen as a pool of employment for young Shia men. The protests spawned a series of violence, including a bomb being set off at a prominent hotel and cases of arson and sabotage using gas cylinders. Despite the Government's tough approach, the violence and hostility continued to grow aggressively in the following months. With alarming frequency, explosions began to rock hotels, cars parked in the capital and elsewhere, shopping centers, car showrooms, restaurants, and small shops near Shia villages. The State Security Court, a particular target of the protesters, continued to hand out sentences. Arson attacks continued throughout 1997, targeting foreign laborers. The unrest resulted in the loss of over fourty lives in Bahrain. The protests and arson attacks continued into 1999, and they seemed endless, but then, on March 6, Emir Shaikh Isa bin Salman suddenly and unexpectedly passed away. His son and the heir apparent, Shaikh Hamad bin Isa al-Khalifa, acceded immediately and sturdily promised a new era in Bahraini politics, and he soon began to make moves to defuse the tension. The violence stopped after a lag of several months, bringing an end to ongoing unrest.

Political Reforms

The 2000s brought hope and optimism for resolution of the protracted social conflict when the present monarch, Shaikh Hamad bin Isa al-Khalifa, acceded to the crown on March 6, 1999.

The National Action Charter

Beginning on November 23, 2000, Shaikh Hamad implemented several substantive reforms and political gestures to bolster support for the new political schema. These reforms were driven by a quest for stability, which was especially significant given the socio-economic challenges of a young population suffering from rising unemployment; Bahrain was also facing domestic pressure to reform its political system quickly. King Hamad established a Supreme National Committee to draft the National Action Charter (NAC). This charter would outline the future structure and principles of Government, leading to the transformation of the country into a constitutional monarchy and would reintroduce the constitutional premise of Government. The committee comprised fourty six leading Bahrainis, including six women and several leading political and private sector critics.

The NAC was put to a referendum on February 14 and 15, 2001. It saw a 90.3% electoral turnout—192,262 out of 217,000 eligible Bahraini men and women voted—resulting in 191,790 (98.4%) people in favor of the NAC, that firmly supported the proposal for a constitutionally grounded monarchy and an elected legislative body. It is essential to highlight the vocal support the referendum received from leading Shia clerics, who emphasized that it was part of a reconciliation effort between the Government and the Shia community. Also, the composition of a new National Assembly was to be announced with the release of the new Constitution by Shaikh Hamad on February 14, 2002, approximately one year after the referendum. The assembly held its first joint sitting on December 15, 2002. Its first term ran until the end of May 2003, and its second term began on October 11, 2003.

Political Societies' Contempt

Despite this outwardly positive depiction, many issues clouded the background. In 2001, when Shaikh Hamad bin Isa al-Khalifa submitted the National Charter for approval by referendum, he assured Bahraini societies that successive reform would be subject to public consultation, and many assumed the way forward would be based on the framework of the 1973 Constitution, which afforded an elected Parliament considerable authority.

Therefore, political activists were disappointed when the King released a new Constitution on February 2002, called for municipal and parliamentary elections two years ahead of what had previously been scheduled, and declared Bahrain a Kingdom without having consulted any of the leading political societies. There was also disappointment that under the new Constitution, there would be an appointed chamber with powers and numbers equal to the elected chamber, with the Speaker of the appointed chamber presiding over joint sessions. The issue with what is known as opposition in Bahrain -both individuals and bodies- is that they continue to repeat the same moves since they were formed. They always assume and rush to conclusions. When they agreed on passing the National Charter, they did not present it to a constitutional expert but consulted prominent civil and criminal lawyers and did not ask for any policy explanatory notes to help decide whether to approve or disapprove. The Shura

Council and its mandate, for example, was mentioned clearly but was somehow overlooked and, therefore, passed by the opposition.

Social Reforms

King Hamad has managed to reach out to his people through several royal gestures to overhaul the damages that have occurred throughout the years and to elevate the aspirations of the Bahraini citizens.

King HAMAD'S SOCIAL REFORMS 1999-2005

- Pardoning of political prisoners
- Royal order for returnees
- Salary bonuses for public employees
- Financial support for the unemployed
- Exemption of electricity bills for 10,000 families
- A reduction of fees at the University of Bahrain
- Sponsorship of orphans
- Exemption of housing installments for families
- Four new townships for 50,000 families
- Financial support for widows
- Ramadan provision for 10,000 families
- Distribution of 30% of Seef Property Company shares
- Financial support for medical students
- Citizenship to Bahraini residents

An Outlook on the Bahraini Situation Before and After Reforms

The Kingdom's initiatives taken since 1999 have laid the foundation for an exceptional start toward the new reforms on all aspects of political, social, economic, and human rights issues. King Hamad's implementation of his reformist vision is interesting as it shows a clear understanding of the domestic problems facing Bahrain's society and an initiative to foster a national consensus behind his liberalization program. It is also important to note that the above revolutionary changes took place prior to the 9/11 terrorist attacks, emphasizing the fact they were born domestically rather than reactively caused by external pressure.

A Chart that Summarizes the Bahraini Situation before and after the Reforms		
Situation	**Before**	**After**
Constitutional Monarchy	NO	YES
Bicameral Legislation	NO	YES
Constitutional Court	NO	YES
Higher Judicial Court	NO	YES
Economic Development Board	NO	YES
Grievance Court	NO	YES
National Audit Court	NO	YES
Human Rights	LITTLE	MORE
Women's Rights	YES	MORE
Parliament Elections	NO	YES
Municipal Elections	NO	YES
Women as candidates	NO	YES
Women Votes	NO	YES
Independent Judiciary	NO	YES
Political Associations	NO	YES
Demonstrations	NO	YES
Free Media	NO	YES
Free Speech	NO	YES
Security Laws	YES	NO
Exiles	YES	NO
Bidoon (non-national residents)	YES	NO

Municipal and Parliamentary Elections of 2002

Two months after the signing of the Constitution, Municipal Council elections were held, for the first time since 1975, on May 9, 2002. During these elections, a total of 306 candidates, including thirty four women, competed for fifty seats in the twelve municipalities.

Voter turnout amounted to 51% of the registered electorate; considered a stark contrast to the 89% of the registered electorate having voted in the referendum over the NAC. For the first round of voting, 51.28% of registered voters went to the polls, with turnout differing by socioeconomic status and along sectarian lines. Fifty-two percent of voters were women, but none were elected. The second round of voting saw a 55% turnout.

This municipal election had unique significance as it was the first in Bahrain's history to be conducted based on universal suffrage, meaning women were allowed to both vote and stand as candidates. The results of the election constituted a landslide for the Shiite al-Wefaq National Islamic Society. Out of the fifty municipal seats, candidates associated with Islamist societies won thirty eight, with the remaining twelve won by independent candidates. Even though a nominal municipal system had been in place for several decades, until 2001, these twelve administrative bodies of the local Government enjoyed little autonomy. In 2001, King Hamad promised to give more autonomy to them. The result was the creation of elected Councils in 2002 to represent the views and interests of each Municipality.

Rising Discontent: Electoral Boycott

After the King's February 2002 announcement, there was speculation that some societies would boycott the municipal elections, but all decided to participate in a gesture of good faith that constitutional issues might be addressed in advance of the parliamentary elections.

Lack of action on constitutional issues in the period between elections, coupled with what many societies have termed arbitrary decrees on issues ranging from housing allocations to trade union laws to electoral laws, led some to argue that the King was not serious about a consultative process.

Citing a lack of movement on the Constitution and the constraints posed by the electoral law, on September 3, 2002, four political societies—al-Wefaq National Islamic Society, al-Amal National Democratic Action Society, al-Tajamo al-Qawmi, and, al-Amal al-Islami—decided to boycott the polls for the legislative elections.

Two nights before election day, the four boycotting political societies held a rally in Manama, and at least 10,000 people attended. The presidents of the societies reiterated their grievances against the Government, including their concerns about the way in which the Constitution was amended and the installation of a 40-member appointed Council with powers equal to those of the elected body, and called into question the legitimacy of the entire process. On October 30, after some debate, the boycotting societies announced they asked their supporters to stay away from the polls again.

In public and private consultations, both the boycotting societies and the Government were ambivalent about the second round; Government efforts to mobilize voters decreased, and the societies seemed uninterested in deciding whether or not to try to enforce another boycott. These factors lend further credence to the notion that election day on October 24 had been a referendum on the King's reform agenda rather than on specific candidates or issues.

These legislative elections took place on October 24 and 31, 2002. The turnout was 53.48% for the first round and 43% for the second. The 10% fall in electoral participation can be ascribed to the aforementioned electoral boycotters. In total, 174 candidates, including eight women, competed for fourty seats. The results of the election saw the lion's share of seats go to Islamist candidates, with no females elected.

The boycotters demanded a contractual Constitution—one agreed upon by the ruler and the ruled. Because, according to the boycotters, talk of anti-reform and the pro-reform camp around the King and the Crown Prince was meaningless. They were much the two sides of the same coin. This approach also implies that the boycotters were not able to distinguish between the different power circles within the Government.

While the ideological side of the boycott was obvious, there was a pragmatic side to it as well: considering Bahrain's majority voting system, it is highly unlikely that the three small societies could have won any seats in the elections -only al-Wefaq did; in fact, they won the municipal elections-. Meanwhile, the boycott had the side effect of stabilizing internal hierarchies within societies, meaning it was harder for politicians to achieve a profile, and many tactical decisions could be postponed. Also, at the time, the leftists still struggled with their communist exile and underground identity, and al-Wefaq barely managed to integrate its returned exiles with the 1990s uprising activists. As soon as signs of possible participation in the next elections surfaced, al-Wefaq split.

Another issue surfaced, as the CoR's internal bylaws were written by those who became part of the political scene. The non-participating opposition societies objected to almost all the bylaws from outside the decision-making arena.

Because of their ideological basis, the strategic options open for the coalition were limited, since they could not recognize the institutions created by the new or amended Constitution of 2002. Therefore, their ability to directly influence legislation was very limited. Any attempts to converse with a member of Parliament was interpreted as a betrayal of the boycotter's ideals. Al-Wefaq, being a mass-integration party stemming from a social movement, had an abundance of auxiliary organizations -women, youth, and human rights- and many locally based branches, that was used as part of their strategy in their campaign for constitutional change in 2004.

2004 Opposition Campaign

The campaign had three distinct (if overlapping) phases: at first, the boycotters' alliance tried to influence public discourse from conference tables. Later, the strategy was built on al-Wefaq's assets as it moved toward a combination of a show of force on the streets and behind-the-doors dialogue with the Government. The third phase was dominated by mass mobilization and the use of majalis and ma'atams.

When the constitutional coalition was launching its campaign, its initial agenda was designed and dominated by the intellectuals of al-Amal al-Watani (Wa'ad). Hence, the campaign started in February 2004 with a conference titled toward a contractual Constitution.

The Government reacted sharply against the meeting, proving that while the event was vital for fostering the coalition's cohesion, it clearly would not achieve a dialogue with the Government on the constitutional question.

The petitioners could confidently expect many signatures since gaining support with religious backing and infrastructure had proven to be easy in the past. Expectations for the constitutional petition were high; it was calculated that at the very minimum, 50,000 signatures should be collected. In April and May 2004, events around the petition movement escalated as it became clear that al-Wefaq had managed to efficiently collect the signatures: young activists had been deployed in every street in every village, while others were touring the shrines. A legalistic squabble between the Government and the campaigners ensued. The Constitution clearly declared that petitions would only be accepted if submitted by a legal body, not a coalition of legal bodies that was itself not registered. Al-Wefaq then announced that it would put together a petition gathering consent from non members to the petition with membership to the political society, which led to its membership to grow noticeably. That was widely welcomed by the society heads but would later be largely regretted in the 2018 legislative elections.

Lebanese Style Protest & Socio-Economic Challenges to the Political Process

The mass demonstrations of Ukraine and Lebanon in February and March 2005 had a strong impact on Bahraini activists. Following the Lebanese example, banners and stickers in national colors were created. Previously, Shiites often sported Iranian or Hezbollah flags and emblems, which infuriated the Government and also alienated Sunnites. The demonstrations for constitutional reform were branded, every participant was given stickers in Bahraini red and white on which was written: *Constitutional reform first*, which sparked a reaction of Sunnites marking every other lamppost with *Bahrain first* stickers.

Two massive rallies were held, one on Sitra island—a traditional stronghold of al-Wefaq—and another one in front of the area's main shopping mall, Dana Mall in the Sanabis area in the heart of the capital. The coalition of boycotters had abandoned dialogue with the Government and resorted to pressure.

The dangers of this strategy were quite apparent to those who adopted it. The mobilization of juveniles for rallies is hard to sustain without risking an escalation into violence. Another constant concern was the sectarian nature of the protests. Street rallies were dominated by Shia youth. Mass demonstrations tended to rally the economic elite and the Sunna parts of the Bahraini populace around the Government. To counter that, Ali Salman and others made use of the majlis structure of the Bahraini society and embarked on a tour through the Sunnites majalis of Muharraq. While this majlis tour was well-received, it still did not add more Sunnites supporters to the campaign, and pressure on the Government did not increase. At the same time, al-Wefaq, as the potential sweeping winner of elections, started to slowly bring back other issues into its discourse.

Legislative Elections 2006

In the period immediately prior to elections, one of the more prominent issues that was raised by the opposition concerned the *Bandargate* allegations and the citizenship law—a high-profile alleged scandal involving a claim by strategic adviser to the Cabinet Affairs Ministry—of corruption and bribes totaling $2.7 million dispersed to manipulate the results of coming elections. What was interesting is that the four leading political opposition societies that boycotted the 2002 elections ultimately decided to participate in the election process despite the announced scandal. A fundamental explanation for the participation of opposition groups in the 2006 elections stems from the provisions of the Political Societies Law No. 25 of 2005. The law tightened the manner in which societies could operate and, most importantly, required them to register to maintain their political status. Besides, they found themselves away from the decision-making circle, while many laws were being passed.

Since the opposition societies had submitted to the registration and procedural requirements of the new law, a debate was sparked amongst key members on whether an elections boycott should be maintained. Registration to vote was seen by many to equate with the implicit acceptance of the Constitution. Compounding, this was an increasingly dominant view that the boycott was distracting political societies away from the real issues of poverty, housing, and employment. The net effect of these factors gave Sheikh Ali Salman the flexibility to ultimately change policy and opt to contest the 2006 parliamentary elections.

This decision resulted in the emergence of a breakaway faction of al-Wefaq called the Haq Movement, headed by Hasan Mushaima, the former vice chairman and co-founder of al-Wefaq. The Haq Movement rejected the legitimacy of the Constitution claiming that the referendum was not identical with the actual text of the Constitution and that the King had reneged on his promise to have a unicameral legislature. Although the Haq movement had only a relatively small number of supporters compared to Al-Wefaq, it nevertheless called on its members to boycott the election. Eventually, al-Wefaq, headed by the cleric Sheikh Ali Salman, secured seventeen of the eighteen candidates fielded, which translated to a 42.5% share of the seats in Parliament. The second election for the Council of Representatives took place on November 25, 2006.

In both these elections, females represented approximately half of the total voters, which indicates they were willing to participate in the decisions of their country. With that level of interest and with women candidates in many districts, there was an expectation that women would be well represented in the Council of Representatives and the Municipal Councils. However, in 2006, only one woman, Latifa al-Quod, succeeded in taking place in the CoR. A study on the small number of female candidates was conducted by the Supreme Council of Women, in cooperation with the United Nations Development Program in 2010. The findings noted that the major political organizations did not nominate women candidates despite their alleged calls for equality.

Furthermore, their chances of success were substantially reduced because most women ran as independents or for less popular societies. The study stated that nineteen (95%) of the female candidates did not belong to any of the political associations, and only 5% represented mainstream political associations. According to the study, other obstacles that led to their failure to make it to political office were the following:

- Being new to politics.
- Their inability to join an electoral alliance.
- Lack of Campaign funding.
- Lack of advice on how to properly manage a campaign.
- Lack of a professional approach.
- Lack of loyal supporters.
- Lack of electoral procedure knowledge.

However, there were more reasons for failure, as identified by the candidates themselves. Almost 30% of female candidates thought their failure in the election was attributable to the influence of religious leadership, which exercised some social and spiritual control over the voters. More specifically, religious leaders argued against women standing for the legislative Council. There is also the suggestion that many people did not want to be represented by women. This attitude is based on the traditional role of women being subservient to men due to religious and cultural reasons. Another 19% of the failed candidates regarded the power of political associations and the obstruction of the electoral process as the crucial factors of their failure, while 9.6% reported mismanagement in their electoral campaign, and 4.8% stated the reason lay in the weakness of electoral financing.

Legislative Elections 2010

The resentment over the handling of the 2006 elections carried over to the November 2010 elections. In December 2008, the Authorities made numerous arrests of Shia demonstrators and accused some of being part of a foreign-inspired plot to destabilize Bahrain. Some were accused of undergoing terrorist training in Syria. On January 29, 2009, the Government arrested three leading Shia activists accused of planning terror attacks and attempting to overthrow the Government, including Abduljalil al-Singace and Hasan Mushaima, both leaders of the unauthorized Haq Movement. They were tried in February and March 2009, but along with other Shia activists, they were pardoned and released in April 2009. Nevertheless, sectarian tensions heightened in 2009. These came to the forefront in October when thousands of demonstrators protested the Government's refusal to review the naturalization law that allows Arab Sunnites to become citizens, claiming it was an effort to change the demographics of the chiefly Shiite population ahead of the 2010 elections.

In February 2010, the Bahrain Centre for Human Rights (BCHR) continued to pressure the Government for reforms regarding freedom of expression, specifically citing threats against the al-Wefaq. The Human Rights Commission issued a set of demands to Bahraini authorities, including the abolishment of the political societies law. Shortly after that, the al-Wefaq legislative bloc demanded -but not through the legislative body- that Parliament names the cabinet rather than appointed by the King. During this period, a meeting between al-Wefaq and the British ambassador prompted harsh criticism from the Shiites, explicitly members of the National Islamic Tribune Society, and provoked protests, including a minor bomb explosion at the British embassy's parking lot, over perceived interference of Britain in Bahrain's internal affairs.

On June 15, 2010, the unlicensed *al-Majlis al-Olamaie* 'Clerics Council' was officially dissolved by the court for not abiding by rules and regulations.

Because of this unrest, an increased number of security forces were visible ahead of parliamentary balloting on October 23 and October 30, 2010, in which 127 candidates participated. Balloting was peaceful, with a turnout of 67% of voters at the polls. Opposition retained their strength in Parliament by winning all eighteen seats -exclusively al-Wefaq- they contested, while independents were second with seventeen. Following the second round in nine constituencies, Sunni Islamists groups added three seats, increasing their representation to five for an overall loss of twelve seats compared to 2006. The National Democratic Action Society (Wa'ad) failed to secure the two seats it contested in the second round one was lost to their allies, al-Wefaq. On November 2, a minor cabinet reshuffle occurred, and the King appointed an additional deputy Prime Minister, Shaikh Khalid bin Abdullah al-Khalifa.

Regional Unrest

Feelings of discontent in Bahrain were running high even before the revolutions in Tunisia and Egypt shook the Arab world. Starting in December 2010, mobilization began to circulate on several social media outlets, including calls for demonstrations to demand political, social, and economic reforms in the Kingdom of Bahrain. In this context a Facebook page called *February 14th Revolution* in Bahrain established to call for mass protests throughout Bahrain on February 14, 2011. This date was intentionally chosen as it marked the 10th anniversary of the referendum of the National Charter, which officially transformed Bahrain into a constitutional monarchy. In other words, the demonstrators wanted to remind the King that he had to abide by what had been approved by popular suffrage.

Inspired by the popular uprisings that swept away the Ben Ali and Mubarak regimes in Tunisia and Egypt, youths began to form new groups. They used Facebook to voice their demands and call for their peers to join the demonstrations on February 14. Like other Arab uprisings, existing organized political groups did not initiate the Bahraini revolt. It was young citizens from an unclear variety of different backgrounds and with differing viewpoints who led the 2011 protests in the Kingdom. The youth movement subsequently started to call itself *The Youths of the February 14th Revolution*, a term for a decentralized and, what seemed like, leaderless organization. In addition to rejecting the political space offered by Parliament, the youth-led uprising was an attempt to find an alternative to the existing political opposition rather than being a proxy of al-Wefaq and, thus, was able to draw many protestors who were not affiliated with existing groups. At the beginning of the protests, it operated as a highly inclusive and loose coalition that united around broad calls for political change without making potentially divisive decisions on more detailed issues. Their demands revolved around the achievement of change and radical reforms in the system of Bahrain, the absence of which had caused continuous unease in the relationship between the people and the ruling family. It made some activists into popular icons who influenced the movement, rather than leaders who command it or were responsible for it. These figures included fourteen high-profile detained political leaders, including former hunger striker Abdulhadi al-Khawaja and Nabeel Rajab, head of the banned Bahrain Centre for Human Rights.

The movement received support from unrecognized political movements, including Haq, al-Wafa, and the Bahrain Islamic Freedom Movement. The support was further strengthened when it gained the endorsement of Shia clergy and politicians of their association, al-Wefaq, through Friday sermons and Mat'am meetups, as well as the support of the National Democratic Action Society (Wa'ad).

Demonstrations began on February 4, 2011, at the Egyptian embassy as a symbol of support for the ongoing popular uprising in Egypt, which eventually culminated in the ousting of

President Hosni Mubarak on February 11, 2011. From then on, the voices of political activists calling to organize demonstrations increased, leading the Ministry of the Interior to take precautionary measures in anticipation of any protests. Starting on February 12, 2011, limited incidents of unrest were reported in various parts of Bahrain. On this day, King Hamad bin Isa al-Khalifa issued a royal decree granting BHD 1,000 (equals to USD 2,645) to each Bahraini family on the occasion marking the tenth anniversary of the National Action Charter. Other concessions were made by the Government, including offering to free some youths who had been arrested in the August crackdown and increase social spending. However, this did not calm rising tensions and discontent.

On February 14, 2011, demonstrations and political rallies erupted throughout Bahrain. These protests varied in size and political orientation, with demands including revision of the Constitution, undertaking political reform, and achieving greater socioeconomic justice. Some were confined to specific locations in Manama and other cities, while others took the form of street marches and rallies. However, the primary location was Manama's GCC Roundabout, widely known as Pearl Roundabout, a monument named after Bahrain's participation in the Gulf Council, highlighting the county's renowned pearl industry, where thousands of civil resisters camped. Later, the Salmaniya Medical Complex, the only full-service public hospital located about two kilometers from the Pearl Roundabout, would also become a massive gathering venue for protestors. Over 6,000 people were estimated to have participated in protests throughout the country that day. According to the Bahrain Independent Commission of Inquiry, a total of fifty five protests of various sizes took place in Bahrain on this so-called *Day of Rage*. The demonstrations assumed prevalent overtones as both Sunni and Shia alike gathered in unprecedented numbers, chanting slogans like No Shia, *No Sunna, only Bahrainis.* An obvious Shia majority was visible to the naked eye. The focus of the planned protest aimed at securing greater political participation and accountability rather than targeting the position of the King or the ruling family in Bahrain

However, in a pattern that was also seen in other countries, the number of protestors swelled after a heavy-handed police response resulted in two deaths on February 14 and 15. On February 15, 2011, King Hamad gave a televised address to the nation expressing his condolences for the two deaths and announced the establishment of a committee headed by Deputy Prime Minister Jawad bin Salem al-Urrayed to identify the reasons for the events of the previous two days. The King also reaffirmed the right of Bahrainis to exercise their freedom of expression and assembly in accordance with the law. This day was also marked by two other announcements: al-Wefaq members of the Council of Representatives announced they would suspend their participation in the Council's sessions, and the General Federation of Bahrain Trade Unions (GFBTU) announced calls for a general strike on February 17.

By the evening of February 16, the number of protests at the Pearl Roundabout continued to increase until they reportedly reached over 12,000 people. Some were calling for the revision of the Constitution, some demanded reforms, and some expressed grievances relating to economic and social disempowerment, while others called for a revolution to bring the Government and the royal family down. At the political level, both the Prime Minister and the Minister of justice gave separate press conferences expressing their regret for the two deaths that had occurred and emphasized that a dialogue, which should happen through the National Assembly, was the solution to the unrest in Bahrain. A meeting was also held between Crown Prince Shaikh Salman bin Hamad bin Isa al-Khalifa and representatives of al-Wefaq, including its secretary-general, Sheikh Ali Salman. Negotiations were not entirely fruitful, and that evening, Sheikh Ali Salman visited the GCC Roundabout and gave a short statement expressing his support for the protest movement and the demands being expressed in the demonstrations.

To stop the movement, on February 17, 2011, orders were issued to the police to regain control of the roundabout and clear the area of demonstrators, and around 1,500 individuals camped in tents. Four battalions, totaling over 1,000, were dispatched to participate in the operation. Police personnel were armed with sticks, shields, sound bombs, tear gas launchers, and shotguns. In retaliation, numerous incidents of violence against police, security patrols, and MoI installations were recorded in various areas, including the King Faisal Highway and the Manama police headquarters. This clash lasted two days and resulted in the death of four protesters, fifty wounded demonstrators, and fourty seven injured police. Thus, this date became known as *Bloody Thursday*. In response, eighteen members of al-Wefaq announced their resignation from the Council of Representatives, despite al-Wefaq's Consultative Council's vote to remain in the CoR while seize their activities as a protest, which was useless since this was the sole decision of their supreme leader, Sheikh Isa Qasim. The rapid mobilization highlighted how quickly the lack of trust felt by many activists toward the Government could assume a more radical stance. On February 18, fueled by heightened public anger over the fatalities, the level of violence and the intensity of confrontation increased and spread to more parts of Bahrain, radicalizing the movement as a result. Instead of appealing for reforms, civil resisters began demanding an end to the al-Khalifas' rule. Anti-Government slogans were heard in the roundabout, *Down, down Khalifa*! These chants were aimed at the Prime Minister, Shaikh Khalifa bin Salman al-Khalifa, rather than at the ruling family itself. Therefore, on February 18, 2011, as the movement expanded and adopted revolutionary goals, King Hamad ordered security forces to withdraw and asked the Crown Prince to start a dialogue and negotiations with the opposition.

On February 19, Government forces pulled back from the GCC Roundabout based on instructions by the Crown Prince, and protestors occupied the location anew. As designated head of the national dialogue, the Crown Prince assembled a negotiations team, in which he included Shia, Sunna, and a member of the ruling family. February 20 saw widespread strikes and demonstrations organized by employees in both the public and private sectors. Estimates have suggested that around 65–75% of employees in Bahrain went on strike. Demonstrations and protests continued throughout the 21st, and this time, thousands of Government supporters gathered at the al-Fateh Mosque in Juffair and again on March 2, 2011, expressing support for the Government and forming the Gathering of National Unity (TGONU). On the same day, the Crown Prince decided to postpone the Formula One races from March 13 to October 30 of the same year. It is a prestigious international event for Bahrain and was considered a pivotal concession to the opposition.

Nevertheless, the number of protesters peaked, reaching approximately 150,000 Bahraini citizens on February 22. This day was dubbed as the *Martyrs' March* in honor of the victims. Due to the march, King Hamad released twenty three of the twenty five defendants accused of being part of the terrorist network in the 2010 trails and pardoned 308 individuals convicted of various crimes relating to state security. The exiled could now return, including leading opposition figures such as the secretary-general of the Haq Movement, Hasan Mushaima. Nevertheless, negotiations with the opposition were still at a standstill, and demonstrations continued. The activists converged on the roundabout and demanded the resignation of the Prime Minister, raising slogans such as The people demand the removal of the regime Step down, Hamad and Down with the Government of Bahrain, and expressed their rejection of calls for a dialogue.

On February 25, 2011, massive anti-Government marches were staged to mourn the protests victims. During these days, hundreds protested outside the Parliament building demanding the resignation of all MPs. In that political sphere, a National Coalition was formed by four political societies: The National Action Charter Society, the National Free Thought Society, the Constitutional Rally Society, and the Islamic Unity Society. The coalition formulated six conditions for negotiations, including the release of political prisoners, formation of an investigative committee into the police repression, and resignation of the current Government. Concessions were made on all demands presented to the Government. The King announced a Government reshuffle in which four cabinet Ministers, who were generally disfavored by the opposition, were replaced: the Minister of Health, the Minister of Housing, the Minister for Electricity and Water Affairs, and the Minister for the Council of Ministers' Affairs. The latter Minister, Shaikh Ahmed al-Khalifa, had come under particularly sharp criticism since the Bandar Report scandal broke out in 2006. As for the other concessions, the political prisoners had already been pardoned and released, and the formation of an investigative committee into the police repression would come in June 2011 as the Bahrain Independent Commission of Inquiry (BICI).

All political societies, community leaders, and social organizations were invited to attend the national dialogue initiated by the Crown Prince, an invitation to which the main opposition parties did not respond to until March 3, 2011. Meanwhile, the hardline Shia faction, reinforced by the return of the leader of the Haq movement, Hasan Mushaima, from exile, hardened negotiation efforts. The faction received support from twenty four civil society organizations, who, in order to break the current impasse, staged a massive protest in front of the office of Prime Minister, demanding his resignation. Later, on March 7, a group of outlawed movements, namely Haq, the 14 February Movement, and the al-Wafa Movement, founded the Alliance for the Republic, a coalition favoring the creation of a republic in Bahrain. These ideological steps were followed by actions. They split with al-Wefaq, taking the decision to expand the action to other repertories than the sit-in at the GCC Roundabout. Haq, al-Wafa and the Bahrain Islamic Movement called for expanding the protests to the Royal Palace and the Financial Harbor before the Peninsula Shield entering the country to protect vital institutions. As protests continued into March, and the hardliners escalated their moves and their religious vocabularies, clashes between Shia and Sunna citizens started to take place. The general level of security & law and order deteriorated significantly throughout the country as more cases of assault against individuals, private and public properties, and incidents of sectarian clashes were reported.

The most significant developments in March 2011 were the following:

— **March 7–10**: Major demonstrations took place outside the US Embassy, the Ministry of Interior, the University of Bahrain, the Information Affairs Authority, and the General Directorate of Nationality, Passport, and Residency.

— **March 10**: A large number of students demonstrated in various neighborhoods and villages across Bahrain, with clashes occurring between Police and anti-Government protesters.

— **March 11**: An increase of demonstrations organized at locations directly affiliated with the Royal Palace, such as the Royal Court. The riot police blocked these protests.

— **March 13**: The University of Bahrain witnessed its most violent clashes, which left many people injured and led to the suspension of classes. Youth groups decided to erect a barricade outside of the Bahrain Financial Harbor complex, blocking the major King Faisal Highway. Protests also continued at the Pearl Roundabout. Several attacks against the police took place.

— **March 14:** Numerous cases of vandalism were reported in various areas of Bahrain, and many attacks against expatriates residing in Bahrain, especially those of Asian descent, took place. Fearing for their lives and property, more citizens organized checkpoints to monitor activity and traffic in their neighborhoods.

Like previous demonstrations, the protesters called for the removal of the ruling family, the resignation of the Government of Bahrain, and the abrogation of the 2002 Constitution. In an attempt to reach a compromise, the Crown Prince introduced a document, presented on March 13, outlining significant concessions in a seven-point initiative partially drawn from the documents presented by the opposition political societies and other documents. He promised the following:

- Fully authorized CoR.
- A Government that represents the well of people.
- Modified constituencies.
- Refined citizenship Law.
- Firm anti-corruption measures.
- State's assets be available for public records.
- Firm anti-sectarian measures.

Despite coming close to an agreement around this set of political reforms, the talks broke down when al-Wefaq refused to enter a formal dialogue unless the Government agreed to a new constitutional arrangement. Soon after, the offer of talks was withdrawn, and due to the increase of violence and the spread of clashes throughout the country, on March 14, 2011, Bahrain requested the assistance of the Peninsula Shield to restore stability.

This assistance came in the shape of the Gulf Council Emergency Forces, also known as the Peninsula Shield Force, with 1,000 men from the Saudi Arabian Royal Guard and 500 men from the United Arab Emirates and State of Qatar military. The next day, King Hamad issued Royal Decree No.18 of 2011, declaring a State of National Safety -a lower form of martial law- throughout the territory of the Kingdom of Bahrain, which lasted until June 1, 2011. In accordance with this decree, Bahraini authorities and law enforcement agencies began to adopt a more forceful approach toward demonstrators and individuals involved in any act causing public disorder. The GCC forces aided the Bahraini Defense Force, and from March 14-18 demonstrators were arrested, including many opposition figures. Harsh clashes between police and protesters were still ongoing but on a smaller scale. In response to the Government's declaration of effective State of National Safety, the General Federation of Bahrain Trade Unions called on another general strike.

Economically, the strikes throughout February and March 2011 had an immense impact on Bahrain's economy. Production of refinery products had slumped as low as 32,000 barrels a day, from 210,000, as the workforce dwindled to about 10%. It was a harsh hit to Bahrain's economy, as petroleum production and refinery account for more than 60% of export receipts, 70% of Government revenues, and 11% of GDP. Other effects included Bahrain's credit rating sinking from A- to BBB, the lowest investment-grade rating, which no longer allowed for the promised $10 billion from Gulf states to build housing and improve infrastructures in the country. Overall, due to the Arab Spring, the economy of Bahrain was affected as the GDP decreased, debt increased, current account balance decreased, Government spending increased, consumption increased, and investments decreased.

On March 18, the Pearl Monument at the center of the GCC Roundabout was demolished, and the roundabout was transformed into a juncture, signifying the end of the 2011 Bahraini uprising. Martial law was lifted on June 1, and shortly thereafter, the King convened a National Dialogue and created an ostensibly independent investigation into the springtime unrest: the Bahrain Independent Commission of Inquiry (BICI). Through these initiatives, the Government hoped to begin a process of reconciliation with the opposition. However, their implementation widened the chasm between the al-Khalifa's and the opposition by casting severe doubt on the credibility of the commitment to reforms.

Iran's Involvement
in Bahrain

Iran's interest in Bahrain's Shia heritage began in 1602 during the Iranian Safavid Dynasty, which is considered the beginning of modern Persian history and is known for the establishment of the Twelver Schools of Shia Islam. The Islamic Regime's de-facto rule over Bahrain lasted until the conquest of the al-Khalifa tribe in 1782, which came on the eastern shores of Bahrain from the nation of Qatar to the east. This subsequently forced many Shia to flee to the northern and western portions of Bahrain, which in turn caused the demographic division of Bahrain's Shia population and is a critical factor in making current conditions ripe for the insurgency.

With the rising prominence of the Ottoman Empire and the subsequent dominance of Sunni Islam, the Shia sect became increasingly isolated, which drastically affected the sentiments of the Shia population in Bahrain. The 1979 Islamic revolution in Iran played a critical role in giving hope to Bahraini Shia opposition and gave rise to the creation of Shia resistance groups throughout the island. Bahraini Shiites became encouraged by the success of the Islamic revolution in Iran, and the relationship between Bahrain's Shia population and the Islamic Regime in the young republic was further cemented when Iranian clerics came to preach in Bahrain. The clerics' visits coincidentally occurred around the same time that a radical Shia group known as the Islamic Front for the Liberation of Bahrain (IFLB) came into prominence. In 1980, IFLB's leadership held a conference in Tehran of which they issued a statement that said: *Imam Khomeini is the leader and axis around which our oppressed peoples should rally if they truly seek freedom, since Imam Khomeini is the summit of jihad and faith and the symbol of challenge and endurance. He is the hope of all the oppressed in the world.*

The IFLB's most overt action against the Bahraini Government took place in 1981 when the insurgent group executed a failed coup attempt that was primarily backed by Iran. Iranian support to the IFLB's coup attempt took several forms, the most notable of which included Tehran's provision of fake Bahraini police uniforms, training, funding, extensive media and propaganda assistance, and weapons. The failure of the attempted coup was followed by the trial of seventy three IFLB members; however, the Bahraini Government was careful in its judicial rulings to not be overly harsh to mitigate further unrest amongst the nation's Shiites. Instead, the more radical members of the IFLB were slowly and systematically deported from Iran, resulting in the gradual dissipation of the group throughout the 1990s and its complete dissolution in 2002. King Hamad managed to mitigate the IFLB supporters' primary grievances by facilitating reforms that increased integration of Shia leaders into the Bahraini political process via the formation of the Council of Representatives.

Starting in the 1980s and through the 1990s, Iran sought to replicate the success of Hezbollah's operations in Lebanon via the implementation of a split-off branch known as Hezbollah al-Hejaz. This group was initially based in Qom, Iran, and was trained alongside

Lebanese Hezbollah with the intent of conducting insurgency support operations in Shia-populated areas of Saudi Arabia, Kuwait, and Bahrain. Hezbollah al-Hejaz is best known for the 1996 bombing of the Khobar Towers in Saudi Arabia, an attack that killed ninteen US service members and injured hundreds. Though they have not since executed an attack of the same magnitude, Hezbollah has maintained a fairly robust presence throughout the GCC and has been an integral part of Iran's operations in the region.

Specifically, in Bahrain, Hezbollah played an active role throughout the 1990s both in terms of combat logistics operations and insurgency support efforts. In 1994, after having received training from the IRGC, Hezbollah al-Hejaz attempted to smuggle Improvised Explosive Devices (IEDs) and weapons into Bahrain at the direction of Iranian intelligence services. In 1996, Hezbollah agents in Bahrain joined an ongoing wave of civil disobedience and disturbances directed against the rulers that included arson and the facilitation of pro-Iranian radio communications from Iranian radio stations. Soon thereafter, Bahraini security forces arrested fourty four Hezbollah operatives, after which a subsequent investigation revealed that Bahraini Hezbollah had been trained by the IRGC and that Iran's intent was to inspire events in Bahrain similar to that of Iran's 1979 Islamic revolution.

Outside of the IFLB and Hezbollah al-Hejaz, Iran's support of dissident groups within Bahrain before late 2010 was primarily geared towards Shia-based political groups. The three most important of these political societies are al-Wefaq, the Haq Movement, and the Bahrain Freedom Movement based out of London. As of Bahrain's elections in 2010, al-Wefaq, the largest of the three crucial opposition political groups, held 18 out of 40 seats on the Council of Representatives.

Unlike al-Wefaq, which is considered to be fairly moderate, the Haq Movement and Bahrain Freedom Movement are fringe Shia political groups within Bahrain that are unlicensed and, therefore, do not have the ability to legally participate in Bahraini elections. The Bahrain Freedom Movement is comprised primarily of former IFLB members; their leader, Saeed al-Shehabi, is currently exiled in London and conducts public outreach activities from abroad, and he was granted the funds for a building to host the movement in London. Members of both groups are often accused of being direct proxies of the Iranian Government or current Hezbollah al-Hejaz sympathizers. This has culminated in accusations that these groups have received training abroad in places like Iran, Iraq, and Syria and has resulted in the subsequent arrest of several key members.

From late 2010, several events have come to pass that have drastically changed the Iranian approach of inspiring an Islamic revolution inside Bahrain. The most significant of these events was the renowned Arab Spring, a revolutionary wave of civil wars, protests, demonstrations, and riots that began to erupt exclusively across the Arab states on December 18, 2010, and continues to the present day. Other, smaller, more isolated yet highly significant events are still taking place.

Beginning in mid-January 2011, the Bahraini Ministry of Interior (MOI) reported an unusual uptick in social disorder, vandalism, and inflammatory rhetoric originating from Shia mosques throughout the island. The MOI was quick to assign blame to Iranian agents and Hezbollah operatives. Such attribution is often a result of overt discrimination against

Shiites, a preference towards maintaining the status quo in favor of the Sunni minority, and a resounding paranoia and perhaps fear of the Republic of Iran and the capability of Iran's intelligence community, IRGC Qods Forces, and sub-state proxies. This particular accusation at this period in time, however, was supported factually by noticeable instances of anti-regime radio messaging, talks of protest and change via social media forums, and a Shia population that appeared to be slowly arming itself and engaging in policing behavior in within densely populated Shia neighborhoods.

Advisor to the Bahraini King for diplomatic affairs, Dr. Mohamed Abdulghaffar, cited before the United Nations on September 25, 2013, that *the Kingdom of Bahrain has been suffering for a long time from the Iranian interference in its internal affairs. There are multiple TV channels that are under Iranian influence, along with several radio stations, newspapers and media institutions that are affiliated with Iran.* Dr. Abdulghaffar's accusation against Iran was particularly applicable in Bahrain from January to early February 2011. Native Arabic and Farsi speakers reported hearing calls from Iran both on the radio and amongst Shia mosques encouraging Bahrain's disparaged Shia population to conduct demonstrations in the streets and to begin policing their own neighborhoods in preparation for an inevitable conflict with the ruling Sunni family. This public messaging campaign within Bahrain coincided with public support for continued unrest from Iranian political circles. Iranian Supreme Leader Khamenei was cited as saying, *the uprising of the people of Bahrain is essentially the same as the uprising of the people of Egypt, Tunisia, Libya, and Yemen. The people of Bahrain only want free elections. Is this too much to expect?*

In addition to public messaging via radio and political statements, suspicions were aroused when Hasan Mushaima, in an interview with Lebanese newspaper *al-Akhbar*, said that Iran would intervene to back the Bahraini opposition if the Saudis intervened to support the ruling family. Mushaima expressed similar sentiments the week before, while he was still in exile in London, during a television appearance on the Iranian channel al-Alam. A significant escalation in demands for change from Bahrain's hardline opposition groups followed. Mushaima led three Shia groups—al-Wafa, Haq, and the Bahrain Freedom Movement—into a *Coalition for an Islamic Republic*, which declared its intentions to end the al-Khalifa rule. In addition, there was evidence to suggest that Iran exacerbated anti-regime sentiments within Bahrain using social media platforms. Post-analysis of the internet's role throughout the duration of the Arab Spring has exemplified the importance of social media platforms such as Facebook, Twitter, and weblogs for popular mobilization. Like other populations in countries affected by the Arab Spring, Bahraini Shiites heavily relied on social media to organize protests, share news about security force movements, and exploit their message to wider audiences throughout the world. Realizing the role that social media was playing in terms of popular mobilization, Bahraini security forces were quick to shut down access to popular social media forums by filtering key websites and, in many cases, slow down internet access in Shia-concentrated locations.

Social Media Activity during Arab Spring Season

January. 2011 - April 2011

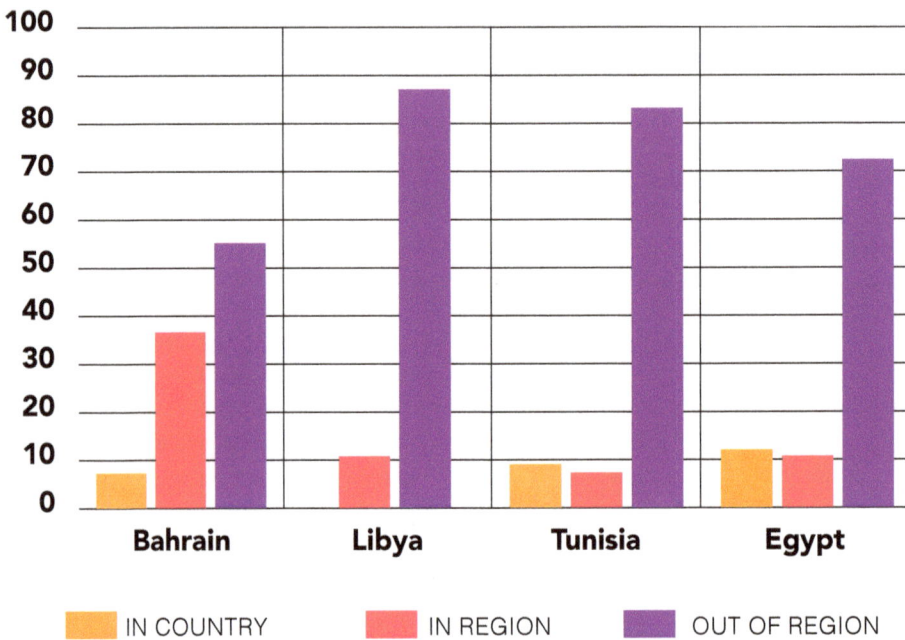

This figure demonstrates the number of clicks on popular social media
by the thousands during the January to April 2011 timeframe.

A Timeline of Iran's Interference in Bahrain

Detailing Iran's involvement and effects on Bahrain's political system:

1919

Internal problems and calls in Iran demanding the appointment of a representative of Bahrain in the Iranian Parliament.

1919

Iran intensified immigration to Bahrain, forcing the Government to issue a nationality law to limit Iranians' access to the nationality.

1922

The British Consulate sent a report that Iranian passport officials had confiscated Bahraini passports pending consideration of Iranian nationals.

1923

The Iranian Consulate in Najaf stressed that all Iranians and citizens in Bahrain should register with the Iranian Consulate there.

1927

Iran protested the treaty between King Abdul Aziz and Britain over Bahrain as a violation of the Persian sovereignty of its boycott.

Iran resorted to another method, sending its customers and immigrants to incite the people of Bahrain against its rulers and stir up sectarian strife in the country.

A memorandum sent by the British political resident stated: *Bahrain has become a base for Iranian conspiracies and Iranian immigration must be stopped.*

1934I

ran objected to Bahrain signing a contract with a foreign oil company, as the agreement was signed 'without Iran's consent.'

1945

The Nairoz Iran newspaper included a speech by Iran's Foreign Minister, who called on the United States to wait for the oil extraction due to Iranian rights in Bahrain.

1946

The Iranian Parliament issued a resolution that determined Iran's exercise of sovereignty and the application of internal postal charges to Bahrain.

1951

The Iranian Ministry of Education issued a decree to teach pupils in schools that Bahrain belongs to Iran.

1957

Iran announced a decision to append Bahrain to the Iranian divisions and allocated two seats in the Iranian Parliament for Bahrain.

1975

The Iranian Government issued a new resolution to include Bahrain as the 14th province to Iranian territory.

Iran formed a powerful class of traders and investors to establish broad popular bases in Bahrain.

Informal Iranian calls to consider Bahrain as a Governorate of Iran.

1979

The slogans of exporting the revolution brought by Iran after its revolution to occupy Bahrain angered the Bahraini officials.

1981

Attempted Coup by the IFLB

1996

Bahrain announced the disclosure of a covert organization called Hezbollah - Bahrain. The Government said the Cell conspired to overthrow the Government and the defendants received training in Tehran, which lead to the decision to reduce diplomatic relations with Iran.

The Bahraini authorities revealed the arrest of members of the Hezbollah - Bahrain and were behind the violence during the uprising, as well as establishing a militia.

Statements by Hussein Shariatmadari, Advisor to the Supreme Leader of Iran Ayatollah Ali Khamenei and the General Supervisor of the Kayhan Press Foundation, in which he stated that *there is a separate account for Bahrain among the GCC countries since Bahrain is part of Iranian territory.*

Assistant Iranian Foreign Minister, Manouchehr Mohammadi, said that *the coming crisis that will paralyze the Gulf region with regard to the legitimacy of the monarchy and traditional regimes that will not be able to survive in the current situation, especially Bahrain.*

2011

Iranian President Mahmoud Ahmadinejad said the entry of Peninsula Shield to Bahrain to counter the popular revolution is *a disgraceful act that will fail,* the official IRNA news agency reported on March 16th, 2011.

President of the Iranian Islamic Shura Council Larijani and Khamenei's advisor warned the rulers of the Gulf states against military intervention in Bahrain and said *they would not pass without paying the price.* The Bahraini Government denounced this statement and withdrew its ambassador for consultation on March 15th, 2011.

A religious incitement from preachers in the Iranian mosques to call for an Islamic republic in the Kingdom of Bahrain occurred, moreover, this is what the euprising aspired to achieve in February 2011.

Tehran expelled Bahraini diplomats, and the Iranian Government organized a demonstration in Tehran in front of the Saudi embassy and the Saudi consulate. Khamenei condemns Saudi aid to Bahrain due to its role in the GCC's Peninsula shield's mission.

Iran lodges a complaint with the United Nations about Bahrain's crackdown on rioters and asks countries of the region to join it in urging Saudi Arabia to withdraw its troops from Bahrain even though it is a GCC force. Bahrain rejects Iran's attempt to internationalize its case.

Declaration of the *Islamic Republic of Bahrain,* which will not hesitate to announce the support of Iran and its symbols, by Hasan Mushaima, Mohamed al-Miqdad and Abduljalil al-Sinqace.

An announcement by the Bahraini Foreign Ministry condemning Iran's continues harassments through their petitions in international assemblies..

More than fifteen statements were made by Salehi, Iran's former Foreign Minister and a supporter of Iran's nuclear organization, shortly after the crisis began in February 2011, and his interventions contributed to the crisis.

Twenty-nine satellite channels were intentionally placed to continue incitement to undermine the stability of Bahrain.

Iran's intervention in political and media support increased. Iran is widely believed to be behind the radical armed opposition that has carried out several bombings in Manama and the daily riots and vandalism against the police, citizens, and residents.

Iran has repeatedly tried to smuggle weapons

to Bahrain during the past three decades and since the 1980s in different ways, exploiting the trade exchange between the two countries.

According to press reports, Iran played a role in the state of affairs of the opposition in the sessions of the National Dialogue, especially their withdrawal in 2011.

Ayatollah Hussein Nouri Hamdani -one of the ayatollahs of the regime- received a group of Bahraini Shia clerics, to promote and declare Jihad in Qom.

One of the movements that emerged after the Iranian revolution was Bahrain Freedom Movement, which is based in London. It took a stand, rejecting the reforms of the King and gave it the name "Khalifian Charter."

Bahraini prominent Sheikh Khalid Mansur, widely known as Mohamed Sanad, a cleric in the Hawza in Qom, on December 26th, 2005, called on the United Nations to issue a referendum on the future of Bahrain. When the authorities stopped him at Bahrain airport, his followers rioted at the airport main hall.

Shiites demanded the Constitution include a clause that grants al-Majlis al-Olamaie full authority over the pursual and implementation of the new and highly debated Family Law.

The Bahraini Foreign Minister's statement on March 26, 2011, What comes from Lebanon, with Iranian support, is pure evil. We may raise the issue to international bodies.

The arrest of members of the military terrorist cell Army of the Imam, that aimed at carrying out terrorist operations in several vital areas in Bahrain. The confessions of the accused are irrefutable evidence of a relationship with Iran through a member of the Revolutionary Guards.

2012

A statement by Ramin Mehmanparast, former Iranian Foreign Ministry spokesman, on Thursday, May 17th, 2012, that the Saudi-Bahraini unity means the demise of Bahrain. The statement coincided with the recall of Iran's Chargé d'Affaires to express its displeasure with a Bahraini statement accusing Tehran of intervening with the jurisdiction of the King.

The Iranian official advised the leaders of Bahrain to change their approach and not complicate the situation with similar initiatives, in reference to the Gulf Union Initiative that may start in Saudi Arabia and Bahrain.

The Bahraini Foreign Ministry summoned the Chargé d'Affaires of the Embassy of Iran to protest the statements made by the president of the Iranian Shura Council, Ali Larijani, and MP Hussein Ali Shahriari on Bahrain.

Iran supports the Bahraini-led opposition, which in turn opposes the Union's initiative with Saudi Arabia, and strongly condemned Peninsula Shield Forcesy intervention in Bahrain in March 2011 to help the PA curb the protest Movement.

The Islamic Republic of Iran claimed through an official statement to be the guarantor of the territorial integrity, and has the right to protect the integrity of the Islamic Republic of Iran. It stated a work in progress to restore the province of Bahrain back to the Islamic nation saying, The people of Bahrain consider themselves Iranian and are reported to want to return to Iran.

Bahrain announced the capture of terrorist cells confirming Iranian claims over the Island..

2013

Iranian President Mahmoud Ahmadinejad's numerous statements, including the statement made on April 14th, 2013, when he received the speaker of the Shura Council in the Sultanate of Oman when he stated his concerns about the situation in Syria and Bahrain, as if the two cases are similar.

Statements made by the secretary general of the Lebanese Hezbollah, when he pledged in a televised interview, indicated to support uprising in Bahrain.

Threats by senior commanders of the Revolutionary Guards and the Iranian armed forces to strike the military bases in Bahrain and the support of sleeper cells in the country.

A joint press announcement by various Iranian political parties condemning what the Shah agreed to letting Bahrain be independent is not binding to the Islamic Republic, hence they encourage the regime to take it back.

Official statements by the Kingdom of Bahrain condemning continues Iranian interferences in the internal affairs of the sovereign and independent state of Bahrain, which is an unusual act and a violation of the sovereignty of Bahrain. said Undersecretary for Regional Affairs and Cooperation Council Hamad al-Amer. The Ministry considered this a reflection of real intentions by Iran to intervene in the affairs of the Gulf Cooperation Council countries. Such threats of aggression constitute a threat to peace in the region under the terms of Article 29 of the Charter of the United Nations, which requires the Security Council to take the necessary measures to maintain international peace and security and instability in the region.

Bahrain Independent Commission of Inquiry (BICI)

Bahrain
Independent
Commission
of Inquiry

BICI Commission Members

Professor M. Cherif Bassiouni Commission Chair	**Dr. Mahnoush H. Arsanjani** Commissioner
Judge Philippe Kirsch Q.C. Commissioner	**Dr. Badra A. al-Awadhi** Commissioner
Professor Sir Nigel Simon Rodley Kbe Commissioner	

In the aftermath of the protests, the Government of Bahrain faced growing international pressure to address the mass alleged abuses committed during the uprising of 2011. In response, on July 29, 2011, King Hamad bin Isa al-Khalifa established the Bahrain Independent Commission of Inquiry (BICI) to investigate Government misconduct and recommend policy and legal changes to prevent a recurrence of such events. The BICI, also known as the Bassiouni Report—named after its Chairman Cherif Bassiouni—consisted of an internationally selected team of prominent jurists and legal scholars who conducted more than 9,000 interviews to investigate the events of 2011.

On November 23, 2011, BICI submitted its final 503-page report to the King of Bahrain, which reported that thirty five people, mostly civilians, had died in the unrest of February–March 2011, including five tortured to death in custody. In all, 2,929 people were arrested, and 4,539 people (3.6%) of the Bahraini workforce were fired from their jobs, 2,464 from the private sector and 2,075 from the public sector. In a televised speech in front of the King, BICI Chairman Cherif Bassiouni stated that the authorities had used excessive force and torture during their crackdown on protesters, whom, he argued, were within their rights to participate in many of the protests. He pinpointed a culture of non-accountability among the security services operating during the state of emergency and accused unnamed officials of disobeying laws designed to safeguard human rights. Overall, the report painted a detailed picture of abuses by the Bahraini security forces and elements of the Authorities, finding a systematic practice of physical and psychological mistreatment, which in many cases amounted to torture.

The BICI contains twenty six recommendations on necessary reforms to the Government of Bahrain—from the security sector to judicial and prosecutorial capacity to labor, media, and educational policy. Following the report, the political leadership of the Kingdom recognized the importance of this process as it represented a critical roadmap for resolving the country's political crisis, and the King publicly accepted the recommendations. The efforts by the Government to implement these reforms are evident when looking at the numbers:

— More than 2,100 arrestees released without charge.

— 4,600 dismissed workers reinstated to their previous employment.

— 1,500 national safety court cases dismissed or charges dropped, and a substantial number of those immediately released.

— Over 240 cases involving alleged criminal acts by police personnel transferred by the police to the Public Prosecution by independent investigations.

— Over 500 students brought back, and all scholarships reinstituted.

— Criminal prosecutors charge more than 50 security force officers and non-commissioned officers.

— Over $26 million marked for financial redress of all those adversely affected by the disorder

— Ten demolished places of Shia worship rebuilt, with construction work ongoing on another seventeen.

— Around 1,500 new policemen and policewomen recruited from all segments of society.

— Several million U.S. dollars spent on training over 5,000 police personnel and around 50% of the judiciary.

However, some activists and international organizations have argued that since the release of the report in 2011, the Authorities failed to address many of the recommendations of the commission adequately. The main areas of concern pertaining to detention and prison sentences for political expression continued. Human rights violations, which have contributed to a growing culture of impunity among security forces, as well as the remainder of protests and the persistence of reports of torture, abuse, and death in detention. Blame has been laid on the Authorities for not creating an environment conducive to national reconciliation. Opposition leaders and prominent members continue to claim to be targeted; for example, at the dialogue, opposition groups were given only thirty five out of 300 places, to which they objected. They demanded more representation, while the Government wanted to give everyone a chance to be represented. At the time the dialogue was held, it could not act as a credible forum for resolving the deep differences between the opposition and the state. In response, the Constitution was amended to enhance the powers of Parliament as follows:

● Parliament has the right to vote no confidence in the Government's four-year work-plan.

● The Speaker of the elected chamber, not the speaker of the appointed chamber, will be the speaker of both houses of the National Assembly when they conduct in joint session.

● The King should consult both Speakers before ending a National Assembly's session.

● MPs will be allowed to question Ministers before Parliament rather than before smaller parliamentary committees as before.

Following are the 26 recommendations provided by the BICI and the actions taken by the Government to implement these provisions:

1715

To establish an independent and impartial national commission consisting of personalities of high standing representing both the GoB, opposition political parties, and civil society to follow up and implement the recommendations of this Commission.

The first BICI recommendation was to swiftly establish a national commission to implement these called the National Commission on the Implementation of the Recommendations of the Bahrain Independent Commission of Inquiry (BICI), chaired by the chairman of the Shura Council and comprised of 19 members. It was convened and began to work on December 8, 2011. In parallel, the Cabinet established a group of Ministers, chaired by the deputy Prime Minister, to coordinate the governmental work and implement the BICI recommendations. It named the Minister of justice, the responsible Minister and established a BICI Follow-Up Unit with permanent staff. This unit issued three public reports, in June 2012, November 2012, and December 2013, along with numerous press statements. Meanwhile, the first deputy Prime Minister chaired a Minister-level committee to coordinate initiatives between ministries to ensure full implementation of the recommendations.

1716

To establish a national independent and impartial mechanism to determine the accountability of those in Government who have committed unlawful or negligent acts resulting in the deaths, torture, and mistreatment of civilians with a view to bringing legal and disciplinary action against such individuals, including those in the chain of command,

military and civilian, who are found to be responsible under international standards of "superior responsibility."

In 2011, all cases of alleged cruel, inhuman, or degrading treatment committed by security officials were transferred from the Ministry of Interior to the Public Prosecutor's Office (PPO). A year later, the PPO established the Special Investigative Unit (SIU) to pursue these cases. The PPO was led by Nawaf Hamza, a public prosecutor.

1717

To place the Office of the Inspector General in MoI as a separate entity independent of the Ministry's hierarchical control, whose tasks should include those of an internal "ombudsman's office," such as that which exists in many other countries. The new office should be able to receive individual or organizational complaints, protect the safety and privacy of the complainants, carry out independent investigations, and have the authority to conduct disciplinary and criminal proceedings as required by CAT, the ICCPR, and the Bahrain Criminal Code to the Prosecutor General. The office should also promulgate and enforce professional police standards and carry out legal and sensitivity training for police officers.

In 2012, King Hamad appointed by royal decree an ombudsman within the MOI to investigate complaints concerning policing and detentions. The office became operational in 2013, and from May 2014 to April 2015, the Ombudsman Office received 908 complaints and requests for assistance. As a result of investigations, 19 police officers were referred to criminal courts, and 14 to disciplinary courts. Overall, the office investigated, independently from the MIO, every case of death of a detainee or inmate and made recommendations that resulted in increased prisoner protections and better policing.

1718

To amend the decree establishing the National Security Agency (NSA) to ensure that the organization is an intelligence-gathering agency without law enforcement and arrest authorities. The NSA should also have an independent office of inspector general to carry out the same internal "ombudsman" functions mentioned above with respect to the MOI. Legislation should be adopted to provide that even during the application of a state of national safety, the arrest of persons should be in accordance with the Code of Criminal Procedure.

In 2011, King Hamad revoked the NSA's law enforcement and arrest powers by royal decree. Since 2011, there have been no verified reports of the NSA officers arresting civilians.

1719

To adopt legislative measures requiring the attorney general to investigate claims of torture and other forms of cruel, inhuman, or degrading treatment or punishment and to use independent forensic experts. Such procedures should guarantee the safety of those raising such claims. Furthermore, the legislation should provide for remedies for any person claiming retribution for having raised a claim of torture or other forms of cruel, inhuman, or degrading treatment or punishment.

In 2012, the cabinet approved legislative amendments giving jurisdiction to the attorney general to investigate claims of torture and other forms of cruel, inhumane, or degrading treatment or punishment. However, the legislation does not require the attorney general to investigate all credible claims of torture. Meanwhile, the SIU continues to investigate allegations of torture and misconduct to implement this recommendation more fully.

1720

To make subject to review in ordinary courts all convictions and sentences rendered by the National Security Courts were fundamental principles of a fair trial, including prompt and full access to legal counsel and inadmissibility of coerced testimony, were not respected be subject to full review in the ordinary courts.

In October 2011, the Government disbanded the National Security Courts (NSC) and transferred all misdemeanor cases that had not yet been completed by the NSC to civilian courts in November 2011. The Supreme Judicial Council, tasked with supervising the work of the courts and the performance of judges, court recorders, and clerks, reviewed all remaining NSC cases. Even though the Government transferred these cases, some testimonies were provided under duress, and it is unclear whether this consideration was accounted for by the civilian courts.

1722

The Commission makes the following recommendations with regard to the use of force, arrest, treatment of persons in custody, detention, and prosecution in connection with the freedom of expression, assembly, and association:

(a) To conduct effective investigations in accordance with the Principles on the Effective Prevention and Investigation of Extra-Legal, Arbitrary, and Summary Executions of all the deaths that have been attributed to the security forces. Likewise, all allegations of torture and similar treatment will be investigated by an independent and impartial body, following the Istanbul Principles. The investigation of both types of alleged violation should be capable of leading to the prosecution of the implicated individuals, both direct and at all levels of responsibility, with a view to ensuring that punishment be consistent with the gravity of the offense.

(b) To establish a standing independent body to examine all complaints of torture or ill-treatment, excessive use of force, or other abuses at the hands of the authorities. The burden of proving that treatment complies with the prohibition of torture and other ill-treatment should be on the state.

(c) To implement an extensive program of public order training for the public security forces, the NSA and the BDF, including their private security companies, in accordance with UN best practices. To ensure future compliance with the Code of Conduct for Law Enforcement Officials and the Basic Principles on the Use of Force and Firearms by Law Enforcement Officials, the security forces should be trained in the human rights dimensions of detention and interrogation, and in particular the obligation to refuse to participate in any actions involving torture and other prohibited ill-treatment.

In 2012, Bahrain amended the penal code on torture, defining and criminalizing such acts and ensuring that the stature of limitation does not apply to crimes of torture. From January to October 2015, 227 cases were referred to the SIU. In May 2015, six Ministry of Interior personnel, including high-ranking officers, received jail terms from one to five years for beating an inmate at Jaw Prison's Reform and Rehabilitation Center to death in November 2014. In January 2016, the SIU was successful in the appeal of two-year sentences for two law enforcement officers in the 2011 death-in-custody case of Isa Saqer, who was heavily tortured until he died from

his wounds. However, security officials facing serious charges of abuse are typically released and not suspended from duty during the duration of their trials.

Other changes made to adopt these recommendations were the establishment of the Prisoner and Detainee Rights Commission (PDRC) and the National Institution for Human Rights (NIHR). The NIHR receives its budget from the Government; however, it has independent administration. In its first annual report in 2014, it named ministries that failed to comply with requests for information or follow-up and recommended the Government schedule a visit by the UN special reporter on torture, among other suggestions for improving human rights conditions.

To implement recommendation 1722c, the Government passed a new police code of conduct in 2012. The MOI issued a handbook to all personnel detailing police guidelines, as well as bringing outside training from bodies such as the United Kingdom's Royal Academy of Police. Another training is done by the SIU aimed at promoting and protecting human rights, especially the rights of detainees or accused persons. The Government of Bahrain claims that over 8,000 police officers and other personnel have received public order training since 2011, and the Bahrain Defense Force and NSA have also received human rights training. Furthermore, to enhance accountability, police activity has been documented by video cameras.

(d) To avoid detention without prompt access to lawyers and without access to the outside world for more than two or three days. In any event, all detention should be subject to effective monitoring by an independent body. Moreover, every person arrested should be given a copy of the arrest warrant, and no person should be held incommunicado. Arrested persons should have access to their legal counsel, and family visits the same as any person detained under the Bahrain Code of Criminal Procedure.

Local and international human rights organizations have reported that arresting officers detain individuals without showing arrest warrants and deny those arrested access to legal counsel. Both the defendants and legal representation have reported difficulty in accessing each other in different stages of the detention and judicial process. To comply with the recommendation and improving the situation, prisoners are given instructions on how to appeal sentences, and prisoner-rights posters have been put on display throughout the prison and detention centers. CCTV cameras have also been installed in police facilities, including prison interrogation rooms and holding cells, and the ombudsman has an office at Jaw Prison to receive prisoner complaints and has complaint boxes in police stations.

(e) The Commission recommends that the GoB establish urgently, and implement vigorously, a program for the integration into the security forces of personnel from all the communities in Bahrain.

From 2012, the Government of Bahrain introduced a community policing program that would recruit 500 new police officers annually from all communities in the country, including the Shia. That year, 577 new police officers graduated from the academy and started working in the community. In October 2015, 504 community officers graduated from the same community policing program, bringing the total number of graduates from the Royal Policy Academy to 1,500. The inclusion of Shia in security forces has been a remarkable improvement.

(f) To train the judiciary and prosecutorial personnel on the need to ensure that their activities contribute to the prevention and eradication of torture and ill-treatment.

At least 2/3 of the judiciary and prosecutorial personnel received training in protecting human rights in criminal procedures according to the Government of Bahrain. Regular training programs were provided by the American Bar Association and the International Institute for Higher Studies in Criminal Studies. Bahrain's judicial system is making efforts to refrain from relying on confession-based evidence that might have been obtained by coercion or under duress, which is consistent with Article 15 of the United Nations Convention Against Torture.

(g) There should be an audiovisual recording of all official interviews with detained persons.

CCTV cameras have been placed in all police stations, interrogation rooms, temporary detention rooms, and prisons as of 2014.

(h) To review convictions and commute sentences of all persons charged with offenses involving political expression, not consisting of advocacy of violence, or, as the case may be, to drop outstanding charges against them.

According to the BICI, in 2011, 2,929 were arrested. Of these, 2,488 were released without charge. The remainder were charged with crimes not related to the exercise of the right to freedom of expression.

(i) To commute the death sentence imposed for murder arising out of the events of February/March 2011, in light of the preference of Article 6 of the ICCPR for the abolition of the death penalty and the concerns regarding the fairness of trials conducted by the National Safety Court.

Following the recommendation, the death sentences of four individuals detained for the death of police officers in the spring of 2011 were commuted.

(j) To compensate and provide remedies for the families of the deceased victims in a manner that is commensurate with the gravity of their loss. In this connection, the Commission welcomes the Royal Decree-Law N0. 30 of 2011 for the establishment of the National Fund for the Reparation of Victims on 22 September 2011.

(k) To compensate and provide remedies for all victims of torture, ill-treatment, or prolonged incommunicado detention. In this connection, the Commission welcomes the Royal Decree-Law N0. 30 of 2011 for the establishment of the National Fund for the Reparation of Victims on 22 September 2011.

These two recommendations were implemented through the establishment of a new Civil Settlement Office (CSO) that approved $26 million to be used as compensation to citizens and residents negatively affected in 2011. The CSO received 421 applications relating to 2011, and 193 were selected for settlement. Beyond these, the Government has continued to offer compensations for damages caused by the police.

1723

The Commission makes the following recommendations with regard to demolition of religious structures, termination of employees of public and private sectors, dismissal of students, and termination of their scholarships.

(a) To ensure that the remaining dismissed employees have not been dismissed because of the exercise of their right to freedom of expression, opinion, association, or assembly.

(b) To use all its powers to ensure that public corporations and other employers who dismissed employees for failure to appear for work at the time of the demonstrations treat them in a way that is at least equal to that provided by the GoB to civil servants.

Public-sector employees dismissed from their jobs in February and March 2011, a total of 4,624 workers, have been reinstated or had their cases resolved, even though some had to return in lower-level positions or posts outside their field of expertise and had to sign loyalty pledges. Only 49 of the 2,462 private-sector employees' cases remained unresolved. Which was more due to their small- or medium-sized business employer going out of business, or something similar.

(c) To reinstate all students who have not been criminally charged with an act of violence and to put in place a procedure whereby students who were expelled on legitimate grounds may apply for reinstatement after a reasonable period of time, and to adopt transparent and fair standards for disciplinary measures against students and to ensure that they are applied in a fair and impartial manner.

In compliance with this recommendation, both the University of Bahrain and Bahrain Polytechnic reinstated 419 students and re-awarded scholarship, and in return, students signed loyalty pledges. Only those who were charged with violence were not readmitted; however, procedures have been put in place to reinstate even these students.

(d) To follow up on the statement by HM King Hamad to the effect that the GoB will consider rebuilding, at its expense, some of the demolished religious structures in accordance with administrative regulations.

The Government of Bahrain pledged to rebuild all 30 Shia mosques mentioned in the BICI Report. By February 2016, 22 had been completely reconstructed, four completely restructured but not opened, and one was ongoing. The remaining mosques have not yet been reconstructed due to ongoing legal matters.

1724

The Commission makes the following recommendations with regard to media incitement issues:

(a) To consider relaxing censorship and allowing the opposition greater access to television broadcasts, radio broadcasts, and print media. The continuing failure to provide opposition groups with an adequate voice in the national media risks further polarizing the political and ethnic divide.

In terms of the media, new regulations were approved by the Cabinet in September 2015 in which all written, audio, video, and electronic news content had to respect Bahrain's sovereignty, its rulers, a form of governance, its establishments, and authorities. However, these regulations have not resulted in increased access of opposition to media outlets, and restrictions on media and speech were increased. The *al-Wasat* newspaper, for example, of the country's seven dailies, it is known to be the only opposition-sympathizing newspaper. It was first suspended and later shut down. Other examples of censorship in 2014 and 2015 include multiple individuals charged with crimes and sentenced to jail in relation to social media posts that criticized the Government. In February 2015, the new pan-Arab al-Arab TV station launched its programming, which featured an interview with an opposition leader, and the station was shut down permanently only hours later.

(b) To establish professional standards for the media and other forms of publications that contain an ethical code and an enforcement mechanism designed to uphold ethical and professional standards in order to avoid incitement to hatred, violence, and intolerance without prejudice to internationally protected rights of freedom of expression.

A Higher Commission for Media and Communication was established in 2012 to implement this recommendation. This commission contained ten members with authority to formulate a national media strategy, monitor content, and receive complaints. Another body that was established was the Ministry of State for Information Affairs to centralize media regulations further. Within this governmental body lies the Information Affairs Agency, who, alongside the Bahraini Journalists Association, introduced codes of ethics for audiovisual and print media. This code set guidelines for responsible journalism as well as the rights of journalists and press houses.

(c) To undertake appropriate measures including legislative measures to prevent incitement to violence, hatred, sectarianism, and other forms of incitement that lead to the violation of internationally protected human rights, irrespective of whether the source is public or private.

In 2012, several laws and amendments appeared to strengthen the protection of freedom of expression, for example, Penal Code Article 168, which criminalizes the act of broadcasting false news. The amendment included that "the act has to be deliberate and damaging to public order, public security or public health, and must cause actual injury." Article 169, however, was amended to stipulate that laws of freedom of expression must be "compatible with the values of a democratic society." The use of language used is broad, allowing for various interpretations, but also allows for possible infringement on freedom of expression.

Other measures taken to lessen and prevent violence related to sectarianism occurred in 2014, with the ban of Sunni cleric and Bahrain Quran Society Chairman Adel Hasan al-Hamad from delivering sermons by the Ministry of Justice and Islamic Affairs under the allegation that he incited sectarian hatred. Similarly, in 2015, the Ministry of Justice and Islamic Affairs briefly suspended Sunni cleric Jassim al-Saeedi from preaching for inciting sectarian hate, and several other opposition members, including Ali Salman and Ibrahim Sherif, were arrested and imprisoned based on speeches they delivered. Human rights organizations and international observers have voiced concerns regarding laws being applied selectively to paint political speech as sectarian or accuse opposition members of stoking sectarian tensions.

1725

The Commission makes the following recommendations with respect to better understanding and appreciation of human rights, including respect for religious and ethnic diversity:

(a) To develop educational programs at the primary, secondary, high school, and university levels to promote religious, political, and other forms of tolerance, as well as to promote human rights and the rule of law.

In-service training courses for educators were provided by the Government to raise awareness about human rights, including political and civil education, children's rights, and forms of combatting violence. It also offered teachers other school activities such as lectures on religious and ethnic tolerance. The Government reviewed school textbooks and curriculums with assistance from UNESCO's International Bureau of Education.

HumanRights

In 2001, King Hamad bin Isa al-Khalifa launched a reform project in which the promotion and protection of human rights were reaffirmed as an essential part of the Kingdom's strategy to develop state institutions and national legislation. This is exemplified in the National Action Charter and the Constitution of 2002, as well as in the subsequent constitutional amendments, which were approved by the legislature in 2012 in response to the outcomes of the National Dialogue that took place from July 2, 2011, to July 25, 2011.

The Kingdom of Bahrain signed and ratified a number of regional and international agreements and conventions, including the Arab Charter on Human Rights, the International Convention on the Elimination of all Forms of Racial Discrimination, the International Covenant on Civil and Political Rights (ICCPR), and the International Covenant on Economics, Social and Cultural Rights (ICESCR). The Kingdom also ratified the Convention on the Elimination of Discrimination Against Women (CEDAW), the Convention Against Torture (CAT), the Convention on the Rights of the Child, the Optional Protocol to the Convention on the Rights of Children with regards to child involvement in armed conflicts, the Optional Protocol to the Convention on the Rights of the Child regarding child sale, prostitution, and pornography, and the Convention on the Rights of Persons with Disabilities.

However, the Government's response to the 2011 unrest in Bahrain has put the Kingdom's human rights practices under criticism. To begin with, none of the demonstrations that occurred during the period under investigation by the BICI Commission were approved by the relevant authorities in accordance with Decree Law No.18 of 1973 on the Organization of Public Meetings, Rallies and Assemblies. During the February and March 2011 unrest, clashes between the Shia and Sunna residents of several neighborhoods occurred, and incidents of violence were also reported at the al-Sakhir Campus of the University of Bahrain. As the overall security situation in Bahrain deteriorated, the residents of many neighborhoods set up checkpoints and roadblocks to Inspect cars and individuals in those areas. Many incidents of violence occurred at these checkpoints, which was the Government's response to the unrest triggered in 2011 in Bahrain that put the Kingdom's human rights practices under criticism.

Much of this deterioration can be traced back to the unrest of 2011 and the political dissent that has persisted until today, specifically on the use and accountability of security forces, but also on related issues such as suppression of free expression and prison conditions. For example, related to the uprising, the Government, along with several of the Gulf States, has increasingly used laws allowing jail sentences for insulting the King to silence opponents. On six occasions -every month of March- since the revolt began, the UN Human Rights Council has issued statements condemning the Government's human rights abuses. This is not to say that Bahrain has not experienced any success or improvements in terms of human rights, as recent legislation has proved an equalizing victory for Bahraini women, for example. Also, the United States, Britain, and eight other EU countries have sometimes opposed these statements on the grounds that Bahrain has sought to address international concerns on this issue. These can be found in the actions taken following the recommendations put forward by the Bahrain Independent Commission of Inquiry (BICI).

Several organizations are chartered as human rights groups; however, since their political calls during the time of the uprising and their leading or supporting demonstrations, the Authorities has since characterized most of them and their leaders as advocates for members of the opposition. The most prominent are the Bahrain Human Rights Society, the Bahrain Transparency Society, and the Bahrain Center for Human Rights (BCHR) and its offshoot, the Bahrain Youth Society for Human Rights (BYSHR). The latter organization was llegally closed but informally remains active. Some of the leaders of these organizations have been repeatedly arrested by the authorities for different committed violations. Most notable was the outcry against the arrest of Nabeel Rajab, Sheikh Isa Qasim, and Sheikh Ali Salman.

In 2012, the Government of Bahrain made significant technical steps toward improving the electoral system of the country by issuing two constitutional amendments limiting the ability of the King to cease the activity of the National Assembly and allowing the elected lower house to hold a vote of no confidence in the Prime Minister. In 2013, in line with the BICI report, the King issued a decree restructuring the National Institution for Human Rights (NIHR) to investigate human rights violations. In October 2016, King Hamad issued a decree enhancing the NIHR's powers, including the ability to make announced visits to detention centers and request formal responses by the various ministries to NIHR recommendations. Other improvements and their effectiveness are explained in the BICI chapter of this report.

It was also in the year 2013 that the King decreed penalties for those involved in terrorism more stringent, along with banning demonstrations in Manama, allowing legal actions against political associations suspected of having violent or terrorist tendencies, and gave security services increased powers in the name of combating terrorism. Two vast areas that human rights activists have focused on are directly involved with the mentioned amendment. First, the acclaimed unlawful arrest of human rights activists, and second, the revocation of citizenships by the Authorities .

Many human rights organizations and activists have condemned the Bahraini Government for the arrest of members of the opposition and Bahraini activists, claiming they were unlawful arrests. However, as per the laws previously mentioned, the arrests made were, in fact, in accordance with the law. Meanwhile, the revocation occurred after the radicalization of certain opposition groups and multiple terrorists' attacks took place in Bahrain, for example, the July 17 vehicle bombing in the exclusive Sunni neighborhood of Riffa, which was claimed by the al-Ashtar radical opposition group, although they claimed it was staged by the Government. This followed by attacks on the police in a Shia village that left one officer dead and three others injured by another attack on the home of a member of Parliament. Furthermore, Bahraini oppositionists launched their own so-called *Tamarod*, 'rebellion,' calling for the overthrow of the al-Khalifa, in emulation of the Tamarod campaign that opposed the military in Egypt, on August 14, 2011. In response, the Government moved forward with new restrictions. The result was a decree in late July 2013, which was issued with the strong support of Parliament imposing new penalties for terror instigators, including the revocation of citizenship, which was an augmentation of the 2006 Law of Protecting Society from Terrorist Acts. It has been claimed that because the 2006 anti-terror law contains a broad and ambiguous definition of terrorist acts and incitements to such acts that includes freedom of expression, assembly, and association, Bahraini officials have utilized their increased authority to deprive the nationality of political and human rights activists alongside alleged violent extremists. In February 2015, the Government released a list of the names of seventy two persons whose citizenship were revoked by the Ministry of Interior; as many as fifty of these individuals were human rights defenders, political activists, journalists, academics, or religious scholars, while twenty were linked to extremist groups like al-Qaeda and ISIL. According to www.anabahraini.org, since 2012, there have been a total of 985 citizenship revocations in the Kingdom of Bahrain.

However, the tightening of security measures, as well as the decision to make these amendments, stems from the significant increase in terrorist acts in the years following the unrest in Bahrain, an aspect that media outlets have neglected. Many of those arrested were considered to have been involved in the matter or have radicalized demonstrators and supporters, urging them to take harsher actions.

Accountability Measures

It is important to note that the Kingdom of Bahrain signed and ratified numerous regional and international agreements concerning human rights, including the Arab Charter on Human Rights, the International Covenant on Civil and Political Rights, the International Convention on the Elimination of all Forms of Racial Discrimination, and the International Covenant on Economic, Social and Cultural Rights. Bahrain has also ratified other treaties, namely the Convention on the Elimination of all Forms of Discrimination Against Women, the Convention on the Rights of the Child and the Optional Protocol to the Convention on the Rights of the Child, the Convention against Torture, and the Convention on the Rights of Persons with Disabilities. While, on paper, the Kingdom's commitment to human rights appears robust, the reality is different. The numerous accountability measures implemented by the Government— from the Office of the Ombudsman to the Independent Commission of Inquiry—reaffirm the Kingdom's goal of transparency; however, more effective actions toward transparency must be taken. For example, Bahrain's National Institution for Human Rights received a "B" rating from the International Coordinating Committee of National Institutions based on its decision-making board that includes members of the Government. Many ambitious initiatives have been taken by the Government, but the accountability mechanisms that allow these to function as independent and impartial bodies still need some further improvement.

It has been claimed that the office of the Ombudsman is not sufficiently independent from the Government and, as such, fails to challenge the norms of impunity among Bahrain's security forces. The ombudsman is a public advocate, an official who is charged with representing the interests of the public by investigating and addressing complaints of maladministration or a violation of rights. The ombudsman is usually appointed by the Government or by Parliament but has a significant degree of independence. While the Office of the Ombudsman has a hotline through which citizens can report police abuse, citizens hesitate to call in fear of retaliation. The Special Investigations Unit, which is charged with investigating torture allegations, is also not independent enough from the attorney general and Public Prosecution Office, and thus the Government. While these mechanisms are extraordinary initiatives, in their present form, they are insufficient and will have to be restructured to function independently. To achieve long-term and sustainable improvement in the human rights situation in Bahrain, the Government will have to improve upon these existing agencies.

Detainment, Torture, and Censorship

Since the initial protests of 2011, the Kingdom of Bahrain has experienced persistent political unrest. This dissent was met initially with a heavy-handed response from the Government and the Peninsula Shield forces, and there were numerous allegations from domestic and international human rights organizations of torture and other cruel, inhuman treatment. The Constitution prohibits the harming of an accused person either physically or mentally; however, detainees in recent years were exposed to a variety of torture, degrading and inhuman treatment by security officials. The Commission on Prisoner and Detainee Rights has confirmed allegations of physical assault of detainees by prison officials. There are a few instances of detainee deaths in the past years; however, these are officially attributed to a physical struggle during arrest. Activists claim that prison conditions are harsh and sometimes life-threatening due to overcrowding, lack of sanitation or medical care, and physical abuse. The spike in arrests since 2011 has led to a rapid increase of prisoners and detainees, whereas facilities and numbers of prison officials have virtually remained the same. Overcrowding is a serious issue and only further complicates sanitation, that has been later addressed.

The Government only provided prison access to the semi-Governmental National Institution for Human Rights (NIHR) and the Commission on Prisoner and Detainee Rights, along with the Office of the Ombudsman. It operates within a general framework that includes respect for human rights and the consolidation of justice, the rule of law, and the public confidence, in line with Recommendation 1717 and Recommendation 1722 Paragraph (d) in the report by the Bahrain Independent Commission of Inquiry (BICI) and Special Investigative Unit.

This initiative sparked an outcry from local and international human rights groups that were skeptical of the objectivity of these domestic mechanisms. These groups, though, have made significant strides for prisoner rights. The National Institution for Human Rights, for example, conducted unannounced visits at prisons or detention facilities in 2014 and posted reports about these surprise visits on its website.

Arbitrary arrest and detention are both prohibited in the Constitution, but various human rights organizations reported detainments of individuals without notifying them of the legal authority of the arresting officer, the reasons for the arrest, or the charges. The Government disputes such claims, including those that the Ministry of the Interior often conducted arrests at private houses without a proper arrest warrant.

The Government has officially acknowledged detaining some high-profile, politically engaged, and anti-Government individuals on a legal basis. The Bahraini Constitution protects freedom of speech and press, with a few reservations pertaining to Islam, national unity, and inciting sectarianism. The Government, however, limited freedom of speech and press through the prosecution of individuals for libel or slander, and that includes journalists. The law forbids any speech that upsets public order or morals, which implies any repercussions for voicing criticism of domestic political or social issues in public. This explains the detention of activists and opposition members, such as Nabeel Rajab, Abdulahi al-Khawaja, and Sheikh Ali Salman. Besides arresting individuals who overtly oppose Government policy, the Bahraini Government also restricts media outlets from employing journalists who have insulted Bahrain or other Gulf or Arab states. Freedom of the press is an issue that still needs to be better addressed by the Government.

Overall, there is a legal system in place to protect against infringement of personal freedoms and the presence of torture, abuse, or unlawful detainment, and the Government respects these laws. That is why the BICI condemnation of the instances where this was not the case has been addressed and new regulations implemented.

Prisons in Bahrain	
Ministry responsible	Ministry of Interior
Prison administration	General Directorate of Reformation and Rehabilitation
Head of prison administration (and title)	(Brigadier) Abdulsalam Yousif al-Oraifi
Director General	
Prison population total (including pre-trial detainees / remand prisoners)	3 485 2017 (via U.S. State Department human rights report)
Prison population rate (per 100,000 of national population)	234 based on an estimated national population of 1.49 million at 2017 (United Nations figures)
Pre-trial detainees / remand prisoners (percentage of prison population)	25.7% (2017)
Female prisoners (percentage of prison population)	c. 4.7% (2015)
Juveniles / minors / young prisoners incl. definition (percentage of prison population)	c. 3.4% (2015 - under 18)
Foreign prisoners (percentage of prison population)	c. 23.7% (2015)
Number of establishments / institutions	4 (2015 - Dry Dock detention centre, Jau prison, women's detention centre, reform and rehabilitation centre for women.)
Official capacity of prison system	c. 3 455 (2015)
Occupancy level (based on official capacity)	c. 110.2% (2015)

Prison Population Trend		
Year	Prison population total	Prison population rate (per 100,000 of national population)
1993	305	56
1995	439	77
1997	911	150

Female Prison Population			
Year	Number of female prisoners	Percentage of total prison population	Female prison population rate (per 100,000 of national population)
2003	101	23.11%	12.7
2009	57	11.4%	4.8
2015	178	c. 4.7%	c. 13.2

General Prison Population 2003 - 2015

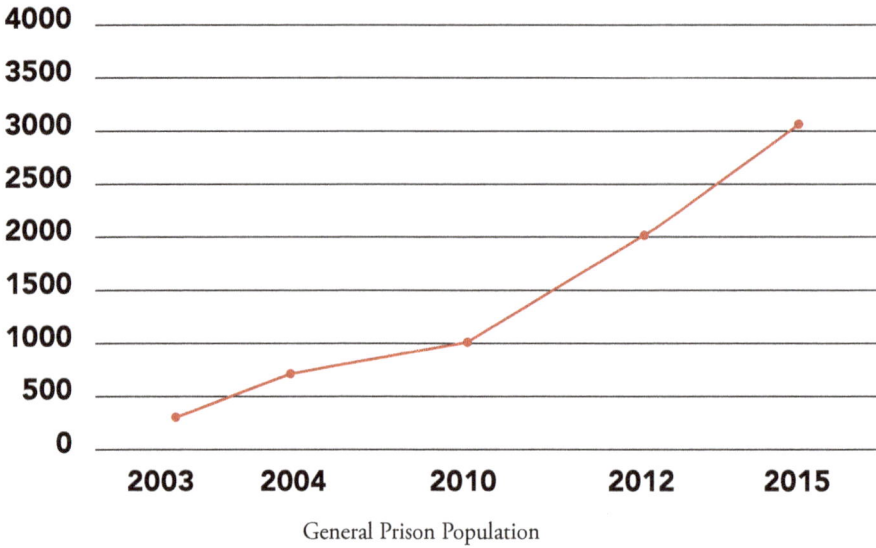

General Prison Population

Female Prison Population 2003 - 2015

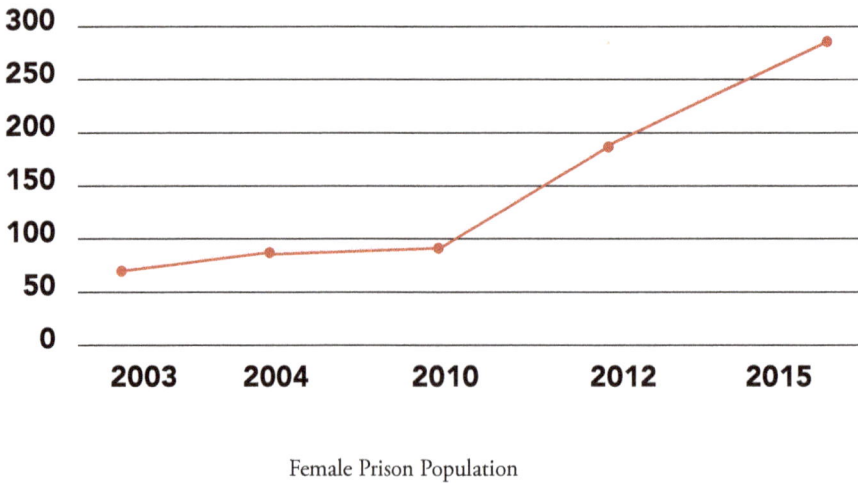

Female Prison Population

Number of Citizenship Revocations in the Kingdom of Bahrain

2012 - 2019
(a total of 434 Revocations)

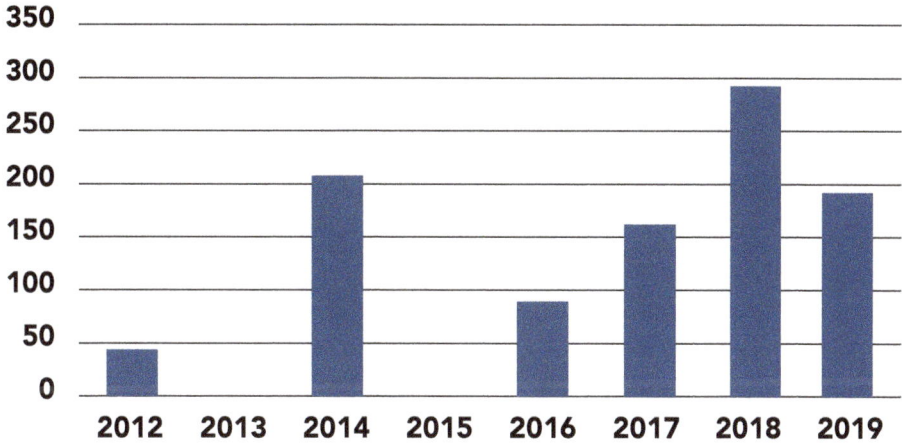

Execution Sentences

36 Execution Sentences since 2011

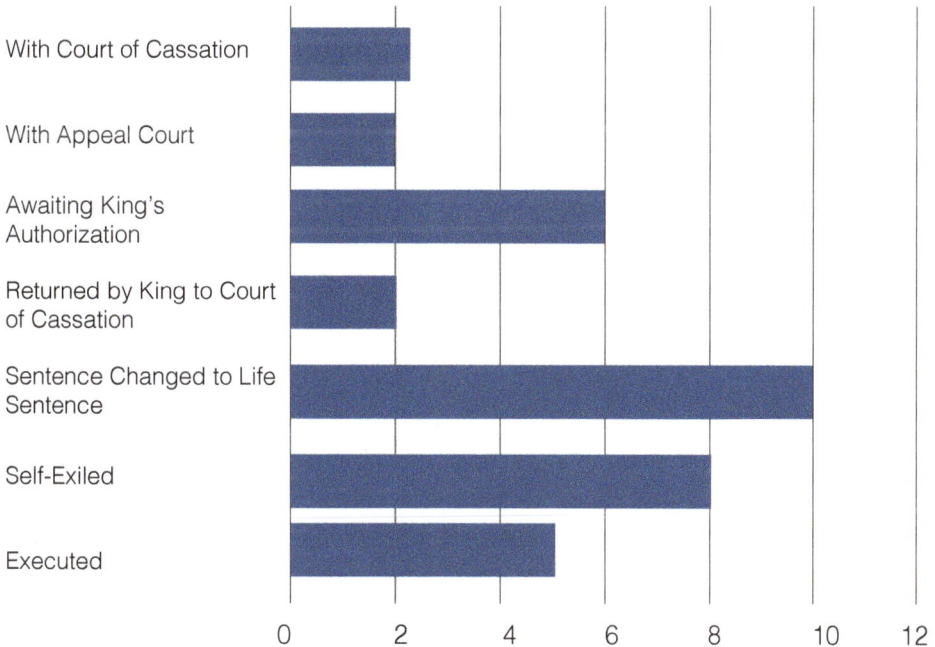

Migrant Workers

Migrant workers make up a significant portion of the Kingdom of Bahrain's population, mainly hailing from South Asian countries. Over half of the country's population are expatriates. The last census indicated that 823,610 migrant workers formed 55% of the total and that roughly half of these expatriate workers were non-Muslim. At the turn of the 20th century, Bahrain's population was diverse—ethnically, religiously, socioeconomically, and in terms of tribal affiliation—but it was distinctly Bahraini. The population of foreigners residing in Bahrain was deficient, a number that would change rapidly with the development of the oil industry and, subsequently, the growth of the Bahraini economy. Today migrant workers are the backbone of Bahrain's service driven economy.

Only private-sector workers have the right to unionize; however, this is prohibited in the public sector, military services, and domestic workers. Nonetheless, public-sector employees can join trade unions in the private sector even though these unions cannot bargain on their behalf. Forced labor is illegal, but this is difficult to enforce. The labor law covers foreign workers, with the exception of domestic workers. Thus, instances of debt bondage are common. A 2012 amendment to the labor law stipulated that domestic workers have the right to see the terms of their employment, and the Labor Market Regulatory Authority (LMRA) has taken steps to reduce the vulnerability of migrant workers. Migrant workers are now permitted to change the employer associated with their visa without employer permission or in the presence of their passport to aid workers in situations of debt bondage. Additionally, the LMRA has threatened employers who withheld passports with both administrative and criminal violations and has prohibited accused employers from hiring new workers.

In complement to the official and social attempts to properly regulate and sustain the existence of migrant workers, several establishments took further steps to improve these efforts:

— Migrant Workers Protection Society (MWPS) was established in 2005 as a registered non-governmental organization in Bahrain that works exclusively to support expatriate workers of all nationalities.

— Labour Market Regulatory Authority (LMRA) Expat Protection Center.

— National Institute for Human Rights (NIHR).

Religious Freedom

As a predominantly Muslim country where the ruling family belongs to the Sunnite sect of Islam, the Sunna-Shia schism appears on a localized level. Sectarian differences are a primary source of tension but are not new to the island Kingdom and have long been a fundamental aspect of the diverse Bahraini identity. However, in relation to other countries in the region, Bahrain is one of the most tolerant toward non-Muslim religious minorities. The Shura Council has Christians and Jews as appointed members. Until May 2021, the head of the National Institute for Human Rights (NIHR) was Maria Khoury, who represented the Christian minority in the country.

The Constitution does not explicitly protect freedom of religion but provides freedom of worship, and the Government generally respects the right of citizens and foreign residents to practice their religion. Members of non-Muslim religious groups that practice their faith privately do so without Government interference and are permitted to maintain places of worship and display symbols of their religion.

The Constitution provides for freedom of conscience, the inviolability of places of worship, and the freedom to perform religious rites and hold religious parades and meetings in accordance with the customs observed in the country, and it states that Islam is the official religion and *Sharia* 'islamic law' is a principal source for legislation.

No restrictions are imposed on non-Muslims' right to choose, change, or practice their religion of choice, including the study, discussion, and promulgation of those beliefs. Instead, in declaring Islam as the state religion and Islamic law as a source of legislation, the Constitution implies that Muslims are forbidden from changing their religion. Although no laws are criminalizing the conversion of a Muslim to another religion, such a restriction is imposed by the family and society in general. A religiously mixed marriage will not be allowed by the Sunnite and Shiite religious bodies that register marriages in the case of a Muslim woman wanting to marry a man from another faith.

The law imposes no restriction on the right to choose, change, or practice one's religion, though it prohibits discrimination on the basis of religion or creed, including by private actors, and it does not specifically target blasphemy, apostasy, or proselytizing. The law does not prohibit, restrict, or punish the importation, possession, or distribution of religious literature, clothing, or symbols, and no imposition on religious dress code exists. However, the construction of places of worship requires approval from several national and municipal entities.

Bahrain is home to nineteen officially registered Churches, with half of them located in the Capital area. In 1906, the National Evangelical Church became the first church to offer services in the country officially.

Although the number of Jews is as little as thirty seven, a synagogue and a cemetery have long existed. Their very small number is attributed to the 1984 hostility wave against them caused by of the Palestinian-Israeli conflict. Many of the families fled to London and New York to escape the hostility that was directed at them. Their shops in the Manama *Souq* 'market,' were looted, and their houses were attacked. The King met with the leaders of these families in New York and London in August of 2008, gave them their citizenships back, and offered them a safe return, as well as granting them the houses, shops, and lands they had left behind.

Women's Rights

The question of women's rights is one that remains relevant to the world over but has specific resonance in the Arabian Gulf. As over half the population of the island is not, in fact, Bahraini, there is no single culture or religion that guides the women's rights climate. Thus, women's rights are best understood through a localized perspective that considers each socio-religious or ethnic group individually.

Women have the right to initiate a divorce, but this request can be refused by both Shia and Sunna religious courts. In early August 2017, the Unified Family Law was unanimously passed by the Shura Council and was subsequently ratified by the King. This law is a remarkable victory for Bahraini women as it prevents the prior disparities between the Shia and Sunna courts that often made divorce proceedings difficult and dangerous for women. Sharia is the basis for family law in both the Sunna and Shia courts, and before this monumental piece of legislation, only Sunnite family law was codified. It as well rectifies the previous issue of which court has jurisdiction in divorce proceedings for Sunna-Shia marriages. Meanwhile, civil society is leading a campaign to increase the minimum age of marriage for females, even though the Sharia is clear that a female can marry once she enters puberty.

Women can own, inherit property and represent themselves in all legal matters. As per Sharia law, proportions of inheritance are dependent on whether the woman is Shia or Sunna and whether or not there is a direct male heir. The particulars of inheritance laws can often be circumvented by more aware families through wills and other legal tools. In terms of reproductive rights, family planning is encouraged in Bahrain, and information on this is freely available. However, women are required by health centers to obtain spousal consent prior to undergoing sterilization. It is the only family planning service that requires any consent. The minimum age for marriage is fifteen years old for girls and eighteen years old for boys; however, Sharia courts can permit marriages at even younger ages. Despite legal leeway, the Government has made efforts to decry child marriage and raise awareness regarding the dangers of early marriage.

Furthermore, women are legally protected against discrimination in the workplace, and wage discrimination is also forbidden. In the political domain, since the beginning of the 2002 election preparations, a Political Empowerment Program was established with a series of tours and field visits by Shaikha Sabeeka bint Ibrahim al-Khalifa, Chairwoman of the Supreme Council for Women. In October 2002 to mosques and shrines in the five governorates, which resulted in an increase in women's participation rate in the elections. Later, during the 2006 preparations for legislative elections, the Council's General Secretariat created a comprehensive program for women's political empowerment under the slogan *Together we build the country*. The program was implemented in cooperation with the United Nations Development Program. It focused on providing all information needed regarding technical support and intensified practical training for every woman who expressed an interest in being part of the political sphere.

After these two experiences, the Political Empowerment Program was established to support women's participation in the 2010 elections and was based on the following three main aspects: partnership, awareness, and quality training. The program was a success, and it was seen in the elections' runoffs in 2011, with four women being elected to the chamber of the National Assembly.

The Supreme Council for Women continued to implement its Political Empowerment Program for Bahraini women in the 2014 and 2018 elections. It is one of the continuous programs in its work plan with national expertise. It succeeded in achieving notable results, with three women being elected to the Council of Representatives, and six others in 2018. In addition to the intense competition of women in all their constituencies and making it to the runoffs.

Summary of Accomplishments by Bahraini Women in Politics

Shura Council, Women Representation 2018

Female members at the Shura Council in 2018 reached nine, with 22.5% of representation of the total members.

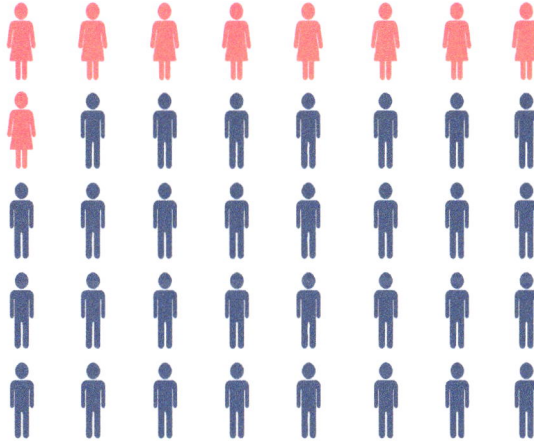

Council of Representatives, Women Representation 2018

Female members at the Council of Representatives increased from one to six from 2006 - 2018, with 15% representation of the total members.

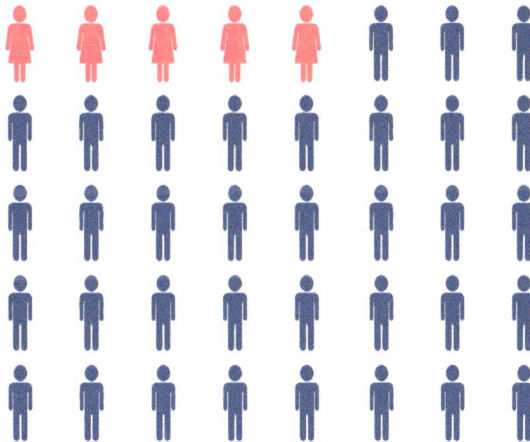

Summary of Accomplishments by Bahraini Women in Politics

2004

The issuance of Law No. (11) for the year 2004 for mandatory pre-marital health checks, which led to the reduction of hereditary blood diseases.

2005

The amendment of the Passport Law: the deletion of the article that required the approval of the husband for the wife to apply for a passport. Married women can apply for passports without their husbands' permission.

The amendment of Law No. (13) for the year 2005 to alter several civil and commercial articles of the Evidence Law promulgated by Decree-Law No. (14) for the year 1996 to make the process of proving a women's financial contribution towards the family during marriage easier and more efficient.

Amend the law of Sharia court procedures so that Sharia cases are given "urgent" status to ensure cases are fast-tracked.

The issuance of Law No. (34) for the year 2005 to establish the Alimony Fund and the amendment of this law by Law No. (33) for the year 2009 to allow the children of Bahraini women who are married to non-Bahrainis to benefit from this fund, provided that the woman and her children reside in Bahrain.

2006

The amendment of Law No. (18) for the year 2006 that governs social security to ensure that children of Bahraini women who are married to non-Bahrainis are treated like their Bahraini counterparts concerning welfare services.

2009

The issuance of Law No. (19) for the year 2009 that issued the Family Law (Part 1) that governs family relations, marriage, divorce, and child custody.

The issuance of Law No. (35) for the year 2009 to treat the non-Bahraini wife of a Bahraini and the children of Bahraini women who are married to a non-Bahraini like a Bahraini citizen concerning fees for Government-provided health and education services and residency.

2010

The issuance of Law No. (19) to amend Article No. (80) of the Social Security Law promulgated by Legislative Decree No. (24) for the year 1976 to state that grandchildren of a deceased grandparent from either parent have the right to their grandparents' previously entitled pension as it would have been given to their parent.

2012

The issuance of Law no. (36) for 2012 on the promulgation of the Labor Law in the Private Sector, regarding the implementation of the law provisions on working men and women in an equal manner without discrimination as per their job positions.

2014

Approval of His Majesty the King of Law No. (47) for the year 2014 to amend some rules of the Cassation Court law issued by Law Decree No. (8) for the year 1989 to allow cassation with regards to the final sentences of the Sharia courts, equal to sentences of civil court, with the exception of divorce cases.

Issuance of Royal Decree No. (59) for the year 2014 regarding the conditions of the

Women in Government (2010-2015)						
Position	2010	2011	2012	2013	2014	2015
Minister	4	4	4	4	5	3
Undersecretary	2	4	4	5	5	7
Members of CoR	1	4	4	4	3	3
Members of Shura	11	11	11	11	9	9
Members of Municipal Councils	1	1	1	1	9	9
Judges	20	17	23	21	23	21

appointment of Shura Council members, including text on the adequate representation of women.

Issuance of Decree-Law No. (70) for the year 2014 to amend some of the rulings of the Decree-Law No. (5) for the year 2002 regarding the ratification of CEDAW, including the reformulation of some of the reservations of the Kingdom of Bahrain, stating that the Kingdom is committed to implementing Articles 2 and 15, Paragraphs 4 and 16 without prejudice to Islamic Sharia Law.

2015
Issuance of Decree-Law No. (22) for the year 2015 amending the provisions of the proceedings law before the Sharia courts issued, ensuring the mandatory referral of the domestic disputes to the Family Reconciliation Office before being presented to Sharia Courts.

Issuance of Decree No. (23) for the year 2015 amending the provisions of the Court of Cassation law issued, which accepts the appeal to the Court of Cassation with judgments issued by Sharia courts.

Issuance of Decree No. (24) for the year 2015 amending the provisions of the Judicial Authority Law issued No. (42) for the year 2002.

Issuance of Law No. (17) for the year 2015 with regards to the protection from domestic violence. In that respect, the Supreme Council for Women launched the National Strategy for the Protection of Women from Domestic Violence in November 2015.

Achievements at Ministerial Decisions and Circulars Level

2003

Offer social allowance to women employees.

2004

Decision No. (12) for the year 2004 that states the right of Bahraini women to benefit from state-provided housing services and grants divorced and widowed women the right to apply for housing services from the state.

Establish women complaints offices in each Governorate.

2005

Allocate social centers to be the location for parents to meet with their children in cases of parent separation.

2006

Decision No. (28) for the year 2006 concerning social security that added the categories of widows, divorcees, abandoned wives, and unmarried women to the beneficiary group.

Amendment of marriage contract template to grant the two parties the right to state special conditions to organize marriage rules between them, especially the conditions that women are allowed to state, such as accommodation, education, jobs, and financial contributions.

2008

Decision No. (1) for the year 2008 regarding the equal treatment of diplomatic women to their male counterparts with regard to allowances.

Decision No. (56) for the year 2008 with regard to allowing the employment of two people for the employment of one Bahraini woman to encourage the employment of Bahraini women in the labor force.

2011

The issuance of a circular from the Ministry of Finance regarding appropriations, regulations, and instructions for the implementation of the state budget for fiscal years 2011–2012, which included a special provision regarding the application of the principle of equal opportunities and gender-sensitive budgeting.

2013

Cabinet's order No. (77) for the year 2013 regarding the approval of the regulations on the salaries and allowances for the employees of the Civil Service Bureau, granting married female employees the right to receive the same allowance as married male employees, which guarantees equality between men and women in terms of social allowance.

Decision No. (16) for the year 2013 regarding specifying the duties, occasions, and jobs that women are not permitted to work in during the night.

2014

Cabinet's decision on January 11, 2014, on the approval of draft law to amend some of the provisions of the nationality law of 1963, to allow the children of Bahraini women married to non-Bahraini men to obtain the Bahraini nationality according to certain conditions, and to transfer it to the legislative authority according to constitutional procedures.

Cabinet's decision on January 19, 2014, on the approval of the representatives' proposal to establish a sports center for women.

Decision of Civil Service Bureau No. (4) for the year 2014 to establish permanent equal opportunity committees at all ministries and governmental entities.

Issuance of a circular by the governor of the Central Bank of Bahrain to ensure the approval of the requests of women in all financial institutions to open accounts for their children, in light of numerous irregularities observed by the Central Bank. This was stated as a condition for the continuation of the license and the adoption of the Central Bank of the financial institutions operating in Bahrain.

2015

The issuance of the Decision No. (84) for the year 2015 by the Ministry of Justice, Islamic Affairs regarding the establishment of the Family Reconciliation Office, which defined the rules and procedures necessary to carry out the functions of the office, ensuring the mandatory referral of family disputes to the office before being presented to Sharia courts.

The issuance of Decision No. (909) for the year 2015, dated October 1, by the Ministry of Housing, which stated in Article (3) that divorced, abandoned, widowed women without children or unmarried orphan women can be granted temporary housing.

2011 - 2021

The National Dialogue convened on July 2 and ran until July 30, 2011. The dialogue lasted until July 25 and included members of more than 300 civil & political societies, accompanied by both houses of the National Assembly. On July 28, the King announced that the measures agreed upon in the dialogue process would be implemented. Al-Wefaq dismissed these advances and continued to call for the resignation of what they referred to as the King's Government, while Bahraini youth took to the streets in a renewed surge of anti-Government protests, resulting in small-scale but constant clashes with security forces. These protests could not be compared to the flare of violence months earlier, yet they were deadly for at least one civilian.

On September 24, 2011, legislative bi-elections were held in Bahrain to take on the 18 seats vacated in February by al-Wefaq as an act of protest against the crackdown by the Bahraini authorities in the early part of 2011. On election day, turnout was reported to be as low as 17%. It was caused by a boycott from the Shia electoral-factions, heightened security and tensions, and several arrests of people accused of attempting to disrupt the elections. The result of these elements was found in the limited number of opposition members in Parliament after these elections. However, in the second round of voting on October 1, Sawsan Taqawi, became the first woman to hold a leadership position in the House, a positive step towards reconciliation.

Bahrain Independent Commission of Inquiry (BICI) published a 513-page report on November 23, 2011 in which Chairman Cherif Bassiouni stated that the Government used excessive force and torture during its crackdown on protesters.

In a televised speech, at the presence of the King, Cherif Bassiouni pinpointed a culture of non-accountability among the security services operating under the State of Emergency and accused unnamed officials of disobeying laws designed to safeguard human rights.

Overall, the report painted a detailed picture of abuses by the Bahraini security forces and elements of the Government, finding a systematic practice of physical and psychological mistreatment, which in many cases amounted to torture.

In response to the BICI report, the King pledged to initiate reforms, and he established a National Commission to oversee their implementation. Specific reforms included the revocation of arrest powers from the national security apparatus, legislative amendments that expanded the definition of torture and lifted the time limits for the prosecution of cases, pledges to rebuild Shia houses of worship that were destroyed by the security forces during the crackdown, and the reinstatement of workers dismissed on the grounds of political expression. Despite these reforms, al-Wefaq refused to participate in the BICI initiatives, saying the commission had no real jurisdiction . Therefore, the measures that were mainly taken failed to address the roots of

Bahrain's political and economic inequalities. In addition, they took place against a backdrop of continuing clashes and daily low-level violence between protesters and security forces.

2012

Tensions in Bahrain continued to escalate in the absence of meaningful or credible dialogue initiatives, and Crown Prince Shaikh Salman, the spearhead of Bahrain's reforming elite, changed his course of action after being failed by those he stood up for—the opposition. A flight to the extremes occurred among both loyalists and opposition groups as radical elements, and advocates of violence outdid advocates for compromise and consensus over engagement.

Thus, in mid-January 2012, King Hamad bin Isa al-Khalifa announced a political reform agenda that would convey more power to the country's Council of Representatives, including the ability to approve or reject Government programs. He also revealed proposed amendments to the Bahraini Constitution, including the extra jurisdiction of the Shura Council to monitor the Government, the right of members of CoR to question cabinet Ministers, and the right to subject cabinet Ministers to votes of no confidence. These reforms were based on recommendations made at the 2011 national dialogue. There was progress made in reforming the police and judiciary, as well as in the realms of education and media. However, the political opposition continued to express skepticism that real change would be implemented in the future despite the reforms and the King's assertion that the country was ready for reform.

On February 6, a group calling itself the Patriotic Independent Gathering, led by a former health and education Minister, was launched for the promotion of reconciliation. Still, on February 13 and 14, the first anniversary of the uprising, Shia demonstrators once again violently clashed with the police; the opposition was in the front seat. This conflict continued onto March 9, 2012, when tens of thousands protested in one of the biggest anti-Government rallies since December, called for by prominent Shia cleric Sheikh Isa Qasim.

In spring 2012, ahead of the Formula One Grand Prix, clashes broke out, and various parts of the country were affected once again. Outside the capital, Manama, police fired tear gas and stun grenades at protesters in an attempt to disperse the crowds, while protesters hurled Molotov cocktails at security forces. On May 6, authorities arrested Nabeel Rajab, and detained him for twenty four days. Later, in July, he was rearrested and sentenced to two years in prison. Meanwhile, the Government braced for attempted disruptions and deployed armored vehicles to the streets of Manama to ensure secure conditions for the 2012 Grand Prix. However, daily clashes between Shiites and security forces took place, and by the end of April 2012, the death toll had risen to over fifty. On June 26, 2012, the Government announced it would compensate the families of seventeen people who had been killed in the unrest and would pay out US$2.6 million from a fund established in November 2011 under BICI's recommendation. Later, in September and October, the implementation of more reforms was announced, including toleration of dissent, a crackdown on torture, and fair trials in line with UN recommendations on human rights, and in October, the National Assembly commenced renewed dialogue with the opposition. That month, the Interior Ministry declared all rallies and gatherings unlawful as they *have been associated with violence, rioting, and attacks of public and private property.*

Across the political spectrum, radical voices were being empowered while Bahrain's political middle ground was being marginalized. Elements of the opposition were growing more violent, with an increase in arson attacks carried out by members of the 14th of February youth movement, while calls from the extreme loyalist groups to crush the opposition also intensified. The 'Bahrain Thirteen,' a group of thirteen Bahraini activists, was convicted by a military appeals court on September 28, 2012. Together, these trends were redrawing the political landscape of Bahrain by weakening the moderate wing of the Government and the opposition, whose leadership was vital in building support for political reform and reconciliation. Even though a 'Declaration of Principles of Nonviolence' was issued by six opposition political societies on November 7, it was of no value since the same societies never issued any statement condemning the increasing violence but encouraged them through other means. Rival factions and individual groups became increasingly vocal critics of Government policy and started to make political demands of their own. Vigilante groups started to form to take local law and order enforcement into their own hands, as they no longer had trust in the Government's ability to resolve the issue.

While the Government could no longer rally the Sunni street behind it, the same can be said for the predominantly Shia opposition. Al-Wefaq and the opposition political societies have been damaged by their failure to show substantive results from their decision to engage with the authorities. Their effectiveness came from the sporadic, uncoordinated, and unpredictable nature of their tactics and their ability to organize massive demonstrations at short notice. Their decentralized nature made it harder for the Government to reach out to them or to prevent individual acts of violence. This shift in Bahrain's political landscape holds great significance. The speed with which the initial demonstrations for political reform escalated into calls for a revolution among a significant portion of the demonstrators testifies to the low confidence in the Government's ability to reform itself. As a result, since 2001, the year the National Action Charter was established and reforms promised, there has been an increase in political opposition movements, a rise in political opposition societies, and, consequently, a decrease in Government support, marking the swelling discontent and distrust in the Government's implementation of reforms—an attitude that reached its peak in 2012.

The Bahrain Political Landscape 2001 - 2012

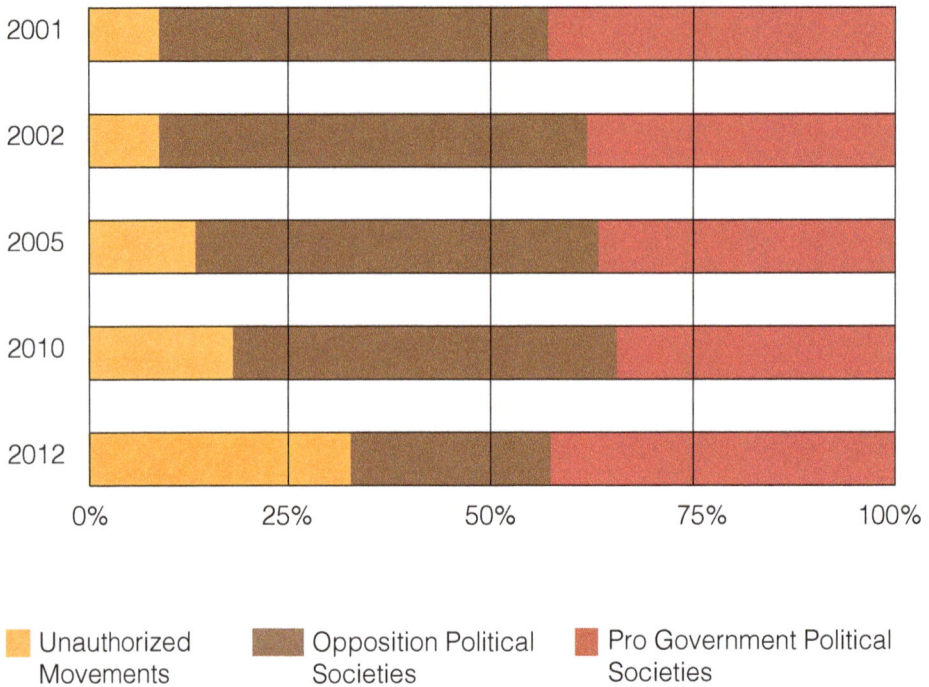

2001			
2002			
2005			
2010			
2012			

0%   25%   50%   75%   100%

- Unauthorized Movements
- Opposition Political Societies
- Pro Government Political Societies

2013

In this environment, the convening of a new National Consensus Dialogue and the naming of the Crown Prince as 'First Deputy Prime Minister' did little to raise confidence in a political breakthrough. The National Dialogue aimed at resolving roughly two years of political deadlock following the uprising. Nevertheless, encouraged by the United States and other allies, the Bahraini Government pressed for negotiations between pro and anti-Government groups. Opposition groups, chiefly al-Wefaq, were reluctant, especially as they rejected the structure of the dialogue and were wary that talks would not lead to a meaningful change. However, they caved to pressure, and by February 10, negotiations between the Government and the opposition began. They did not last long.

On February 14, 2013, violent demonstrations marked the second anniversary of the Bahraini uprising. The protests went on for several days and involved firebombs, gasoline bombs, as well as the throwing of steel rods and stones. By the third week of February 2013, Bahraini authorities announced they had uncovered an Iranian-backed terror plot targeting military and civilian installations as well as certain public figures. In response, six suspects linked with the terror cell, named *Jaysh al-Imam* 'Army of the Imam,' were arrested in Bahrain and Oman.

Reconciliation talks weakened later in the month when negotiations reached a stalemate, reportedly over the demand from opposition groups to have an official representative of the

Organized Militia parade in the village of Sanabis

King involved. In response, the King then appointed the Crown Prince, as he was seen as a reformer, as deputy Prime Minister in March 2013. Still, al-Wefaq, along with other opposition political societies leaders, announced a two-week boycott of the dialogue on May 22, 2013. The reasons for this collective action was the slow pace of the dialogue and a reported crackdown by security forces, where arrests and scores of homes were raided, including that of the prominent Shia cleric Sheikh Isa Qasim. Following the two-week boycott, Bahrain's opposition rejoined national reconciliation talks, while near-daily clashes in Shia neighborhoods between protesters who were frustrated with the slow pace of reform and security forces occurred. By June 2013, rights groups said at least eighty people had been killed in Bahrain since the unrest had begun in February 2011.

However, in September 2013, opposition groups indefinitely suspended their participation after al-Wefaq leader, Khalil al-Marzouq, was detained for thirty days on charges of inciting terrorism. On December 25, the Government attempted to resume talks despite the ongoing boycott by al-Wefaq and four other Shia groups, and on January 9, 2014, the dialogue was indefinitely suspended. Later that month, the Crown Prince held meetings with the opposition groups in a failed attempt at reconciliation, and on February 9, 2014, al-Wefaq unveiled a blueprint to start a dialogue, too, yet this was not sent to the King by the traditional means, but communicated through social media. However, only days later, the group called for demonstrations to mark the third anniversary of the uprising, which killed the initiative before it started.

2014

At the beginning of 2014, there was new hope in the Kingdom of Bahrain that a political consensus might finally be reached. The Crown Prince met directly with opposition leaders in January, but despite the hopes for the revival of national reconciliation talks, no discussions took place over the next two months, and deadly violence rose to a level not seen since the peak of the uprising. On February 15, 2014, thousands joined a demonstration, again organized by al-Wefaq, and it was claimed to be one of the biggest staged since 2011. On April 4, 2014, just two days ahead of the annual Formula One Grand Prix, protesters marched in Bahrain again, calling for democratic reforms in the Kingdom. Despite the rise in violence, Bahraini opposition said the Government must make significant changes in its domestic security policy if the National Dialogue were to succeed. They claimed that police routinely targeted innocent civilians and used tear gas in Shia neighborhoods.

In June 2014, al-Marzouq was cleared of charges of instigating violence; however, he and Sheikh Ali Salman were charged on July 11th with violating the foreign contracts law. Later that month, the Ministry of Justice moved to ban the political society, al-Wefaq.

Legislative elections were set to take place on November 22, 2014. By the time of elections, there was little progress made toward reconciliation between the Government and the opposition, demonstrations continued to take place, and prominent opposition activists, such as Ibrahim Sherif, were arrested. Most meaningfully, a significant opposition boycott took place again. It included four political societies; al-Taqadomi, Wa'ad, al-Wehdawi, and al-Wefaq. This time, the rationale of the boycott was the opposition's claim that the election would be a farce and the results would be fully controlled by the ruling authority. Bahrain opened fourty nine polling stations on the morning of November 29, 2014. All indications were that pro-Government candidates had won the most seats in Parliament. However, despite the boycott by the main opposition, as many as thirteen independent Shia candidates managed to win seats in the legislative body, and three of these thirteen candidates were women. Other winners included candidates from Sunni Islamist blocs, such as the Muslim Brotherhood's al-Menbar Islamic society. In total, only six MPs were elected, leading to second round scheduled for thirty four of the polling stations.

Meanwhile, civil unrest continued to break out in Shia villages and around the Shia mosque in Manama. A police officer was killed in an explosion in early 2014. During this month, activist Zainab al-Khawaja was sentenced to three years in prison, and Sheikh Ali Salman, the leader of the Shia opposition, was arrested while attending an anti-Government demonstration. His arrest sparked protests that lasted three months.

2015

By the 2014 elections, most Bahrainis were tired of all political societies, which seemed to prioritize ideology over common good. As a result, 90% of the Council of Representatives seats went to independent candidates. In late 2015, two liberal societies, the Justice and Development Society and the al-Watan Society, announced their closure, citing struggles to maintain consistent support.

The collapse in active left-wing support created significant tensions within these organizations between those who remained ideologically committed to boycotting and those who felt they were going in the wrong direction and desired compromise. On June 16, 2015, al-Wefaq's secretary-general, Ali Salman, was sentenced to four years imprisonment, accused of promoting disobedience and inciting hatred.

Its weekly street rallies to demonstrate relevance had been banned since Bahrain expanded its terror legislation to include a total ban on sit-ins and gatherings in Manama in 2013. Only a few days later, Nabeel Rajab was sentenced on January 20, 2015, to six months in prison for Online comments made in 2014, and activist and former leader of the National Democratic Action Society (Wa'ad) Ibrahim Sharif was released after four years in prison. However, on July 12, 2015, only three weeks after his release, he was rearrested again for other cases within the same scope.

At this time, the religious opposition society al-Wefaq was also in turmoil. It had emerged in a time of political reform; however, with the standstill in the process of negotiations and little Government engagement, no compromise was sufficient to bring it back to the political negotiation table. The power hog of al-Wefaq weakened the opposition coalition. Under the pressure of increasing sectarianism, the smaller leftist political societies participating in the seven-party opposition coalition—Wa'ad, al-Minbar al-Taqadumi, and al-Tajamu al-Qaumi— suffered defections, especially of Sunnis. They distanced themselves from al-Wefaq and moved toward the creation of a new democratic alliance. However, due to deprivation of leadership due to arrests, the opposition coalition was struggling to have an impact on the field, politically.

Similarly, Sunni Islamist societies seemed affected by the political turbulence. The leadership of Bahrain's Muslim Brotherhood and Salafi political societies were challenged by a new, predominantly Sunni mobilization —National Unity Assembly—that emerged in reaction to the Shia political uprising. However, this political formation failed to constitute an institutionalized political force, and not a single member was elected in the 2014 legislative elections.

The Muslim Brotherhood saw its political space narrowed in line with the Gulf turn against the movement after 2011. Its Government Ministers were replaced, and due to the reorganization of electoral districts, their parliamentary representation was reduced to one seat in the 2014 elections. The Salafi political society did better, maintaining a Minster and a small Parliamentary coalition of two members and affiliated independents. Still, there was a general decline in Bahrain's once-influential Islamist political societies, both Shia and Sunna, with independents playing more significant roles within the Council of Representatives.

2016

This decline was further enabled by the amendment to the country's political society law banning the mixing of politics and religion. The amendment was issued by King Hamad bin Isa al-Khalifa on June 11, 2016 through a decree. According to the amendment, in an effort to remove religion from politics, members of Bahrain's political societies were no longer allowed to give religious speeches or guidance. It was a blow for opposition groups such as al-Wefaq. With judges, diplomats, and military actors already blocked from politics by the fundamental law of 2005, the amendment further shrank the pool of influential figures who could seek involvement in political societies. Religion played an essential role for al-Wefaq, with clerics such as Sheikh Ali Salman controlling rhetoric by taking a sectarian stance. One of the several crimes Sheikh Salman was accused of was inciting religious hatred. The Government also later used this law to further crackdown on the opposition.

On June 14, 2016, the al-Wefaq Islamic Society was suspended by courts orders and was accused of inciting violence and civil tensions that had a significant repercussion on the political landscape of Bahrain. On July 17, 2016, the religious Shiites' main political front in the country was shut down. International actors and human rights bodies widely condemned this suspension. For example, on July 7, 2016, the European Parliament adopted a resolution on human rights abuses by Bahraini authorities, which were already being tackled as response to the BICI recommendations, and on August 2016, a UN-appointed panel accused the authorities of carrying out a systemic campaign of harassment against the country's Shia populace.

As part of the amendment to the 2005 Political Societies Law, Bahraini authorities charged Sheikh Isa Qasim, the spiritual leader of the majority opposition, with illegal fundraising and money laundering gathered from the Shia community. The Government also revoked his citizenship on June 20, 2016, which led to mass demonstrations, reminding everyone of the unfortunate events of 2011.

On June 21, the village of Duraz -home to Sheikh Isa Qasim-, became a sieged village. At all its nine main entrances and sixteen sub-entrances, there were checkpoints, and thorough searches were conducted, and only registered residents of Duraz were allowed an entry.

2017

Clashes with the Shiite villages in Bahrain continued into 2017, and so did the clampdown on the opposition. January was marked by Bahrain's execution of three Shia prisoners convicted of killing three law enforcement officers in a bomb attack in 2014—the first execution in six years. On March 7, 2017, the Ministry of Justice announced the commencement of legal procedures for the closure of the National Democratic Action Society (Wa'ad). The supporters of this move pointed to the failure of Wa'ad Society to distance itself from those engaged in violence who were responsible for the killings of more than twenty law enforcement officers. By this action, they were in violation of Article Six of the Political Society Law that stipulates societies must protect the independence and security of the Kingdom and its national unity and reject all forms of violence. Furthermore, the political society had betrayed its secular roots by affiliating with a sectarian organization with an anti-national agenda. By expressing its solidarity with al-Wefaq, it is in breach of Clause Four, Article Seven of the Political Society Law, which bans association or cooperation with any political society that does not respect the principles and articles of the Constitution or the premises of the political command in the Kingdom.

In a solidarity statement with other societies, Wa'ad also announced that it had rejected the 2002 Constitution and considered it illegitimate, which was yet another breach of the law, specifically Article Six of the Political Society Law, which calls for compliance with the principles of the National Charter and the Constitution and respect for the rule of law.

Even before the shut down of Wa'ad, the need for a new political movement to allow any

Wall Mural of Redha al-Ghasra that instates the 'Revolution is our Choice' slogan

future success by liberal and secular elements became evident, given that the old left-wing societies had discredited themselves in the eyes of many Bahrainis. Even relatively liberal societies like the National Coalition and al-Wasat al-Islami joined the Sunni loyalist al-Fateh Coalition and, more recently, ceased to be visibly active. Thus, Bahrain seems to be in dire need of activism from the liberal center of society.

2018

On June 3, a declaration of no value was announced by al-Wefaq's secretary-general, al-Daihi, after being highly criticized for not doing anything aside from giving speeches. Bahrain's declaration came too late and had no content except for some generic political terms and their meanings. That also indicated how the scattered leaders of al-Wefaq were not in agreement on how to proceed, for this declaration was not in line with what al-Ghuraifi had been working on for the previous six months. The declaration did not acknowledge the existence of the King nor the ruling family, and on top of lacking an agreement and not having been presented to the King, it was distributed through social media only, a technique that had been used by the opposition for years. It was widely discredited, and as expected, no response was given.

Duraz Siege, which had started two years earlier, was put to an end, as Sheikh Isa Qasim was sent with members of his family to London by the King to get treatment for cancer. The legislative elections took place as planned, with a chief setback for the opposition due to being not allowed to participate nor vote. Many people felt they were not presented well in the Council of Representatives hence crossed the boycott and participated, especially the Shiites. A woman won the speaker's seat for the first time in the Middle East, along with a majority of first-timers. Political associations harvested five seats only, the lowest on record so far.

2019

The year began with everyone looking forward to the new Council of Representatives and its new set of young members. Devastation soon hit the crowds when they realized they had made a big mistake electing people with no political background.

In April, a court sentenced 138 Shiites and revoked their citizenship for plotting to form a terrorist group with links to Iran's Revolutionary Guard. They received prison terms varying from three years to life for having tried to re-build the Bahrain Hezbollah, similar to the Shiite militia active in Lebanon. Out of the 138 people, sixty nine were given life sentences for terror-related activities.

Bahrainis have reportedly lost their citizenship through court verdicts or executive orders since 2012. Most have been left effectively stateless, and some were deported. On Sunday, April 21, the King reinstated the citizenship of 551 people convicted by courts during a crackdown on dissent. A move that was welcomed by all and one that indicated the opposition had not been doing what they should have to at least assist those who stood by their cause and faced jail time, encouraging the community to overstep and communicate directly with the King and the Authorities for closure.

Three were executed in July; two young men accused of murdering a law enforcement officer, and the third accused of murdering a Mosque Imam. It was notable that opposition leaders refrained from saying anything about the execution resulting doubt about their roles and interests. Many activists started calling for a complete ban of executions in the country, but it is distinguished that some of them called for executions of the royal family prominent members in 2011 making them seem hypo-critic in their approach.

2020

The year 2020 impacted Bahrain massively, as it did the whole world. The global spread of COVID-19 and the Health, Social, Economic, and even Sovereign implications it brought with it, making it a world event like no other, impacting every country on the globe.

The first challenge the state faced was convincing its citizens to avoid visiting infected areas, which was neglected immensely by some 1200 Bahrainis who traveled to the Islamic Republic of Iran. That has created a hurdle for the authorities to fly them back from what was considered a red zone by the WHO at the time. Later in August, Muharram Processions were restricted due to the spread of the virus, which lead to massive discontent from Shia youth, who despite all the strict measures have commemorated the annual procession, claiming it is a first step by the authorities to completely ban the tradition in the future. Knowing that all

Great Britain's Prime Minister, Boris Johnson's tweet over the Bahraini Prime Minister's demise.

Shia Clerks in Iran, Iraq & even Lebanon have taken similar measures to the ones imposed by the Bahraini authorities to protect their societies.

The Government emergency measures included funding of salaries, exemptions of water & electricity bills, and delay of Bank loans made it a bit easier for the community in Bahrain.

Alternative Sentences were implemented following Law No.18/2017. Nabeel Rajab was released as part of the implementation along with 806 others.

The High Criminal Court rules against a sleeper terrorist cell of fifty one members, sentencing them between five years to life.

Prime Minister, Shaikh Khalifa bin Salman al-Khalifa died at the age of eighty four on the 11th of November. He was born on Sunday, November 24, 1935. H.R.H. Prince Khalifa bin Salman bin Hamad al-Khalifa has served as the Prime Minister of the Kingdom of Bahrain since its independence in 1971.

He was the second son of the former ruler of Bahrain, Shaikh Salman bin Hamad al-Khalifa, Ruler of Bahrain from 1942 to 1961. and the uncle of His Majesty King Hamad bin Isa bin Salman al-Khalifa.

Crown Prince, Shaikh Salman bin Hamad al-Khalifa is decreed by the King as the new Prime Minister, while serving as the Crown Prince.

Bahrain, UAE, and Israel signed a historic agreement on the 15th of September, the Abraham accords. Marking the first public normalized relations between an Arab country and the State of Israel since the Israel-Jordan Peace Treaty of 1994.

ABRAHAM ACCORDS: DECLARATION OF PEACE, COOPERATION, AND CONSTRUCTIVE DIPLOMATIC AND FRIENDLY RELATIONS
Announced by the State of Israel and the Kingdom of Bahrain on 15 September 2020

His Majesty King Hamad bin Isa bin Salman al-Khalifa and Prime Minister Benjamin Netanyahu have agreed to open an era of friendship and cooperation in pursuit of a Middle East region that is stable, secure and prosperous for the benefit of all States and peoples in the region. In this spirit Prime Minister Netanyahu of Israel and Foreign Minister Mr. Abdullatif Al Zayani met in Washington today, at the invitation of President Donald J. Trump of the United States of America, to endorse the principles of the Abraham Accords and to commence a new chapter of peace. This diplomatic breakthrough was facilitated by the Abraham Accords initiative of President Donald J. Trump. It reflects the successful perseverance of the United States' efforts to promote peace and stability in the Middle East. The Kingdom of Bahrain and the State of Israel trust that this development will help lead to a future in which all peoples and all faiths can live together in the spirit of cooperation and enjoy peace and prosperity where states focus on shared interests and building a better future.

The parties discussed their shared commitment to advancing peace and security in the Middle East stressing the importance of embracing the vision of the Abraham Accords, widening the circle of peace; recognizing each State's right to sovereignty and to live in peace and security, and continuing the efforts to achieve a just, comprehensive, and enduring resolution of the Israeli- Palestinian conflict.

In their meeting, Prime Minister Benjamin Netanyahu and Foreign Minister Abdullatif Al Zayani agreed to establish full diplomatic relations, to promote lasting security, to eschew threats and the use of force, as well as advance coexistence and a culture of peace. In this spirit, they have today approved a series of steps initiating this new chapter in their relations. The Kingdom of Bahrain and the State of Israel have agreed to seek agreements in the coming weeks regarding investment, tourism, direct flights, security, telecommunications, technology, energy, healthcare, culture, the environment, and other areas of mutual benefit, as well as reaching agreement on the reciprocal opening of embassies.

The Kingdom of Bahrain and the State of Israel view this moment as a historic opportunity and recognize their responsibility to pursue a more secure and prosperous future for generations to come in their respective countries and in the region.

The two countries jointly express their profound thanks and appreciation to President Donald J. Trump for his untiring efforts and unique and pragmatic approach to further the cause of peace, justice and prosperity for all the peoples of the region. In recognition of this appreciation, the two countries have asked President Donald J. Trump to sign this document as a witness to their shared resolve and as the host of their historic meeting.

Prime Minister Benjamin Netanyahu

Foreign Minister Abdullatif Al Zayani

Witnessed by
President Donald J. Trump

The Abraham Accords Declaration signed by US, UAE and Bahrain

2021

In January Prince Salman bin Hamad Al Khalifa Crown Prince, Deputy Supreme Commander, and Prime Minister started making changes in the Government as the new Prime Minister. It consisted of new appointments in the Labour Fund, EDB, NIHR, LMRA, and MoFA. Most are mid-management positions enabling the youth to partake in the Government.

April witnessed the comeback of demonstrations, demanding the release of prisoners due to the spread of coronavirus in jails. The demonstrations continued with concerns of transforming to violent ones. While the authorities continued to handle them calmly and did nothing more than summon some protestors asking them to sign a document confirming they won't do it again and did not use the force of any sort.

A prisoner, Abbas Malallah dies of a stroke in Jau prison, influencing more demonstrations amid the COVID-19 outbreak.

The Council of Representatives passes a law that restricts the members to no more than five minutes of discussion per member in a general discussion and forbids the Council to criticize or undermine the Government or its representatives in a public session, igniting widespread discontent.

Demonstrations were held post an official visit by the Israeli Foreign Minister Yair Lapid in September.

Conclusion

The ensuing conflict between the east, the west, and the Middle East is partly a result of the uncommon understanding of terms and what they are intended for when stating them; and on top of these terms is politics.

Politics is the sum of activities associated with the governance of a country or area. That includes the debate between parties having power. Derived from Greek's *Politikos* from *politēs* 'citizen', from *polis* 'city' which leads to the practice of public affairs; and throughout the years of ancient and modern times, the Western civilization strove to instate that understanding of the term into their daily lives.

In Arabic, where it is the official language in the Middle East, the term that is widely used in correspondence for Politics is *Seyasa*. As a language term, it is derivative from he who cares for a herd or a horse's caretaker, which gives the term a whole different purpose than the western term. It could as well mean the relationship between a ruler and his citizens, which leads to a usual conflict when each chooses to interpret the term the way it suits them -as almost everything else-.

That, by all means, caused a gap towards the outcome of politics in Bahrain. When institutional politics transformed into scattered meaningless efforts of charity and parade like marches, it all goes down to the one-man show complex that the middle east is administered with. In every Society, Community, or even an organization; there is a person who is always right and remains in his seat for life. Even though oppositions in the Middle East seek change and call for it, are committing the same mistake within their internal hierarchy systems; such people exist in every political affiliation in Bahrain. Most of them got into politics during the colonial era and kept on doing whatever it is that they did until today, which led to the exact same results.

While observing the political societies work, it became apparent why the outcome of their efforts is still minimal compared to the amount of press and media releases they produce. Their understanding of politics varies from one person to the other within the same body, their ideological intake on almost everything as well varies.

Rarely a Secretary-General is replaced while still alive or not imprisoned, and a lot of the committees within these societies are headed by a close family member to the man on top. In our observation, we found that some committee heads came to know about press releases and announcements carrying their names only after it was published by the media, sent by their immediate family member from the top management for example.

A similar yet older conflict is that relation between Islam and Politics. Theocratic enthusiasts emphasize that Politics is a significant part of Islam, while at the same time fail to demonstrate that in how they handle their political activities—beside them not being able to provide reliable religious references corresponding to the matter; giving each scholar a chance to include his own ideology into the already diversified political culture. Moreover, lacking the element of righteousness, making them no different than everyone else, and mostly -as well- the ability to transform the religious teachings into a modern manifesto that reflects their understandings.

That does not make Liberals and Leftists better than their religious rivals in both Bahrain and the Middle East, for not a single political society in the Kingdom has its written Manifesto or at least an understanding of what it is. A manifesto is a public announcement made to demonstrate the political group mindset, their intentions and how they are willing to apply all that on the ground and is used to convince and attract new members or even supporters.

The lack of such a fundamental document and the understanding that is defaulted by its existence made the political scene a responsive one. Since the societies do not have a clear vision of how they want things to be, or be done, they became a group of people complaining about the situation rather than finding solutions and push for them to happen and respond to whatever the state pushes towards them in the Council of Representatives and the Municipal Councils.

Repetitive examples were boldly demonstrated throughout the years, and since the first session of the new Council of Representatives in 2002, every society and every politician from within the Council was yet still pushing towards an increase in the public employees' remunerations. To the naked eye, that may seem like a fair demand, yet the implications are catastrophic, and they should be the ones responsible for its consequences.

When such increase takes place, without any consideration of the respective laws, immediate inflation happens by default. Such measures cannot be decided bluntly and without a thorough understanding of the situation, and the direct and indirect implications of such a decision. As a first step there should be an ensemble of laws concerning the welfare and social equality for all, irrespective of their gender, origin, and religion, then form a precise products & services prices monitoring system, minimum wages and properly structured labor unions to be enforced. Only after all that is done, they could start talking about an increase but only if imposed upon all sectors and based on productivity too. Knowing that 60% of the workforce are serving the private sector against 40% in the public sector.

That reflects the pre-existing gap between the understanding of politics, the lack of a clear Manifesto and mostly the role that's required of them to play in and out of the Council of Representatives. Instead of Investing the financial aid the Political Societies received from the state regularly -until stopped early 2018- on new legislations, research, and developing laws, or even propose solutions for the issues they always raise in front of media instead of the Council. They donated these funds to the poor, or even invested them in properties and mixed it with charity money -in the case of some Islamic societies who originally started as charitable funds prior to establishing themselves as political societies-. The Liberal parties, on the other hand, wasted their time in polishing their image in response to the hits they have been receiving since the '60s by the Islamist's and the state by conducting local and international conferences that initially were paid for by the Government they oppose!

It is as well noted that they do not reflect what they call for in reality, such as freedom of speech, limited presidency terms and demonstrating actual achievements eliminating corruption. Most of the political societies chiefs remain in their seats until death -or imprisonment in the case of opposition societies-; beside the habit of instating their immediate family members heading most committees. Women empowerment claims always hit a solid wall when put to the test; it may be accepted from the conservatives but coming from liberals makes it a bit harder to comprehend. As well, they do not tolerate any opinion that's not in line with theirs, either within the establishment or from outsiders, eliminating them politically or agitating the community against them.

It is as well reflected in the outcome of their so-called alliances. During the 2006 elections, an alliance was formed mainly between Wa'ad and al-Wefaq to recover from the boycott they undertook in 2002 that left them outside the political equation. al-Wefaq ended up hogging all the constituencies, including the ones they pledged towards yielding them to their liberal partners. One major Candidate was Ebrahim Kamaluddein, a prominent leader and one of the Godfathers of Wa'ad, with 488 votes against a last-minute candidate *Mulla* 'Religious Scholar' by al-Wefaq, with a landslide win of 2022 votes. Beside the fierce campaign, they ran against him and his family members, despite the agreement and the previous plans.

Even though every alliance between the leftists and the Islamist's collapsed immensely every single time, it is noted that the leftists keep running back to them again and again, despite the single-sided repeated attempts. It all goes down to the backgrounds of the Bahraini community and its relation to religious conservatism.

The whole issue with the scholars from both sects is that they still control the political decision on behalf of the crowds. Their followers believe they speak to them in the name of the Lord, hence can never go wrong. Their opponents from other paths of political orientations failed massively against them. Islamist's have proven to be patient, having their time slipping such teachings in their semi-daily messaging's in shrines and through Iranian based TV and Radio stations, and the state media in case of the Sunnites. Islamist's as well have taken the elite families' role; especially those known in Manama and Muharraq, who historically played a significant mediatory role in any conflict between the people and the ruling family. Their methods were -yet still- covering anything they want to convey with a hint of religion. Taking that power from the cities to the villages; broke the ties between both the crowds and the elites; resulting in total religious control over the masses.

However, that resulted in a more significant issue with leading the crowds. Since there was no agreement on who will be in charge, conflicts started to mount. It came to the surface when Sheikh Abdulamir al-Jamri was sidelined by Sheikh Isa Qasim, and then even more apparent passing it to his successor, Sayyed Abdulla al-Ghuraifi.

The past few years proved that the opposition has no proper leadership. Al-Wefaq, for example, has no clear organizational structured ladder of command; Sheikh Ali Salman was its secretary-general, and since he was imprisoned Sheikh Hussein al-Daihy replaced him, while Sheikh Isa Qasim is the man with the upper hand even though he's not a registered member, but a supreme spiritual leader. Moreover, since he left the country in 2018, one would think that Sayyed Abdulla al-Ghuraifi would be the one to take the lead, but that is not the case as well. Such complexity was demonstrated when the late Prime Minister visited al-Ghuraifi in his Majlis and Qasim issued a statement right after with conflicting directions; their supporters were literally confused, some accused al- Ghuraifi of being a traitor, and others were defending him, and the rest were waiting to cash on it.

Such incidents and many others only state boldly the resemblance they portray with that of their ideology's origins. For it is recognized that all political orientations in the Kingdom were introduced through university students or exiled activists. Hence all adapted ideologies convey nationalist or religious agendas by those who molded them, making most of them -knowingly or unknowingly- sleeper cells serving those whom they owe allegiance to.

Sunnite organized Islamic movements started in Manama in 1910 and evolved ever since varying from Brotherhood, Salafism, and even Sufism. It got to its peak when they gathered heavily to aid the Taliban in the late '70s and then the '80s in Kosovo and then some who served time in the Syrian conflict too. Participating and joining ISIL in recent years was a natural path for this segment as a retaliation for the growing presence of the Iranian influence. It is worth mentioning that the authorities always managed to contain their behavior.

The history of the Shiite Islamic Movements is closely tied to the clerical establishment in the Islamic Republic of Iran, which created a thin red line that's easily shattered; for the Iranian establishment is a political theocratic body with predefined Persian nationalist principles against Arabs, Liberals, Communists, Sunnites and Ruling families in the Gulf. Having their saying wither to participate in elections or boycott it through *Fatwa'a* 'Religious Command', wither or not to have a rally against the local Governments, or even passing a law, even though they are strictly domestic matters. Such interference from across the sea is an intrusion on a foreign state's sovereignty, especially if it comes from Iran, whose officials clearly claims Bahrain as Iran's 14th district. Besides all the claims its spokespersons made throughout the years. 'Guardianship of the Islamic Jurists' became a significant threat to Governments in the Middle East such as Yemen, Iraq, Lebanon, and Bahrain with the conflicts it brings through the Shiites putting the rule of the religious Iranian Supreme leadership above a state's leader one way or another.

Leftists, entailing Baathists, Communists, Socialists, Nationalists amongst others had their share of armed activities. Some served time in the Palestinian – Israeli armed conflicts, others in Yemen, and most joined the Omani front to overthrow the Sultans and Emirs in Oman, Bahrain and the rest of the Gulf states too. All these armed formations had support, one way or another. None of them could have existed without financial, logistics, and political support. That is where Tudeh leftists party of Iran played a major role, serving as a proxy for its Government's regional schema even before the Islamic revolution — linking the Iranian intrusion to every unrest the Gulf region underwent in the last century at least. Besides the escalation that occurred due to the core belief of the Islamic revolution's creed that states the importance of exporting the revolution.

Since a revolution is an overthrow or repudiation and the thorough replacement of an established Government or political system by the governed citizens, there is no such thing as a peaceful revolution. Revolutions are bloody and chaotic. The term became commonly used since the '90s when the local conflicts began to escalate. The protesters took emotional turns most of the times, wrecking facilities -public and private alike- and taking lives along the way. Looking back at each uprising attempt, and every detail will only lead to looking at the same results happening all over again; for the same means and rationales have been re-used every single time.

Peaceful protests became a front for all acts, though most are not exactly peaceful. When an explosion occurred in the area of Sanad in a small branch of the National Bank of Bahrain due to a planted home-made bomb in February 2013. The first response from the opposition was that they were Government agents -an accusation of such sort always surfaced whenever anything of that sort happened.- When Saraya al-Ashtar announced their responsibility, no one said a word, and when five were captured and trailed, they started calling them prisoners of war. Another example was when a group of prisoners fled Jau reform and rehabilitation center -the central prison of the Kingdom- armed men attacked the prison in the isolated southern part of Bahrain, killing one policeman and wounding another, while allowing ten inmates escape. Seven of the prisoners who escaped were serving life sentences. The security forces immediately launched a manhunt for the attackers and the escapees. As usual, the first response from the opposition was that it is a lie and that no one possesses arms in Bahrain, until hours later when Redha al-Ghasra was seen in photos and videos taken of him prior to his escape, holding a rifle while in prison, with a message to the authorities. Until a couple of weeks later where he and his fellow escapees were killed in armed conflict while fleeing to Iran using a boat. Even then, the opposition leaders did not denounce the behavior, nor condemned it; on the contrary, they participated heavily in the burial ceremonies of whom they referred to as martyrs and referring to al-Ghasra as a battlefield leader.

The same conflicting messages were noticed when Wa'ad opposed publicly the 'Separation of Church and State bill' passed by the Parliament. In a clear conflict with what they called for in their public speeches and the 'Civil State Charter' they solely launched. Why would they stand against their beliefs in plain sight?

The same happened when the opposition societies launched a 'Non-Violence Charter' or the 'Manama Charter.' They launch them without abiding by what they declare, nor use it as a ground to move forward.

We cannot neglect the role of media when mentioning the Arab Spring and all it caused mainly by social media and international media alike; it played a key role in agitating the masses in Bahrain during the 2011 unrest creating a new segment of self-proclaimed activists and politicians.

The mind control was evident when the Shiites themselves started repeating after the Iranian media outlets; changing even the way they call areas and refer to streets and empty lots. What used to be known as *Baraha'a* 'open area' or *Dafna'a* 'reclaimed land' became known as *Saha'a* 'Town Square' after the common Lebanese term for a town's square. Which is irrelevant for there are now town squares in all of the Arab Gulf states considering the Bedouin and humbler backgrounds. The same was noticed with the *Qura'a* 'villages', that they started calling *Balda'at* 'Township,' which is a term known for the same used widely in the Levant countries. That was a clear sign of the influence and interference.

One of the highly debatable examples is how the previously mentioned media outlets called the uprising peaceful while at the same time many were dying, the streets where always on fire, and armed attacks were conducted on the police, civilians, houses, and cars. Militias were being formed and freely parading the villages with increasing numbers of young adults who were recruited openly, and not a single opposition society condemned these acts.

The misuse of media led the opposition to lose some credibility internationally as well as locally when spreading untrue rumors and call them news. When the GCC Roundabout was demolished, the leaders of the opposition started telling the international media about white trucks that bagged hundreds of murdered citizens and shipped them away to an unknown location. Two days later, when many started asking who these citizens were, and why their families did not announce their identities, they just kept quiet about it and did not even denounce their statements. Amongst many other examples, Sheikh Isa Qasim got sick, they claimed that he was denied health care and hospital admittance. Hours later he was taken to town's most expensive hospital. The same people who spread the rumors kept quiet and started questioning why that hospital and not another, even though it has been his preferred destination for years. He was sent to be treated in London later with all expenses paid for him and his companions by the King; a gesture that was not utilized wisely by the opposition.

Another example, in April of 2019, the King decreed 551 riot-related prisoners their citizenship's back; instead of a praise, it was received skeptically by the opposition. Rather than capitalizing on it, they raised the issue of Saudi Arabia executing thirty seven terrorist accused prisoners two days later and linked it to dead-end route Shiites are being pushed to.

It is widely notable as well that the civil society started depending on social media as a primary source of information, as a result of the gap between the state official media outlets from one side and the private conventional outlets on the other side. Apps like Whatsapp, Twitter & Instagram became more credible to the audience than the conventional means, while very few still consider newspapers a credible source of information. 2018 CoR members took that to their benefit and focused on these outlets to reach out, but that did not cover up for the mess they created on the floor of the Council. They neglected legislation and focused on their social media press releases thinking it will be in their favor to get reelected or even get appointed to the Shura Council, thinking it is the natural order. Some even released more than five press releases a day via Instagram. Days later the masses figured what it was and started attacking them on the same outlets.

Both the community and the Political bodies should understand that all the changes they want to see will only be done through the legislative bodies and not outside it. In order for them to take advantage of it, is for them to understand how they function and adapt proper manifestos to get the best results; along with assigning deadlines to their goals that match the available resources, and most of all be transparent with the masses. The community, like any other community around the world, wants to be in the know.

On another note, they must focus on the local scene for a solution. It is boldly notable that the opposition in Bahrain depends mainly on weak readings of the regional power equations and count on them to plan their moves. For instance, when Secretary of State John Kerry visited Manama for one last attempt encouraging reconciliation, the response came from al-Wefaq's Khalil al-Marzouq as a shock. Repeating the 1973 National Assembly demands he told Kerry, *We think it is about time the American Naval Base moves out of Bahrain.* Which outlines a significant issue, that is the lack of a clear vision on what the opposition is trying to achieve.

Instead, the existing members and the political associations should carefully re-prioritize and consult with the political elites and the Government alike; they should hire external experts, each in their field. Just so that they do not repeat the mistakes, they did in the past.

What is required of them is to have a proper understanding of their role as members of a legislative body and how to communicate with their constituents.

An end for blaming the Government on every issue must be bluntly established. The main goal for the Council now is to lead the community, for its members to regain the trust of the people in the institution they represent and mainly in their own-selves as individuals and establishments. Only with that, a real reconciliation could take place for the island to recover from a long history of unrest that left its people weary and in an almost irrecoverable shape.

That proves immensely that the Opposition is leaderless, specifically when they announced during the 2011 rallies that the crowds are the leaders. Even though it was a stunt that got everyone around them, it was believed by many. Each believes their idol is the one leader. Which makes sense in a way for the situation as it is today.

One way to move forward was for independents who only represented themselves to try and find ways to reconcile, but all efforts went downhill as they were demonized by the masses and the opposition alike — making it clear that nothing could ever be achieved by one group sidelining others.

The only way out now is by adopting a proper understanding of what is offered on the table, with a clear, unified vision. As well a constant communication must be established between the concerned parties, clear messages should be put forward that the only allegiance is that attributed to the state, and the King just as per the agreed upon national charter. Such misunderstandings created massive allegations locally and regionally and must be put off. Violence must be denounced and desperate measures to match it socially. All that must be led by known citizens chosen as representatives of all groups - even the non-politically affiliated- by the people who could present legitimate precise demands and can put an offer on the table, because no one attends a table without offering something in return.

Bibliography

Timeline

1. Bahrain profile – Timeline. BBC. Web. Accessed 20 December 2018. https://www.bbc.com/news/world-middle-east-14541322

2. Rabea'a, Ali, 2010. Gutted Experiment, Democratic Life in Bahrain, p. 10-151

3. Black boxes found after 143 die in gulf crash. The Telegraph. Web. Accessed 24th February 2018. https://www.telegraph.co.uk/news/worldnews/middleeast/bahrain/1367597/Black-boxes-found-after-143-die-in-Gulf-crash.html

4. Highlights of Bahrain-US FTA. Customs Affairs. Web. Accessed 13th January 2018. http://www.customs.gov.bh/fta.php

5. State Department, Country Report. Bahrain. Web. Accessed 1st May 2019. https://2009-2017.state.gov/j/drl/rls/hrrpt/2001/nea/8246.htm

6. Shura Council Vision. (2019, June 4). Retrieved from Shura Council: http://www.shura.bh/en/Council/Pages/ShuraVision.aspx

Kingdom Of Bahrain

1. Kingdom of Bahrain, 2019. E-Government Portal. Web. Accessed 28 January 2018. https://www.bahrain.bh/wps/portal

2. United States, 2011. CIA World Factbook: Bahrain. The World Factbook. Central Intelligence Agency Web. Accessed 20 January, 2018 https://www.cia.gov/library/publications/the-world-factbook/geos/ba.html

3. Gulf Labour Markets and Migration, 2014. Bahrain: Foreign Population by Country of citizenship, sex, and migration status (worker/family dependent). Gulf Research Center. Web. Accessed 10 July 2017 http://gulfmigration.eu/bahrain-foreign-population-by-country-of-citizenship-sex-and-migration-status-worker-family-dependent-selected-countries-january-2014/

4. 4.Ibid

5. 5.Ibid

6. 6. Toumi, H., 2013. *Bahrain grants citizenship to 240 UK citizens*. Gulf News. Accessed 15 September 2017. http://gulfnews.com/news/gulf/bahrain/bahrain-grants-citizenship-to-240-uk-citizens-1.1182895

Constitution

1. Constitution of the Kingdom of Bahrain. Web. Accessed on 11th September 2017. http://www.legalaffairs.gov.bh/102.aspx?cms=iQRpheuphYtJ6pyXUGiNqq6h9qKLgVAb

2. United States Department of State. *Background Note: Bahrain*. 2011. Web. Accessed 26 August 2017.

3. "Constitution of Bahrain." *University of Richmond Constitution Finder*. Web. Accessed 26, August 2017.

4.   Institute for Democracy and Electoral Assistance (IDEA), Constitutional History of Bahrain, Constitution Net. Web. Accessed 20 August 2017.

5.   Bakri, Nada. 'Bahrain's Opposition says King's Measures Fall Short'. The New York Times. Accessed 15, Jan 2012 http://www.nytimes.com/2012/01/16/world/middleeast/bahrains-King-announces-constitutional-reforms.html

6.   Katzman, K., 2010. *Bahrain: Reform, Security, and US Policy* (Vol. 95, No. 1013). Diane Publishing.

7.   Niblock, T. ed., 2015. Social and Economic Development in the Arab Gulf (RLE economy of Middle East). Routledge.

8.   Wright, S., 2010. Fixing the Kingdom: Political evolution and socio-economic challenges in Bahrain.

9.   Bahrain King ratifies unified family law (2017, July 20). Retrieved from http://www.tradearabia.com/news/MISC_327810.html

10.   Mechantaf, K., 2010. The Constitutional Law and the Legal System of the Kingdom of Bahrain. Hauser Global Law School Program, New York University School of Law.

11.   Human Rights Watch, 2011, July 5. Bahrain's Human Rights Crisis. Retrieved from https://www.hrw.org/news/2011/07/05/bahrains-human-rights-crisis

12.   Almehzel, M., 2005. Call for women's poll quota in Bahrain rejected. Gulf News. Retrieved from http://gulfnews.com/news/gulf/bahrain/call-for-women-s-poll-quota-in-bahrain-rejected-1.275768

13.   Ali Radhi, H., 2003. "Judiciary and Arbitration in Bahrain: A Historical and Analytical Study", p.10-13.

Ruling Family

1.   Constitution of the Kingdom of Bahrain. Web. Accessed on 11th September 2017. http://www.legalaffairs.gov.bh/102.aspx?cms=iQRpheuphYtJ6pyXUGiNqq6h9qKLgVAb

2.   Kingdom of Bahrain Ministry of Foreign Affairs, 2018. H.M. The King. Accessed on 21, August 2017.

3.   House of Khalifa Royal Family of Bahrain News and Information, 2015. Bahraini Royal Family History. Retrieved from http://houseofkhalifa.com/royal-family-history/

4.   Kingdom of Bahrain's Office of the First Deputy Prime Minister, 2018. HRH Prince Salman bin Hamad Al Khalifa: Biography'. Retrieved from http://www.fdpm.gov.bh/en/biography.html

5.   Kingdom of Bahrain Ministry of Foreign Affairs, 2018. HRH The Prime Minister. Accessed on 21, August 2017.

6.   Ali Radhi, H., 2003. "Judiciary and Arbitration in Bahrain: A Historical and Analytical Study", p.20-29.

7.   House of Khalifa Royal Family of Bahrain News and Information, 2015. Bahraini Royal Family History. Accessed 20 December 2017. http://houseofkhalifa.com/royal-family-history/

8. Ali Radhi, H., 2003. "Judiciary and Arbitration in Bahrain: A Historical and Analytical Study".

Government

1. Constitution of the Kingdom of Bahrain. Web. Accessed on 11th September 2017. http://www.legalaffairs.gov.bh/102.aspx?cms=iQRpheuphYtJ6pyXUGiNqq6h9qKLgVAb

2. "Bahrain." *Political Handbook of the World 2012*, edited by Tom Lansdorf, 101-7. Washington, DC: CQ Press, 2012. http://library.cqpress.com/phw/phw2012_Bahrain.

3. Court of the Crown Prince, 2017. 'HRH Prince Salman bin Hamad Al Khalifa'. Web. Retrieved from http://crownprince.bh/en/About-his-Royal-Highness

4. Kingdom of Bahrain, 2017. The Government of Bahrain's Cabinet'. Bahrain E-Government Portal. Web. Accessed 30 December 2018 https://www.bahrain.bh

Municipal Councils

1. Constitution of the Kingdom of Bahrain. Web. Accessed on 1st September 2017. http://www.legalaffairs.gov.bh/102.aspx?cms=iQRpheuphYtJ6pyXUGiNqq6h9qKLgVAb

2. Kingdom of Bahrain, Ministry of Works, Municipalities Affairs and Urban Planning, 2015. 'Capital Municipality: Historical view'. Web. Accessed on 17, September 2017. http://websrv.Municipality.gov.bh/manama/pages/History_en.jsp

3. Ibid

4. Ibid

5. Ibid

6. "Bahrain making advanced sustainable development strides." Financial Services Monitor Worldwide 3 Oct. 2016. Business Insights: Essentials. Web. 25 July 2017.

7. Bahrain News Agency, July 2017. 'Cabinet: premier praises fruitful Executive-Legislative cooperation'. Accessed on 5 August 2017. http://www.bna.bh/portal/en/news/793254

8. The National Democratic Institute for International Affairs, 2002. 'Bahrain's October 24 and 31, 2002 Legislative Elections'. p.1-15.

Shura Council

1. Bahraini Parliamentary Codes found in the National Action Charter. Web. Accessed 10 December 2017. http://www.legalaffairs.gov.bh/

2. Shura Council specialties and duties. Web. Accessed 4 Feb 2019. http://www.shura.bh/en/GENSEC/Pages/Specialties_Tasks.aspx

3. Constitutional Amendments, 2012. Web. Accessed 4 Feb 2019. http://www.legalaffairs.gov.bh/115.aspx?cms=iQRpheuphYtJ6pyXUGiNqmbRlZXuwQXF

Council Of Representatives

1. Constitutional Amendments, 2012. Web. Accessed 4 Feb 2019. http://www.legalaffairs.

gov.bh/115.aspx?cms=iQRpheuphYtJ6pyXUGiNqmbRlZXuwQXF

2. Kingdom of Bahrain, Council of Representatives, 'Legislation and Oversight'. Web. Accessed 11 December 2017. https://www.nuwab.bh/legislative-and-oversight/?lang=en

3. Katzman, K., 2010. *Bahrain: Reform, Security, and US Policy* (Vol. 95, No. 1013). Diane Publishing.

4. Niblock, T. ed., 2015. Social and Economic Development in the Arab Gulf (RLE economy of Middle East). Routledge.

5. Inter-Parliamentary Union (IPU), 2015. Bahrain: Majlis al-Nuwab (Council of Representatives). Accessed 18 December 2017.

6. Kingdom of Bahrain Supreme Council of Women, 2015. 'Bahraini Women in Numbers 2015', p. 3-34.

7. 2014 Elections Archive. Al-wasat Newspaper. Web. Accessed 3 January 2018. http://www.alwasatnews.com/elections/2014/

8. 2010 Elections Archive. Al-wasat Newspaper. Web. Accessed 3 January 2018. http://www.alwasatnews.com/elections/2010/

9. 2006 Elections Archive. Al-wasat Newspaper. Web. Accessed 3 January 2018. http://www.alwasatnews.com/elections/2006/

10. 2002 Elections Archive. Al-wasat Newspaper. Web. Accessed 3 January 2018. http://www.alwasatnews.com/elections/2002/

11. Kingdom of Bahrain's Elections Portal. Web. Accessed 10 January 2018. http://www.vote.bh/

12. Elections Archives. Al-Aayam Newspaper. Web. Accessed 10 January 2018. https://elections.alayam.com/

13. Election Guide. Election for Bahraini Council of Representatives. Web. Accessed 10th Feb 2019. http://www.electionguide.org/elections/id/3119/

Political Affiliations

1. Duverger, M., 2012. 'Political party', Encyclopedia Britannica. Web. Accessed 10 July 2018. https://www.britannica.com/topic/political-party

2. Citizens of Bahrain, April 2016. Bahrain's Political Societies. Web. Accessed 11 July 2017. https://www.citizensforbahrain.com/index.php/entry/bahrain-s-political-societies

3. Silent majority Cambridge Advanced Learners Dictionary 1995. Web. Accessed 22 Feb 2017. https://dictionary.cambridge.org/dictionary/english/silent-majority

4. Mudaires, Falah, 2004. Political Movements & Groups in Bahrain 1938-2002. P.10-170

5. Ministry of Justice, Political Societies Buearu Booklet, 2010.

6. Dissolvement of two Political Societies. Web. accessed 10 March 2019. https://www.alayam.com/alayam/Parliament/545479/News.html

7. 2014 Elections Archive. Al-wasat Newspaper. Web. Accessed 7 January 2018. http://www.alwasatnews.com/elections/2014/

8.   "Political Party | Definition, Types, Functions, Examples ..." Insert Name of Site in Italics. N.p., n.d. Web. 03 Aug. 2019 https://www.britannica.com/topic/political-party.

9.   "Structural Equation Modeling In Practice: A Review And ..." Insert Name of Site in Italics. N.p., n.d. Web. 03 Aug. 2019 http://aboomsma.webhosting.rug.nl/csadata/anderson_gerbing_1988.pdf.

10.   "How Libertarians Sucked In 2016 - The Unshackled." N.p., n.d. Web. 03 Aug. 2019 https://www.theunshackled.net/recourse/how-libertarians-sucked-in-2016/.

11.   Act#68 2019. Official Gazette, Issue 3432. 15 August 2019. Page 4.

Political Unrest

1.   Al Qassim, W., 2007. An Analysis of Bahrain's Reform Process, 1999-2005: Elite Driven Reform, Developmental Challenges, and Strategic Opportunities (Doctoral dissertation, Durham University).

2.   Ibid

3.   Kaiksow, S.E., 2009. Threats to British" Protectionism" in Colonial Bahrain: Beyond the Sunni/Shia Divide, p.46.

4.   Ibid

5.   Al-Rumaihi, M.G., 1973. *Social and Political Change in Bahrain Since the First World War* (Doctoral dissertation, Durham University).

6.   Al-Jamri, M., 2010. Shia and the State in Bahrain: Integration and Tension. *Alternatif Politika*, p.11.

7.   Khūrī,F, 1980. Tribe and State in Bahrain: the transformation of social and political authority in an Arab state. University of Chicago. p.125.

8.   Kaiksow, S.E., 2009. Threats to British" Protectionism" in Colonial Bahrain: Beyond the Sunni/Shia Divide, p.46.

9.   Al-Rumaihi, M.G., 1973. *Social and Political Change in Bahrain Since the First World War* (Doctoral dissertation, Durham University).

10.   Ibid, p.310

11.   Kaiksow, S.E., 2009. Threats to British" Protectionism" in Colonial Bahrain: Beyond the Sunni/Shia Divide, p.87.

12.   Ibid, p.88

13.   Al-Rumaihi, M.G., 1973. *Social and Political Change in Bahrain Since the First World War* (Doctoral dissertation, Durham University).

14.   Kaiksow, S.E., 2009. Threats to British" Protectionism" in Colonial Bahrain: Beyond the Sunni/Shia Divide, p.94.

15.   Khuri, F.I., 1980. Tribe and State in Bahrain.

16.   Al-Jamri, M., 2010. Shia and the State in Bahrain: Integration and Tension. *Alternatif Politika*, p.12.

17.   Wright, S., 2006. Generational change and elite-driven reforms in the Kingdom of Bahrain.

18. Zahlan, R.S., 2016. The Making of the Modern Gulf States: Kuwait, Bahrain, Qatar, the United Arab Emirates and Oman (Vol. 10). Routledge.p.52

19. Seccombe and Lawless; 1986 cited in Louër, L., 2008. The political impact of labor migration in Bahrain. *City & Society*, *20*(1), p.33.

20. Louër, L., 2008. The political impact of labor migration in Bahrain. *City & Society*, *20*(1), p.34.

21. Louër, L., 2008. The political impact of labor migration in Bahrain. *City & Society*, *20*(1), p.35.

22. Zahlan, R.S., 2016. The Making of the Modern Gulf States: Kuwait, Bahrain, Qatar, the United Arab Emirates and Oman (Vol. 10). Routledge.p.52

23. Rumaihi, M.G., 1976. Bahrain: Social and Political Changes Since the First World War. Bowker. P.197

24. Zahlan, R.S., 2016. The Making of the Modern Gulf States: Kuwait, Bahrain, Qatar, the United Arab Emirates and Oman (Vol. 10). Routledge.p.52

25. Ibid, p.53

26. Ibid, p.53

27. Ibid, p.53

28. Louër, L., 2008. The political impact of labor migration in Bahrain. *City & Society*, *20*(1), pp.32-53.

29. AlShehabi, O.H., 2013. Divide and Rule in Bahrain and the Elusive Pursuit for a United Front: The Experience of the Constitutive Committee and the 1972 Uprising. Historical Materialism, 21(1), pp.94-127.

30. Al-Rumaihi, M.G., 1973. *Social and Political Change in Bahrain Since the First World War* (Doctoral dissertation, Durham University).

31. Ibid

32. Ibid

33. Ibid

34. Al-Rumaihi, M.G., 1973. *Social and Political Change in Bahrain Since the First World War* (Doctoral dissertation, Durham University).

35. Louër, L., 2015. The Arab Spring Effect on Labor Politics in Bahrain and Oman. Arabian Humanities. Revue internationale d'archéologie et de sciences sociales sur la péninsule Arabique/International Journal of Archaeology and Social Sciences in the Arabian Peninsula,

36. Ibid

37. Al-Shehabi, O., 2012. Political Movements in Bahrain: Past, Present, and Future. Jadaliyya.

38. Ibid

39. Khalaf, A., 1985. Labor Movements in Bahrain. Middle East Report, 132, pp.24-9.

40. Al-Shehabi, O., 2012. Political Movements in Bahrain: Past, Present, and Future. Jadaliyya.

41.   Khalaf, A., 1985. Labor Movements in Bahrain. *Middle East Report*, *132*, pp.24-9.

42.   Khalaf, A., 2000. Unfinished Business: Contentious Politics and State-Building in Bahrain. University.

43.   Al-Shehabi, O., 2012. Political Movements in Bahrain: Past, Present, and Future. *Jadaliyya*.

44.   ibid

45.   Khalaf, A., 1985. Labor Movements in Bahrain. *Middle East Report*, *132*, pp.24-9.

46.   Al-Shehabi, O., 2012. Political Movements in Bahrain: Past, Present, and Future. *Jadaliyya*.

47.   Khalaf, A., 1985. Labor Movements in Bahrain. *Middle East Report*, *132*, pp.24-9.

48.   Khalaf, A., 2000. Unfinished Business: Contentious Politics and State-Building in Bahrain. University.

49.   Nakhleh, Emile A., 1976. Bahrain. Political Development in a Modernizing Society.

50.   Louër, L., 2008. The political impact of labor migration in Bahrain. *City & Society*, *20*(1), pp.32-53.

51.   Khalaf, A., 1985. Labor Movements in Bahrain. *Merip Reports*, *132*(May), pp.24-29.

52.   Ibid, p.1.

53.   Zahlan, R.S., 2016. The Making of the Modern Gulf States: Kuwait, Bahrain, Qatar, the United Arab Emirates and Oman (Vol. 10). Routledge. p.60

54.   Ibid, p.61.

55.   Khalaf, A., 1985. Labor Movements in Bahrain. *Merip Reports*, *132*(May), pp.24-29.

56.   Zahlan, R.S., 2016. The Making of the Modern Gulf States: Kuwait, Bahrain, Qatar, the United Arab Emirates and Oman (Vol. 10). Routledge. p.61.

57.   Al-Mdaires, F., 2002. Shicism and political protest in Bahrain. *Digest of Middle East Studies*, *11*(1), pp.20-44.

58.   Ibid, p.35.

59.   Ibid

60.   Louër, L., 2013. Sectarianism and coup-proofing strategies in Bahrain. *Journal of Strategic Studies*, *36*(2), pp.245-260.

61.   Ibid, p.245.

62.   Ibid, p.247.

63.   Al-Mdaires, F., 2002. Shicism and political protest in Bahrain. *Digest of Middle East Studies*, *11*(1), pp.20-44.

64.   Louër, L., 2013. Sectarianism and coup-proofing strategies in Bahrain. *Journal of Strategic Studies*, *36*(2), pp.245-260.

65.   Ibid

66.   Ibid

67.   Bahrain Independent Commission of Inquiry, Bassiouni, M.C. and Rodley, N.S., 2011. *Report of the Bahrain Independent Commission of Inquiry*. Manama: Bahrain

Independent Commission of Inquiry.

68.   Al Qassim, W., 2007. An Analysis of Bahrain's Reform process, 1999-2005: Elite Driven Reform, Developmental Challenges, and Strategic Opportunities (Doctoral dissertation, Durham University).

69.   Ibid.

70.   National Democratic Institute, 2002. 'Bahrain Elections Report', p.10.

71.   Niethammer, K., 2006. Voices in Parliament, Debates in Majalis, and Banners on Streets: Avenues of Political Participation in Bahrain. p.15.

72.   Ibid, p.15

73.   Ibid, p.15

74.   Ibid, p.15

75.   Ibid, p.15

76.   Gengler, J.J., 2011. Ethnic Conflict and Political Mobilization in Bahrain and the Arab Gulf (Doctoral dissertation, University of Michigan).

77.   Katzman, K., 2010. *Bahrain: Reform, Security, and US Policy* (Vol. 95, No. 1013). Diane Publishing.

78.   Al Gharaibeh, F., 2011. Women's empowerment in Bahrain. *Journal of International Women's Studies*, *12*(3), p.96.

79.   Ibid, p.106.

80.   Ibid, p.106.

81.   Ibid, p.107.

82.   Ibid, p.107.

83.   Al-Baker, Abdulrahman, 1971. From Bahrain to Exile "Saint Helen", p.6-7

84.   Rabea'a, Ali, 2010. Gutted Experiment, Democratic Life in Bahrain, p. 10-151

85.   Amiz Nanji & Farhad Daftary, (2007) *"What is Shi'a Islam?" The Institute of Ismaili Studies*, (London, UK: Institute of Ismaili Studies), 8.

86.   Geneive Abdo, (2013) "The New Sectarianism: The Arab Uprisings and the Rebirth of the Shi'a-Sunni Divide" *The Saban Center for Middle East Policy at Brookings*, (Washington, DC: Brookings), 9.

87.   Jadaliyya Reports, (2013) "Gerrymandering in Bahrain: Twenty-One Persons, One Vote," Jadaliyya جدلية, http://www.jadaliyya.com/pages/index/10275/gerrymandering-in-bahrain_twenty-one-persons-one-v (accessed 7 Jul. 2018).

88.   U.S. Embassy, (2014) "Bahrain Off Limits Areas," *Google Maps*, https:// *maps.google.com/maps/ms?msid=216471892140116171495.0004ca e74799a7cdb9fb6&msa=0&ll=26.23769,50.578995&spn=0.220492,0.307 274&dg=feature (accessed 7 Jul. 2018).*

89.   Geneive Abdo, (2013) "The New Sectarianism: The Arab Uprisings and the Rebirth of the Shi'a-Sunni Divide," *The Saban Center for Middle East Policy at Brookings*, (Washington, DC: Brookings), 10.

90. Hasan Tariq Alhasan, (2011) "The Role of Iran in the Failed Coup of 1981: The IFLB in Bahrain," *Middle East Journal*, Vol. 65, No. 3, 603-17.

91. Kevin Downs, (2012) "A Theoretical Analysis of the Saudi-Iranian Rivalry in Bahrain," *Journal of Politics & International Studies*, Vol. 8, 214.

92. Ibid.

93. Ibid.

94. Claire Beaugrand, (2010) "The Return of the Bahraini Exiles (2001-2006): The Impact of the Ostracization Experience on the Opposition's Restructuring, *Mapping Middle Eastern and North African Diasporas, BRISMES Annual Conference*, (London, UK: University of Leeds), 5.

95. Kenneth Katzman, (2011) "Bahrain: Reform, Security, and U.S. Policy," *Congressional Research Service*, (Washington, DC: GPO), 2.

96. Scott Modell & David Asher, (2013) "Pushback: Counter the Iran Action Network," *Center for a New American Security*, (Washington, DC: CNAS), 17.

97. Toby Matthiesen, (2011) "The History of Hizbullah Al-hijaz," *Arabia Today*. Web. Accessed 8 Jul. 2018. http://arabia2day.com/featured/the-history-of-hizbullah-al-hijaz/

98. The Israeli Intelligence & Heritage Commemoration Center, (2013) "Bahrain as a Target Preferred by Iran for Terrorism and Subversion," *The Meir Amit Intelligence and Terrorism Information Center*, (Israel: IDF), 14.

99. Ibid.

100. The Israeli Intelligence & Heritage Commemoration Center, (2013) "Bahrain as a Target Preferred by Iran for Terrorism and Subversion," *The Meir Amit Intelligence and Terrorism Information Center*, (Israel: IDF), 15.

101. Sarah Beckerman, (2014) "Bahrain," *The National Democratic Institute*. Web. Accessed 8 July 2018. https://www.ndi.org/bahrain

102. Official Nuwab Web Page of Bahrain, (2014) "Council of Representatives members". Web. Accessed 8 Jul. 2018 http://www.nuwab.gov.bh/CouncilMembers/Pages/default.aspx

103. Geneive Abdo, (2013) "The New Sectarianism: The Arab Uprisings and the Rebirth of the Shi'a-Sunni Divide," *The Saban Center for Middle East Policy at Brookings*, (Washington, DC: Brookings), 12.

104. Claire Beaugrand, (2010) "The Return of the Bahraini Exiles (2001-2006): The Impact of the Ostracization Experience on the Opposition's Restructuring, *Mapping Middle Eastern and North African Diasporas, BRISMES Annual Conference*, (London, UK: University of Leeds), 6.

105. Ali Alfoneh, (2012) "Between Reform and Revolution: Sheikh Qassim, the Bahraini Shi'a, and Iran," *American Enterprise Institute for Public Policy Research*, No.4, (Washington, DC: AEI), 7.

106. Kenneth Katzman, (2011) "Bahrain: Reform, Security, and U.S. Policy," *Congressional Research Service*, (Washington, DC: GPO), 3.

107. The central hub and organization center for Bahraini civil unrest in the early 2011

timeframe.

108. Yasmine Ryan, (2011) "The tragic life of a street vendor," *Al Jazeera*. Web. Accessed 10 July 2018. http://www.aljazeera.com/indepth/features/2011/01/201111684242518839.html

109. Ibid.

110. Kareem Fahim, (2011) Slap to a Man's Pride Set Off Tumult in Tunisia," *The New York Times*. Web. accessed 10 Jul. 2018. http://www.nytimes.com/2011/01/22/world/africa/22sidi.html?pagewanted=1&_r=2&src=twrhp

111. Ibid.

112. Seth Jones, (2013) "The Mirage of the Arab Spring: Deal With the Region You Have, Not the Region You Want," *Foreign Affairs*, Vol. 92, No. 1, 55-64.

113. The name for Bahrain's public security forces and special security forces.

114. Yasser al-Chazli, (2013) "Adviser to Bahrain King: GCC basis of balance in region," *Al-Monitor*, http://www.al-monitor.com/pulse/tr/security/2013/11/bahrain-gcc-balance-unrest-iran.html# (accessed 12 Jul. 2014).

115. Hanif Zarrabi-Kashani, (2014) "Iran and the Arab Spring: Then and Now," *Muftah.org*, http://muftah.org/iran-arab-spring-now/#.U8H_uvldVyI (accessed 12 Jul. 2018).

116. Maha Taki & Lorenzo Coretti (2013) "The role of social media in the Arab uprisings – past and present," *Westminster Papers in Communication and Culture*, Vol. 9, Issue 2, 1.

117. Sean Aday, et al., (2012) "New Media and Conflict After the Arab Spring," *United States Institute of Peace*, (Washington, DC: USIP), 12.

118. Ibid, 13.

119. Mudaires, Falah, 2004. Political Movements & Groups in Bahrain 1938-2002. P.11-30

120. "Shia And The State In Bahrain: Integration And Tension ..." .p., n.d. Web. 04 Aug. 2019 http://www.acarindex.com/dosyalar/makale/acarindex-1423869241.pdf.

121. "Louer Bahrain - Pdf Free Download - Vibdoc.com." N.p., n.d. Web. 04 Aug. 2019 https://vibdoc.com/louer-bahrain.html.

122. "Bahrain - The Constitutional Experiment." N.p., n.d. Web. 04 Aug. 2019 http://countrystudies.us/persian-gulf-states/42.htm.

123. "Fixing The Kingdom: Political Evolution And Socio-economic ..." N.p., n.d. Web. 04 Aug. 2019 http://qspace.qu.edu.qa/bitstream/handle/10576/10759/No_3_Fixing_the_Kingdom.pdf.

124. "Bahrain's October 24 And 31, 2002 Legislative Elections ..." N.p., n.d. Web. 04 Aug. 2019 https://www.ndi.org/sites/default/files/2392_bh_electionsreport_engpdf_09252008.

125. "House Foreign Affairs Committee Tom Lantos Human Rights ..." N.p., n.d. Web. 04 Aug. 2019 https://humanrightscommission.house.gov/sites/humanrightscommission.house.gov/files/documents/Leslie%20Campbell%2C%20Lantos%20Commission%2C%20Bahrain%20briefing.

126. "Bahrain: The Political Structure, Reform And Human Rights ..." N.p., n.d. Web. 04 Aug. 2019 https://www.eurasiareview.com/28022011-bahrain-the-political-structure-reform-an.

127. "Report Of The Bahrain Independent Commission Of Inquiry ..." N.p., n.d. Web. 04 Aug. 2019 https://slidelegend.com/report-of-the-bahrain-independent-commission-of-inquiry_.

128. "Bahrain's Uprising: Regional Dimensions And International ..." N.p., n.d. Web. 04 Aug. 2019 https://www.stabilityjournal.org/articles/10.5334/sta.be/.

129. Dr. Ali Fakhro's Speech. Official Gazette, Issue 1008. 23 January 1973. Page 29.

Regional Unrest

1. Kinninmont, J., 2012. *Bahrain: Beyond the Impasse*. Chatham House/Royal Institute of international Affairs.

2. Ibid, p.7

3. Bahrain Independent Commission of Inquiry. Bassoni, M.C. & Rodley, N.S., 2011. *Report of the Bahrain Independent Commission of Inquiry*. Manama: Bahrain Independent Commission of Inquiry, p. 65.

4. Ibid, p. 67.

5. Ibid, p.70.

6. Ulrichsen, K., 2014. The Uprising in Bahrain. Routledge Handbook of the Arab Spring: Rethinking Democratization.

7. Bahrain Independent Commission of Inquiry. Bassoni, M.C. & Rodley, N.S., 2011. *Report of the Bahrain Independent Commission of Inquiry*. Manama: Bahrain Independent Commission of Inquiry, p.83.

8. Ibid; p.74.

9. Nepstad, S.E., 2013. Mutiny and nonviolence in the Arab Spring: exploring military defections and loyalty in Egypt, Bahrain and Syria. Journal of Peace Research, 50(3), pp.337-349.

10. Estimates cited by the Bahrain Independent Commission of Inquiry, p.83

11. Bahrain Independent Commission of Inquiry. Bassoni, M.C. & Rodley, N.S., 2011. *Report of the Bahrain Independent Commission of Inquiry*. Manama: Bahrain Independent Commission of Inquiry, p.89

12. Ibid, p.89

13. Ibid, p.92

14. Ibid, p.92

15. Kinninmont, J., 2012. Bahrain: Beyond the Impasse. Chatham House/Royal Institute of international Affairs.

16. Meijer, R. & Danckaert, M., 2015. The Dynamics of a Conflict. *Arab Spring: Negotiating in the Shadow of the Intifadat*

17. Zartman, I.W.ed., 2015. Arab Spring: Negotiating in the Shadow of the Intifadat. University of George Press.

18. Ulrichsen, K., 2014. The Uprising in Bahrain. Routledge Handbook of the Arab Spring: Rethinking Democratization.

19. Meijer, R. & Danckaert, M., 2015. The Dynamics of a Conflict. *Arab Spring: Negotiating in the Shadow of the Intifadat*, p.232

20. Kerr, S. & Wigglesworth, R., 2011. Protests take economic toll on Bahrain. The Financial Times Limited, 2017. https://www.ft.com/content/13614288-53e5-11e0-8bd7-00144feab49a

21. Central Intelligence Agency, World Fact book: https://www.cia.gov/library/publications/the-world-factbook/geos/ba.html

22. Kerr, S. & Wigglesworth, R., 2011. Protests take economic toll on Bahrain. The Financial Times Limited, 2017. https://www.ft.com/content/13614288-53e5-11e0-8bd7-00144feab49a

23. Ibid, p. 1.

24. Personal Interview with Dr. Ali Fakhro - 13th April 2017

25. Personal Interview with Ali Rabea'a - 13th April 2017

26. Personal Interview with Saeed al-Asbool - 13th April 2017

27. Personal Interview with Jassim Murad - 13th April 2017

Iran's Involvement in Bahrain

1. Iran's Involvement In Bahrain | Small Wars Journal. N.p., n.d. Web. 04 Aug. 2019 https://smallwarsjournal.com/jrnl/art/iran%E2%80%99s-involvement-in-bahrain.

2. The Middle East, Westernized Despite Itself: Middle East ..." N.p., n.d. Web. 04 Aug. 2019 https://www.meforum.org/290/the-middle-east-westernized-despite-itself.

3. J. B. Kelly. "The Persian Claim to Bahrain." International Affairs (Royal Institute of International Affairs 1944-) 33, no. 1 (1957): 51-70. Accessed July 2, 2021. doi:10.2307/2604468.

4. Wagner, W. (1956). Bahrein Islands—A Legal and Diplomatic Study of the British-Iranian Controversy. By Fereydoun Adamiyat. New York: Frederick A. Praeger, Inc., 1955. pp. 268. American Journal of International Law, 50(2), 456-457. doi:10.2307/2194977

5. Wagner, W. J. The American Journal of International Law 50, no. 2 (1956): 456-57. Accessed July 2, 2021. doi:10.2307/2194977.

6. Longrigg, S. H. International Affairs (Royal Institute of International Affairs 1944-) 31, no. 4 (1955): 531. Accessed July 2, 2021. doi:10.2307/2604911.

7. Khadduri, Majid. Middle East Journal 10, no. 1 (1956): 87-89. Accessed July 2, 2021. http://www.jstor.org/stable/4322782.

8. Johnson, D. H. N. The Modern Law Review 19, no. 2 (1956): 230-31. Accessed July 2, 2021. http://www.jstor.org/stable/1090665.

9. Parker, C. F. The Modern Law Review 19, no. 2 (1956): 229-30. Accessed July 2, 2021. http://www.jstor.org/stable/1090664.

10. "International Law and Relations." The American Political Science Review 49, no. 2 (1955): 580-89. Accessed July 2, 2021. doi:10.2307/1951839.

11. Parker, C. F. The Modern Law Review 19, no. 2 (1956): 229-30. Accessed July 2, 2021. http://www.jstor.org/stable/1090664.

12. "International Law and Relations." The American Political Science Review 49, no. 2 (1955): 580-89. Accessed July 2, 2021. doi:10.2307/1951839.

13. Alhasan, Hasan Tariq. "The Role of Iran in the Failed Coup of 1981: The IFLB in Bahrain." Middle East Journal 65, no. 4 (2011): 603-17. Accessed July 3, 2021. http://www.jstor.org/stable/41342743.

Bahrain Independent Commission Of Inquiry

1. ADHRB – BIRD – BCHR "Shattering the Façade. A Report on Bahrain's Implementation of the Bahrain Independent Commission of Inquiry (BICI) Recommendations Four Years On", Washington, 2015, p. 29: http://www.adhrb.org/2015/11/shattering-the-facade-a-report-on-bahrains-   implementation-of-the-bahrain-independent-commission-of-inquiry-bici-four years-on/ [Accessed on 25 November 2017].

2. Bahrain Independent Commission of Inquiry, M. Cherif Bassiouni, and Nigel S. Rodley. *Report of the Bahrain Independent Commission of Inquiry*. Manama: Bahrain Independent Commission of Inquiry, 2011.

3. Bahrain Independent Commission of Inquiry. Bassoni, M.C. & Rodley, N.S., 2011. *Report of the Bahrain Independent Commission of Inquiry*. Manama: Bahrain Independent Commission of Inquiry, p.29.

4. BICI Follow-up Unit, 2014. Moving Beyond 2011: A Special Report Detailing the Government of Bahrain's Implementation of the Recommendations of the Bahrain Independent Commission of Inquiry, p.4-5.

5. Kinninmont, J., 2012. *Bahrain: Beyond the Impasse*. Chatham House/Royal Institute of International Affairs.

6. Sadiki, L. ed. 2014. Routledge Handbook of the Arab Spring: Rethinking democratization. Routledge, p.137

7. U.S. Department of State, Legislative Affairs, 2016. Steps Taken by the Government of Bahrain to Implement the Recommendations in the 2011 report of the Bahrain independent Commission of Inquiry. Washington Printing Office, 2016. (Serial Set 20520)

8. Kepel, Gilles, 2004. The war for Muslim Minds. Belknap Harvard. P.70-77.

9. Ibid, p.197-240.

10. "Shattering The Façade - Americans For Democracy & Human ..." N.p., n.d. Web. 04 Aug. 2019 http://www.adhrb.org/wp-content/uploads/2015/11/Shattering_the_Facade_Web.pdf.

11. "Bahrain's Uprising: Regional Dimensions And International ..." N.p., n.d. Web.

04 Aug. 2019 https://www.stabilityjournal.org/articles/10.5334/sta.be/.

12. "Bahrainis Complain Of Government Tear Gas Attacks On ..." N.p., n.d. Web. 04 Aug. 2019 https://www.voanews.com/world-news/middle-east-dont-use/bahrainis-complain-gover.

13. "Bahrain's Uprising: Regional Dimensions And International ..." N.p., n.d. Web. 04 Aug. 2019 https://www.stabilityjournal.org/articles/10.5334/sta.be/.

14. "Sab 01 - Parliament (publications) - Parliament Uk ..." N.p., n.d. Web. 04 Aug. 2019 https://slidelegend.com/sab-01-Parliament-publications-Parliament-uk_5ba7cf15097.

15. "Bahrain Monitor - A Monthly Newsletter On The Human Rights ..." N.p., n.d. Web. 04 Aug. 2019 http://www.bahrainmonitor.org/reports/p-035-01.html.

16. "Report Of The Bahrain Independent Commission Of Inquiry ..." N.p., n.d. Web. 04 Aug. 2019 https://slidelegend.com/report-of-the-bahrain-independent-commission-of-inquiry_.

17. "H.con.res.431 - 107th Congress (2001-2002): Condemning The ..." N.p., n.d. Web. 04 Aug. 2019 https://www.congress.gov/bill/107th-congress/house-concurrent-resolution/431.

18. "Failing Grade: A Report Card On The Status Of Bahrain ..." N.p., n.d. Web. 04 Aug. 2019 http://adhrb.org/wp-content/uploads/2012/11/Failing-Grade-20121.pdf.

19. "The National Commission Assigned To Follow-up The Bici ..." Insert Name of Site in Italics. N.p., n.d. Web. 04 Aug. 2019 http://www.biciactions.bh/wps/portal/BICI/%21ut/p/c5/04_SB8K8xLLM9MSSzPy8xBz9CP0os3gLAxNHQ093A3eLMEc/dl3/d3/L2dJQSEvUUt3QS9ZQnZ3LzZfT0FISUdHRzBHT0Q5OTBJUFA/indexd5f5.html?WCM_GLOBAL_CONTEXT=/wps/wcm/connect/egov+english+library/bici/progres.

Human Rights

20. Neumann, R.E., 2013. Bahrain: A Very Complicated Little Island. *Middle East Policy*, *20*(4), pp.45-58. Bahrain Independent Commission of Inquiry, M. Cherif Bassiouni, and Nigel S. Rodley. *Report of the Bahrain Independent Commission of Inquiry*. Manama: Bahrain Independent Commission of Inquiry, 2011.

21. Department of State, Bureau of Democracy, Human Rights and Labor, Country Report on Human Rights Practices for 2016, Bahrain, pp. 128-134 (DoS Country Report), p.8.

22. http://www.state.gov/j/drl/rls/hrrpt/humanrightsreport/index.htm?year=2016&dlid=265492

23. Neumann, R.E., 2013. Bahrain: A Very Complicated Little Island. *Middle East Policy*, *20*(4), pp.45-58.

24. Ibid

25. Ibid

26. Bahrain Institute for Rights and Democracy (BIRD), 2015. Convention Against Torture (Bird "Victims Suffer"). Web. Accessed 11 September. 2017. http://birdbh.

org/wp-content/uploads/2017/05/2017.03.15-BIRD-Submission-to-CAT.pdf

27. Department of State, Bureau of Democracy, Human Rights and Labor, Country Report on Human Rights Practices for 2016, Bahrain, pp. 128-134 (DoS Country Report) p.10. Web. Accessed 11 September. 2017. http://www.state.gov/j/drl/rls/hrrpt/humanrightsreport/index.htm?year=2016&dlid=265492

28. BIRD's report pertaining to the Convention Against Torture (Bird "Victims Suffer"). Web. Accessed 11 September. 2017. http://birdbh.org/wp-content/uploads/2017/05/2017.03.15-BIRD-Submission-to-CAT.pdf

29. Department of State, Bureau of Democracy, Human Rights and Labor, Country Report on Human Rights Practices for 2016, Bahrain, pp. 128-134 (DoS Country Report), p.3. Web. Accessed 11 September 2017. http://www.state.gov/j/drl/rls/hrrpt/humanrightsreport/index.htm?year=2016&dlid=265492

30. Ibid, p.7.

31. Ibid, p.15.

32. Ibid, p.15.

33. See BICI Chapter or Bahrain Independent Commission of Inquiry, Bassiouni, M.C. and Rodley, N.S., 2011. *Report of the Bahrain Independent Commission of Inquiry.* Manama: Bahrain Independent Commission of Inquiry.

34. International Religious Freedom Report (USCIRF 2017), p.129. http://www.uscirf.gov/sites/default/files/2017.USCIRFAnnualReport.pdf

35. Department of State, Bureau of Democracy, Human Rights and Labor, Country Report on Human Rights Practices for 2016, Bahrain, pp. 128-134 (DoS Country Report), p.39. http://www.state.gov/j/drl/rls/hrrpt/humanrightsreport/index.htm?year=2016&dlid=265492

36. Ibid, p.40.

37. Ibid, p.40.

38. Ibid, p.40.

39. International Religious Freedom Report (USCIRF 2017), p.129. Web. Accessed 13 September. 2017.http://www.uscirf.gov/sites/default/files/2017.USCIRFAnnualReport.pdf

40. Department of State, Bureau of Democracy, Human Rights and Labor, Country Report on Human Rights Practices for 2016, Bahrain, pp. 128-134 (DoS Country Report), p.32. http://www.state.gov/j/drl/rls/hrrpt/humanrightsreport/index.htm?year=2016&dlid=265492

41. Ibid, p.32.

42. Ibid, p.34.

43. Bahrain Supreme Council for Women. Web. Accessed on 1st July 2018. http://www.scw.bh/en/SupportCenter/Databases/Statistics/Pages/default.aspx

44. Ibid

45. Ibid

46. Ombudsman. About. Web. Accessed on 14th April 2019, http://www.ombudsman. bh/en/about/

47. Habib Toumi, Gulf News. *Bahrain is home to 19 churches.* Web. Accessed on 1st May 2019. https://gulfnews.com/world/gulf/bahrain/bahrain-is-home-to-19-churches-1.932485

48. Khedouri, Nancy, 2007, *From our beginning to present day*, p. 25-30.

49. Updated list of executions in Bahrain. Salam For democracy & Human Rights. Web. Accessed 31. July.2019. https://salam-dhr.org/wp-content/uploads/2019/02/ جدلية- المحكومين-بالإعدام-في-القضايا-السياسيةpdf

50. "About Human Rights - Ministry Of Foreign Affairs." Insert Name of Site in Italics. N.p., n.d. Web. 04 Aug. 2019 https://www.mofa.gov.bh/Default. aspx?tabid=135&language=en-US.

51. Katzman, Kenneth. "Bahrain: Reform, Security, And U.s. Policy *." Current Politics and Economics of the Middle East, vol. 7, no. 2, Nova Science Publishers, Inc., Apr. 2016, p. 195.

52. "Annual Report - Uscirf - Slidelegend.com." N.p., n.d. Web. 04 Aug. 2019 https:// slidelegend.com/annual-report-uscirf_5b25f361097c4758178b4582.html.

53. "Convention On The Rights Of The Child | Convention Rights ..." N.p., n.d. Web. 04 Aug. 2019 https://www.liquisearch.com/convention_on_the_rights_of_the_child.

54. "Human Rights Without Frontiers Int'l - Hrwf." N.p., n.d. Web. 04 Aug. 2019 http://hrwf.eu/wp-content/uploads/2015/01/Christians-in-Bahrain.pdf.

55. "Supreme Council For Women - Political Empowerment." N.p., n.d. Web. 04 Aug. 2019 https://www.scw.bh/en/SupportCenter/CenterServices/TrainingPrograms/ PoliticalEmp.

56. "Bin Shams: "bahraini Women Are The Main Driver Of Bahrain ..." N.p., n.d. Web. 04 Aug. 2019 http://www.bipa.gov.bh/en/bin-shams-bahraini-women-are-the-main-driver-of-bahrai.

57. "Supreme Council For Women - Legislative Achievements." N.p., n.d. Web. 04 Aug. 2019 https://www.scw.bh/en/WomenFiles/Pages/File6.aspx.

58. "Bahrain." *World Prison Brief Data*. Web. 05 June. 2019 https://www.prisonstudies. org/country/bahrain

2011-2021:

1. Lansford, T. ed. 2014. Political Handbook of the World 2016-2017. Cq Press.

2. Ibid, p. 114

3. Bahrain Country Review 2017, Country Watch publications, 2017. Available URL: http://www.countrywatch.com/Intelligence/CountryReviews?CountryId=13

4. Sadiki, L. ed. 2014. Routledge Handbook of the Arab Spring: Rethinking democratization. Routledge, p.137

5. Lansford, T. ed. 2014. Political Handbook of the World 2016-2017. Cq Press.

6.   Sadiki, L. ed. 2014. Routledge Handbook of the Arab Spring: Rethinking democratization. Routledge, p.137

7.   Bahrain Independent Commission of Inquiry. Bassoni, M.C. & Rodley, N.S., 2011. *Report of the Bahrain Independent Commission of Inquiry*. Manama: Bahrain Independent Commission of Inquiry, p.298

8.   Sadiki, L. ed. 2014. Routledge Handbook of the Arab Spring: Rethinking democratization. Routledge, p.137

9.   Ibid, p.137

10. Ibid, p.138

11. Ibid, p.26

12. Human Rights First, Bahrain Timeline 2010-2016, Available at: http://www.humanrightsfirst.org/sites/default/files/HRF-Bahrain-timeline-hires-spread.pdf

13. Lansford, T. ed. 2017. Political Handbook of the World 2016-2017, Cq Press, p.114

14. Ibid, p.114

15. Sadiki, L. ed. 2014. Routledge Handbook of the Arab Spring: Rethinking democratization. Routledge, p.139

16. Human Rights First, Bahrain Timeline 2010-2016, Available at: http://www.humanrightsfirst.org/sites/default/files/HRF-Bahrain-timeline-hires-spread.pdf

17. Gengle, J., 2012. The (sectarian) politics of public-sector employment in Bahrain. Religion and Politics in Bahrain, May 27.

18. Ashoor, M. 2012. The Bahrain Political Landscape: The National Action Charter, Manama Document and Lulu Charter, Wordpress. Accessed on 28.10.2017

19. Sadiki, L. ed. 2014. Routledge Handbook of the Arab Spring: Rethinking democratization. Routledge, p.139

20. Ibid, p.139

21. Louër, L., 2008. Transnational Shia Politics. Columbia University Press. p.11-17.

22. Ibid, p.61-65

23. Ibid, p.243-260

24. Lansford, T. ed. 2017. Political Handbook of the World 2016-2017, Cq Press, p.114

25. Ibid, p.114

26. Bahrain Country Review 2017, Country Watch Publications, 2017, p.29

27. Ibid, p. 29

28. Sadiki, L. ed. 2014. Routledge Handbook of the Arab Spring: Rethinking democratization. Routledge, p.139

29. Diwan, K.S., 2016. *Bahrain faces Austerity Without Protest*. The Arab Gulf States in Washington. http://www.agsiw.org/bahrain-faces-austerity-without-protest/

30. The Economist, 13 June 2016. http://country.eiu.com/article.aspx?articleid=1414307125&Country=Bahrain&topic=Politics&subtopic=_4

31. The Rise and Fall of Bahrain's Left-Wing https://www.citizensforbahrain.com/index.

php/entry/the-rise-and-fall-of-bahrain-s-left-wing

32. Ibid

33. Bahrain News Agency, 2017. http://bna.bh/portal/en/news/788452

34. The Rise and Fall of Bahrain's Left-wing https://www.citizensforbhrain.com/index.php/entry/the-rise-and-fall-of-bahrain-s-left-wing

35. Bahrain sentences 138 individuals on terror charges http://english.alarabiya.net/en/News/2019/04/16/Bahrain-sentences-138-individuals-on-terror-charges.html

36. Bahrain's King reinstates citizenship of 551 tried in courts. BBC. Web. Accessed 2nd May 2019. https://www.bbc.com/news/world-middle-east-48011493

37. I am Bahraini, Nationality is my right. Revocation of citizenship in #Bahrain (Up today). Web. Accessed 1 May 2019. http://www.anabahraini.org/

38. Bahrain holds elections with ban on opposition groups. Reuters. Web. Accessed 10 December 2018. https://www.reuters.com/article/us-bahrain-politics-election/bahrain-holds-elections-with-ban-on-opposition-groups-idUSKCN1NT038

39. Bahrain's King reinstates citizenship of 551 tried in courts. BBC. Web. Accessed 2nd May 2019. https://www.bbc.com/news/world-middle-east-48011493

40. Bahrain executes three men the day after US reinstates federal death penalty. CNN. Web. Accessed 31 July 2019. https://edition.cnn.com/2019/07/27/middleeast/bahrain-executions-intl/index.html

41. Stephen Zunes. "Bahrain's Arrested Revolution." Arab Studies Quarterly 35, no. 2 (2013): 149-64. Accessed July 2, 2021. doi:10.13169/arabstudquar.35.2.0149.

Conclusion

1. Politics. Wikipedia. Web. Accessed 05 July 208. https://en.wikipedia.org/wiki/Politics

2. What does politics mean? Definitions.net. Web. Accessed 05 July 208. https://www.definitions.net/definition/politics

Index

Al-Haydariya Platoon 178
Ali Abdulla 76, 78
Ali Ahmed 15, 104, 105, 108, 112
Ali al-Aradhi 121
Ali al-Asheeri 112
Ali al-Aswad 112
Ali al-Durazi 116
Ali al-Muhannadi 75
Ali al-Muqla 74, 76, 78, 120
Ali al-Nasouh 80
Ali al-Noaimi 125
Ali al-Samaheji 104
Ali al-Shuwaikh 80
Ali al-Uttaish 116, 120
Ali bin Khalifa al-Khalifa 66
Ali bin Mohamed al-Rumaihi 67
Ali bu Farsan 120
Ali Ishaqi 124
Ali Kamaluddein 147
Ali Mansour 76
Ali Mattar 105
Ali Rabea'a 308
Ali Salman 13, 16, 108, 153, 208, 209, 215, 216,
   223, 247, 252, 255, 276, 277, 278
Ali Shamtoot 116
Ali Zayed 113, 125
al-Khalifa 12, 13, 14, 16, 23, 27, 28, 30, 32, 33,
   43, 44, 49, 52, 54, 57, 59, 60, 61, 62, 66, 67,
   71, 89, 99, 150, 183, 187, 198, 208, 209, 210,
   218, 222, 223, 224, 226, 229, 231, 239, 251,
   262, 272
alliance 28, 197, 214, 217, 277
Al-Menbar al-Watani al-Islami Society 157
al-Qafilah newspaper 193
al-Wafa Movement 175, 177, 224
Al-Wasat Al-Arabi Society 169
Al-Watan Society 166
Al-Wefaq National Islamic Society 153, 180
ambassador 13, 15, 166, 218, 234
amendment 48, 54, 90, 246, 252, 260, 264, 277,
   278
Amin Hassan 76
Amir Salman 75
Ammar Abbas 124
Ammar Qamber 124
Anas bu Hindi 121
anti-colonialist 194
anti-government 15, 194, 225, 254, 272, 274,
   276
Arab 12, 15, 19, 28, 30, 33, 34, 36, 37, 43, 49, 52,
   53, 54, 55, 146, 148, 161, 162, 163, 169, 181,
   190, 194, 195, 196, 197, 202, 206, 207, 217,

221, 225, 226, 230, 231, 232, 246, 251, 253,
   255, 298, 300, 301, 302, 303, 304, 305, 306,
   307, 308, 309, 312, 313, 314
Arabia 12, 13, 16, 23, 26, 27, 34, 35, 36, 37, 158,
   167, 176, 183, 204, 230, 234, 235, 305
Arabic 23, 37, 39, 53, 60, 99, 146, 231
Arab League 33, 34, 206
Arab Nationalism 161, 162, 163, 181, 194, 195,
   196
Arab Spring 19, 28, 49, 226, 230, 231, 232, 302,
   306, 307, 308, 309, 312, 313
Arbitration Court 184
arrest 15, 16, 192, 194, 196, 204, 209, 230, 234,
   242, 243, 244, 252, 254, 271, 276
Assembly 12, 23, 32, 33, 34, 43, 44, 46, 52, 54,
   55, 65, 87, 89, 90, 93, 94, 96, 99, 148, 150,
   160, 161, 163, 165, 179, 180, 192, 202, 204,
   206, 210, 222, 240, 252, 262, 272, 277
asylum 13, 33
authority 28, 65, 192, 204, 210, 241, 246, 253,
   254, 266, 276, 301
Aymen Tawfiq al-Moayyed 67
Aziza Kamal 81, 83

B

Bab al-Bahrain 209
Bader al-Dowseri 79, 81, 125
Bader al-Tamimi 81, 83
Badriya Ebrahim 82
Bahrain 1, 10, 12, 13, 14, 15, 16, 19, 20, 21, 23,
   26, 27, 28, 29, 30, 31, 32, 33, 34, 35, 36, 37,
   38, 39, 43, 44, 46, 47, 52, 53, 54, 55, 59, 60,
   61, 62, 65, 71, 72, 93, 94, 95, 96, 99, 143, 144,
   145, 146, 147, 148, 149, 150, 155, 156, 175,
   176, 177, 179, 181, 183, 184, 186, 187, 188,
   190, 193, 194, 196, 197, 198, 202, 204, 206,
   207, 208, 209, 210, 211, 212, 213, 214, 215,
   217, 218, 221, 222, 223, 224, 225, 226, 227,
   229, 230, 231, 232, 233, 234, 235, 236, 237,
   239, 241, 243, 244, 245, 246, 251, 252, 253,
   254, 255, 256, 259, 260, 261, 262, 264, 265,
   267, 271, 272, 273, 274, 275, 276, 277, 278,
   279, 280, 297, 298, 299, 300, 301, 302, 303,
   304, 305, 306, 307, 308, 309, 310, 311, 312,
   313, 314
Bahrain Centre for Human Rights 217, 221
Bahrain Culture and Antiquities Authority 28
Bahrain Financial Harbor 225
Bahrain Freedom Movement 175, 179, 207,
   230, 231
Bahrain Independent Commission of Inquiry
   222, 224, 226, 239, 241, 252, 303, 307, 309,

Director 13,256
dispute 13,34,206,207
district 75
divers uprising 186
domestic violence 95,96,265
Dubai 188,209
Duraz 149,209,279

E

East India Company 183
Ebrahim Ahmed 75
Ebrahim al-Doy 74
Ebrahim al-Hammadi 120
Ebrahim al-Nefaie 124
Ebrahim bin Mousa 147
Ebrahim Busandal 108
Ebrahim Fakhro 75,147
Ebrahim Ismail 75
Ebtisam Hejris 116
Economic Development Board 31,61,212
economy 23,30,31,71,187,208,226,260,298,
    300
education 29,31,50,60,61,72,148,186,187,
    190,193,198,202,247,264,266,272
Egypt 15,19,48,157,161,162,169,170,173,
    176,194,196,206,221,231,232,252,307
Egyptian embassy 221
elections 12,14,15,16,19,44,48,49,51,53,72,
    81,89,95,99,100,132,143,144,145,148,
    149,153,154,155,156,157,158,160,162,
    164,165,166,169,170,172,173,175,193,
    197,206,210,213,214,215,216,217,230,
    231,262,271,276,277,280,300,314
electoral 48,52,53,71,96,99,143,204,210,
    213,214,217,252,271,277
Elite's Charter 150
Eman al-Qahtani 81
Eman al-Qallaf 82
emir 28,43,44,60,61,65,89,99,186,202,208
Environment Committee 46,100
equality 47,48,50,51,53,55,197,216,266
Essam bin Abdulla Khalaf 66
exile 148,153,179,194,214,224,231
ex-officio 99
explosions 13,209

F

Fadhel Abbas 76
Fadhel al-Oud 82
Fadhel al-Sawwad 124
Fadhel Isa 78
Faeqa bint Saeed al-Saleh 67

failed coup 16,28,207,229
Faisal Shabeeb 82
Falah Hashim 125
Farid Ghazi 105
Fasht al-Dibal 13
Fatima Abbas 80,124
Fatima Salman 78
Fawzia Zainal 99,100
Fdawiya 192
Financial and Economic Affairs Committee 46,
    100
Flag 22
Formula One 223,272,276
Fouad Seyadi 154
Free National Thought Society 173
free-trade agreement 14,30

G

Gathering of National Unity 223
GCC 12,13,16,33,37,206,222,223,224,226,
    230,234,306
GDP 23,30,31,226
General Federation of Bahrain Trade Unions
    222,226
General Federation of Workers in Bahrain 198
Ghazi al-Dowseri 78
Ghazi al-Hamar 79
Ghazi al-Murbati 78,80,82
Ghazi al-Rahma 121,125
governance 43,55,94,246
government 10,12,13,14,15,16,19,20,28,30,
    31,32,36,37,43,44,46,48,49,50,51,55,
    60,65,71,72,90,94,95,96,99,100,144,
    145,147,175,176,177,180,183,186,187,
    188,190,192,193,194,196,198,202,204,
    206,207,208,209,210,211,213,214,215,
    217,222,223,224,225,226,229,230,233,
    234,239,240,241,242,243,244,245,246,
    247,251,252,253,254,255,261,262,264,
    272,273,274,275,276,277,278
Gulf Air 14,198,206
Gulf Cooperation Council 12,13,33,54
Gulf of Bahrain 12

H

Hadi al-Modarrissi 12,155
Hadi al-Mosawi 112
Hague 13
Haider Hassan 109
Hamad al-Dowseri 80
Hamad al-Fadalah 75
Hamad al-Kooheji 124

O

oil 12, 23, 27, 30, 31, 96, 185, 187, 188, 190, 196, 202, 206, 207, 233, 260
Oman 12, 150, 197, 274, 302, 303
Omar Abdulrahman 82
Omran Hussein 74
operation 33, 192, 223
opposition 14, 15, 16, 19, 20, 44, 48, 94, 144, 145, 153, 155, 156, 162, 163, 164, 173, 175, 186, 188, 196, 197, 204, 210, 211, 214, 216, 221, 223, 224, 225, 226, 229, 230, 231, 235, 240, 241, 246, 247, 252, 255, 271, 272, 273, 274, 275, 276, 277, 278, 279, 280, 314
organizations 10, 51, 54, 55, 144, 176, 190, 214, 216, 224, 240, 244, 247, 252, 254, 277
Osama Muhanna 116
Otham al-Rayes 104, 112
Ottoman 12, 183, 229
oust 28
outlook 10, 20, 46, 194, 196

P

Parliament 39, 41, 44, 46, 48, 60, 71, 90, 93, 95, 99, 144, 148, 153, 154, 155, 156, 157, 158, 159, 160, 161, 162, 163, 164, 165, 166, 167, 168, 169, 170, 171, 172, 173, 174, 204, 206, 208, 212, 214, 216, 217, 218, 221, 224, 240, 252, 253, 271, 276, 278, 300, 304, 310
Parliamentary Codes 90, 299
parliamentary elections 49, 89, 99, 100, 148, 153, 154, 157, 162, 165, 166, 169, 170, 175, 197, 210, 213, 216
Pearl-diving 184
pearling 183, 184
Pearl Roundabout 222, 225
Peninsula Shield Force 13, 225
People's Bloc 197, 202, 204, 206, 207
Persia 27
Persian 35, 37, 39, 164, 185, 229, 233
plot 13, 207, 217, 274
political 10, 14, 15, 19, 20, 28, 48, 49, 50, 51, 52, 53, 55, 59, 65, 95, 96, 100, 143, 144, 145, 146, 148, 150, 154, 155, 156, 158, 160, 163, 164, 166, 170, 173, 174, 179, 183, 185, 186, 187, 188, 190, 192, 193, 194, 196, 197, 198, 202, 204, 206, 207, 208, 210, 211, 212, 213, 214, 215, 216, 217, 221, 222, 224, 225, 229, 230, 231, 233, 239, 240, 241, 244, 246, 247, 251, 252, 253, 254, 255, 262, 271, 272, 273, 274, 275, 276, 277, 278, 279, 280, 300, 301, 302, 303, 307
political societies 10, 15, 96, 144, 170, 179, 210,

213, 216, 217, 224, 225, 230, 273, 275, 276, 277, 278
politics 10, 33, 94, 96, 146, 209, 217, 277, 313, 314
Politics 143, 287, 302, 303, 305, 312, 313, 314
poll 14, 185, 298
popular 15, 27, 28, 44, 48, 59, 96, 177, 192, 194, 198, 208, 217, 221, 231, 232, 233, 234
populist 96
Portuguese 23, 27, 183
president 12, 33, 47, 48, 93, 99, 196, 235, 262
private 29, 30, 31, 186, 210, 214, 223, 224, 239, 243, 245, 246, 254, 260, 261, 272
Pro-Government 157, 159, 160, 161, 162, 166, 167, 169, 170, 171, 172, 173, 174
protest 14, 15, 16, 19, 175, 184, 195, 222, 223, 224, 231, 235, 271, 303, 313
public 14, 29, 30, 31, 38, 47, 50, 51, 52, 53, 60, 61, 95, 96, 144, 147, 183, 185, 187, 190, 192, 193, 198, 204, 208, 210, 214, 222, 223, 224, 226, 230, 231, 239, 241, 243, 245, 246, 253, 255, 260, 272, 274, 306, 313

Q

Qarmatians 26
Qatar 12, 13, 14, 16, 23, 34, 59, 206, 225, 229, 302, 303
Qatif 27, 36, 184
Qitat Jaradah 13

R

Radhi al-Mosawi 154
Radhi Aman 77
Ramzi al-Galaleef 78
Rashid bin Abdulla al-Khalifa 66
recommendation 241, 242, 243, 244, 245, 246, 272
Redha al-Ghasra 279
Redha Humaidan 75
referendum 27, 28, 44, 59, 65, 207, 210, 213, 214, 221
reform 14, 19, 20, 30, 44, 65, 71, 94, 145, 146, 185, 188, 194, 210, 214, 215, 222, 251, 256, 272, 273, 275, 277, 307
region 28, 34, 59, 143, 148, 176, 187, 192, 202, 206, 230, 234, 260, 306
religion 28, 39, 43, 47, 48, 51, 52, 53, 55, 94, 260, 261, 277
religious 37, 48, 50, 95, 96, 146, 149, 192, 198, 202, 207, 215, 217, 224, 234, 245, 247, 253, 260, 261, 277, 278
Religious Bloc 145, 179, 202, 204

St. Helena Island 194

strike 15, 147, 188, 190, 193, 196, 198, 204, 222, 223, 226, 236

structure 10, 20, 43, 197, 210, 215, 274, 307

Subah al-Dowseri 80

successor 52, 59, 93, 202

Suez Canal 194

Sukhra 184, 185

Sulfah court 186

Sumaya al-Jowder 116

Sunna 46, 277

Sunni 13, 19, 20, 28, 35, 36, 37, 47, 96, 145, 146, 157, 160, 167, 168, 169, 170, 179, 185, 186, 192, 197, 202, 215, 218, 222, 229, 231, 246, 247, 252, 262, 273, 276, 277, 279, 301, 304, 305

Sunni Islamist 167, 276, 277

Sunnite 94, 143, 183, 185, 260

Supreme National Committee 210

Syria 19, 37, 163, 217, 230, 307

T

Taha al-Junaid 80

Talal al-Bashir 83

Tarbeia Islamic Society 150

Tariq al-Sheikh 76

taxation 181, 184, 185

Tayaar al-Amal al-Islami 178

Tehran 12, 149, 177, 207, 229, 234, 235

temporary committees 101

term 13, 31, 93, 96, 143, 145, 146, 166, 188, 202, 210, 221, 254

Theyab al-Noaimi 77

think tanks 10, 30

Tisgam 184

treaty 12, 233

U

Ukraine 215

underground movements 14

Unitary National Democratic Assembly 163

United Nations 12, 27, 30, 34, 206, 216, 231, 234, 244, 256, 262

United States of America 33, 176

universal suffrage 89, 213

University of Bahrain 29, 211, 225, 245, 251

unrest 10, 15, 16, 19, 20, 27, 30, 33, 34, 44, 47, 49, 89, 144, 145, 147, 150, 160, 162, 174, 180, 186, 192, 196, 204, 207, 208, 209, 218, 222, 223, 226, 229, 231, 239, 251, 253, 254, 272, 275, 276, 305, 306

uprising 19, 27, 28, 148, 154, 177, 179, 180, 185,

186, 196, 198, 214, 221, 226, 231, 234, 239, 251, 252, 272, 274, 275, 276, 277

U.S. 12, 13, 14, 15, 206, 240, 256, 304, 305, 309

Usama al-Khaja 120

Usfurids 26

Uyunid Dynasty 26

V

violent 15, 19, 28, 43, 150, 175, 194, 197, 225, 252, 253, 273, 274

vision 30, 31, 94, 145, 212

vote 12, 14, 28, 46, 48, 51, 53, 72, 89, 90, 96, 99, 100, 202, 213, 216, 240, 252, 280, 300

W

Wa'ad 150, 154, 156, 218, 221, 276, 277, 278

Wael al-Mubarak 66

Waheeb al-Nasser 81

Waheed al-Mannaie 82

Walid Hejres 75, 77

War 13, 33, 146, 187, 190, 196, 202, 206, 301, 302

women 14, 28, 31, 32, 48, 50, 51, 53, 55, 89, 94, 95, 99, 100, 166, 197, 202, 210, 213, 214, 216, 217, 252, 256, 261, 262, 264, 265, 266, 267, 276, 298, 312

Women's Rights 212, 249, 261

Y

Yassein Zainal 82

Yemen 16, 207, 231

Yousef al-Dowseri 75, 77

Yousef al-Rayes 76

Yousef Buzaid 75

Yousef Hashem 74

Yousif al-Hermi 104

Yousif al-Sabbagh 79, 80

Yousif al-Thawadi 80

Yousif Rabie 76

Yousif Zainal 105, 125

Z

Zainab Abdulamir 314

Zayed bin Rashid al-Zayani 67

Zeinab al-Derazi 82

Zeina Jassim 82

www.ingramcontent.com/pod-product-compliance
Lightning Source LLC
Chambersburg PA
CBHW041610260326
41914CB00012B/1444